I0810006

IMAGES
of America

SUMMER ON THE SOUTHSIDE

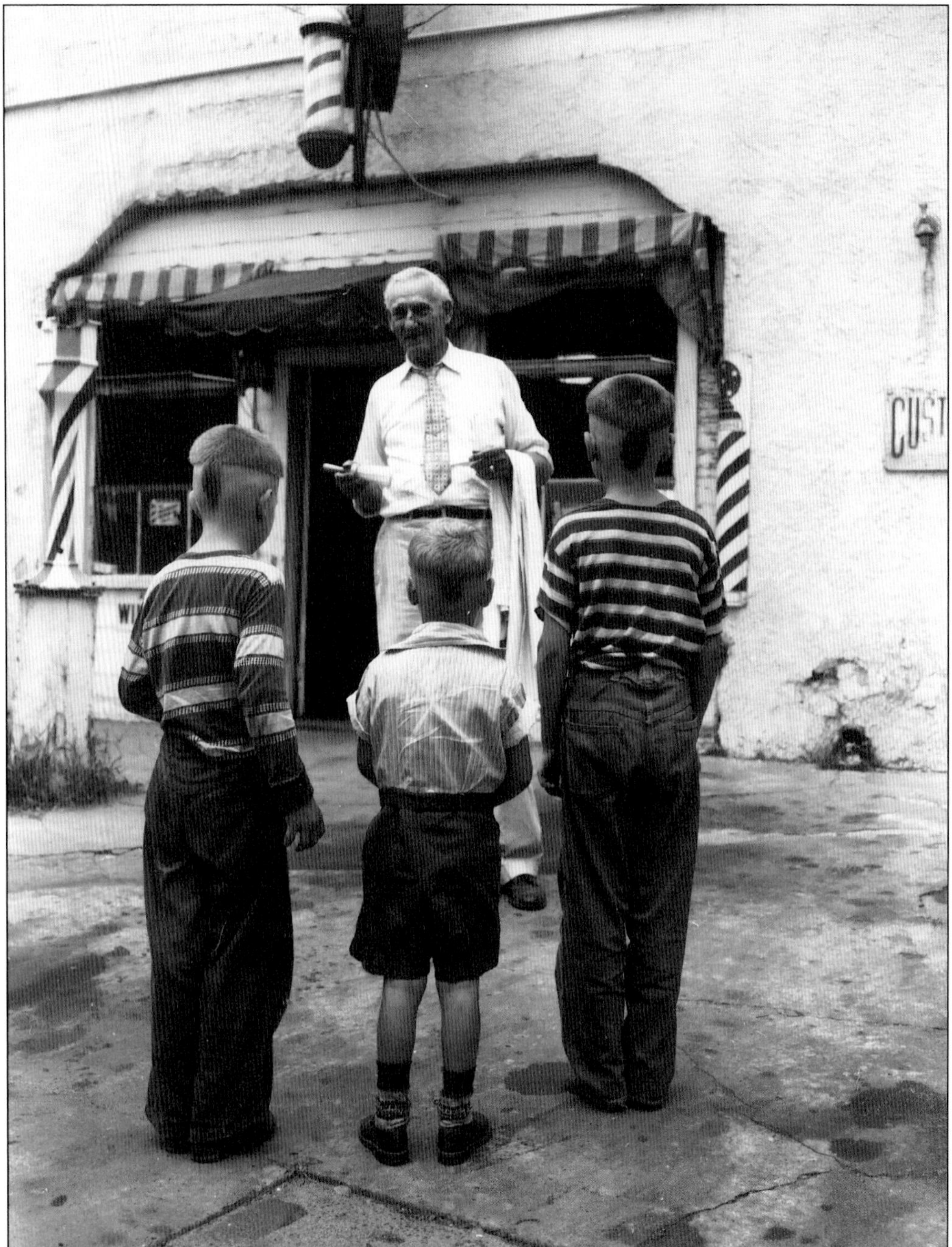

A Berkley barber, Charles H. Hess, gave these three little boys a Davy Crockett haircut on July 8, 1955. These little fellas actually started the fad here by taking advantage of Hess's advertisement for free Davy "Crewcuts" at his 108 East Liberty Street shop. The Davy Crockett haircut was basically a soup-bowl crewcut with a coonskin tail effect in the back. The style received national publicity, as boys across the country convinced their parents they had to have their hair cut to look like the ever-popular Davy Crockett faux fur hats. (Jim Mays, photographer.)

IMAGES
of America

SUMMER ON THE SOUTHSIDE

Amy Waters Yarsinske

ARCADIA
PUBLISHING

ISBN 978-0-7385-6897-3

Published by Arcadia Publishing
Charleston, South Carolina

Printed in the United States of America

Library of Congress Catalog Card Number: 98-86900

For all general information contact Arcadia Publishing at:
Telephone 843-853-2070
Fax 843-853-0044
E-mail sales@arcadiapublishing.com
For customer service and orders:
Toll-Free 1-888-313-2665

Visit us on the Internet at www.arcadiapublishing.com

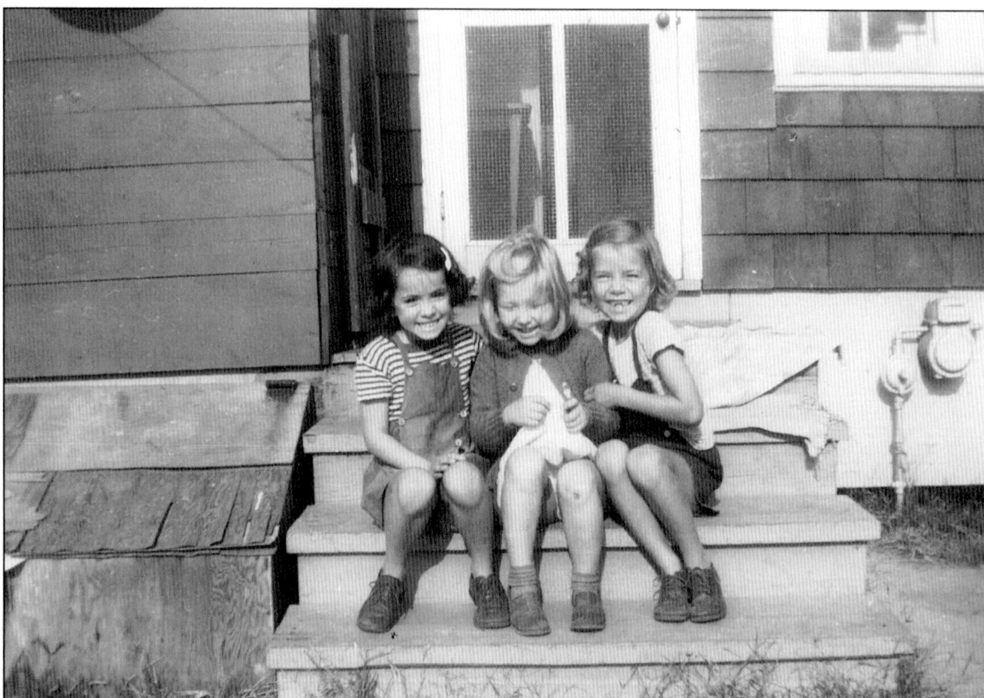

The "Dead End Kids" of Broadcreek Village in Norfolk, (from left to right) Marie Fentress, Sarah Jane Albert, and Marie's older sister Elizabeth, posed on the back stoop of their house in the summer of 1947. Marie was eight years old at the time, while Sarah Jane and Elizabeth were nine. The sisters are the daughters of Herbert Maitland and Helen Lucille Fentress Jr.

CONTENTS

Acknowledgments		6
Introduction		7
1.	Nothing Is So Beautiful as Spring . . .	9
2.	Memorial Days and Wartime Memories	21
3.	Summer Solstice and Dog Days	35
4.	June Bugs and Dragonflies	45
5.	The Boys of Summer	55
6.	To the Mountains and Sea	67
7.	Toiling in the Sun	77
8.	On the Water	87
9.	All the Fun We Had	93
10.	And Those Smiling Faces	99
11.	The Way We Were	107
12.	School Bells and Fall Leaves	123

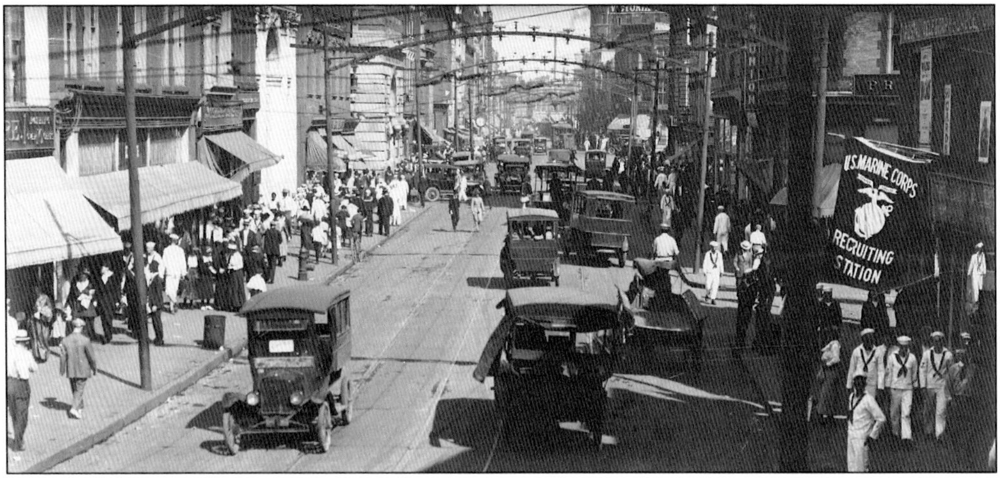

Harry C. Mann chose a warm summer's day in 1918 to take this picture along East Main Street near Commerce Street. Jitney buses were filled with sailors and citizens too hot to continue walking to their destination in downtown Norfolk. This photograph is of particularly high quality, as it was developed from the original 5x7-inch glass plate.

ACKNOWLEDGMENTS

There are numerous individuals and institutions who contributed their knowledge and resources toward the completion of *Summer on the Southside*. I am grateful to all of them but particularly those who lended important pieces of information in addition to their time and, perhaps, a photograph or two. I gratefully acknowledge the contributions of Diana L. Bailey, assistant public affairs officer, United States Army Corps of Engineers, Norfolk District; Edgar T. Brown, historian and genealogist; Harriet Collins, Moses Myers House manager, the Chrysler Museum of Art Historic Houses; Herbert Maitland and Helen Lucille Fentress Jr.; Louis L. Guy Jr., P.E., D.E.E., director, Department of Utilities, City of Norfolk; Peggy A. Haile, city historian, Sargeant Memorial Room, Kirn Library, City of Norfolk; Alice Haines, president, Portsmouth Historical Association; Margaret Forehand Stillman, director, Libraries and Research Service, City of Chesapeake; and Willoughby William Colonna Jr., president, Colonna's Shipyard.

I dedicate this book to my husband, Raymond, and our children, Ashley Nicole, Allyson Emily, and Raymond III. Our children inspired many of the chapter headings in the book. These three special little people, each the child of my heart in their own way, remind me on a daily basis to live life fully and happily. Through their eyes and heightened sense of discovery, I have seen life come alive anew. I will never forget the day my daughter Ashley showed me the moon on a beautiful, clear spring day, or Allyson explained, from her four-year-old perspective, all the insects roaming our yard. As he has grown older and more mobile, baby Raymond has plucked flowers from the wildflower garden and had his nose tickled by their petals. His curiosity is fed by sisters who feel it their duty to take him hand-in-hand on foraging expeditions in the yard, or gleefully teach him to throw a ball. Their smiling faces and joyous laughter serve as a constant reminder of the happiest days of my childhood spent climbing trees, exploring a woods, or laying in tall grass watching clouds take shapes of fairy queens and gilded horses, eagles and Indian braves. It is almost too easy for me to slip into my writing chair and forget . . . until I feel the tug on my arm and look into the countenance of one of my children.

INTRODUCTION

North Carolinian John Thomas Watson (1822-1905) once wrote of summer, " 'Tis true I may have been too hot, / And said some things which I should not. / Your cooler counsels ne'er offend, / But claim my grateful thanks, dear friend, / To Spring and Autumn I express / Regrets for causing them distress.' " This volume is an exploration of history bounded by summer's friends—spring and fall—on either end, with summer as the star attraction. Though it is easy enough to restrict, in terms of geographical bounds, the areas covered in this volume, it is more difficult to place limits on the significant historical impact of the cities and counties comprising the southern portion of Lower Tidewater. Perhaps, for purposes of geographical and historical clarification, it would be helpful to note that we are not in Tidewater, Virginia, when we refer to the region. The part of Virginia between the coast and fall line, which occurs at Richmond on the James River and Fredericksburg along the Rappahannock River, is the area of the state called Tidewater. Those of us living in Hampton Roads reside in Lower Tidewater, the area of Virginia beginning at the mouth of the Chesapeake Bay in the southeast corner of the state. Explorer Ralph Lane's 1585-6 map, engraved by Theodore de Bry, first appeared in 1588 and 1590. Lane's map names the area including Lower Tidewater by its Native American name of Weapemeoc. Thus, those of us living in South Hampton Roads reside on the southside of Lower Tidewater, geographically inclusive of what are now the cities of Chesapeake, Norfolk, Petersburg, Portsmouth, Suffolk, Virginia Beach, and the counties of Isle of Wight and Southampton.

We should be proud of the history of this place called South Hampton Roads. Some of the first explorations outside the English settlement on Roanoke Island took place on the southside in 1585. It was here that the first landing by English settlers took place in 1607 at Cape Henry before Captain Christopher Newport led his expedition to Jamestown. Lower Tidewater is home to two of the oldest, continuously existing municipalities—Norfolk and Isle of Wight—in the Commonwealth of Virginia, established by an Act of Assembly in 1680. Of the three 1680 towns in Lower Tidewater created by the act, commonly known as the Town Act, Norfolk is the only one which held onto its status as a town and, by 1845, an incorporated city. Warwick and Elizabeth City, located on the Peninsula of Lower Tidewater, were absorbed into the cities of Newport News and Hampton, respectively, and did not remain independent towns or cities. Norfolk became only the second of two towns chartered in Virginia before the American Revolution. It is here on the southside that we find the oldest continuously occupied site since the English settled at Jamestown in 1607. The site, Lake Joyce off Chesapeake Beach, was the location of the Chesapeake Indian village of Apasus, shown on the Lane map of 1585. Some of the oldest primary and private schools in the United States and Virginia, dating to the 17th and 18th centuries, are here in Lower Tidewater, several of them on the southside. We have the world's greatest natural harbor, recognized by mariners centuries ago. It is here on the southside that we once found the most beautiful and agriculturally significant dairy and truck farms. And, it is here on the southside, that we earned a reputation as far back as the mid-19th century for having several of the most famous vacation and resort areas in Virginia, the Mid-Atlantic, and the East Coast. We live and work in Lower Tidewater, birthplace of the nation and harbinger of great history.

The considerable contributions of the entire Lower Tidewater area on the history of the Commonwealth of Virginia and the nation go without saying. The book includes images and stories from the cities and counties which have long molded and shaped the historic fabric of South Hampton Roads, more accurately known as southside Lower Tidewater. Though the photographic images in this volume cover 1870 to 1970, there is artwork and narrative that take us back to the 17th, 18th, and early 19th centuries—to simpler times and simpler places.

In our mind's eye of a summer's day long ago are scenes as innocent as when marbles made kings of kids and a man's community contribution was made not for the splashy headlines it would make, but for the satisfaction of his soul. Revisit bright and balmy days when the air was sweet with the perfume of flowers, and the only noise was the chorus of birds and the buzzing of insects or the music of a Memorial Day parade. Summer was a midsummer night's dream that melted into dog days and endless heat waves. It was the season of June bugs and dragonflies in which nothing quite compared to their flights of fancy and whimsical dances. From the first balmy day of spring through the first cool summer's night in September, summer meant vacations to the mountains and sea, and being on the water. The boys of summer came out to play, while so many others toiled in the sun. But, think, in the end, of all the fun we had, of the smiling faces, and of the way we were.

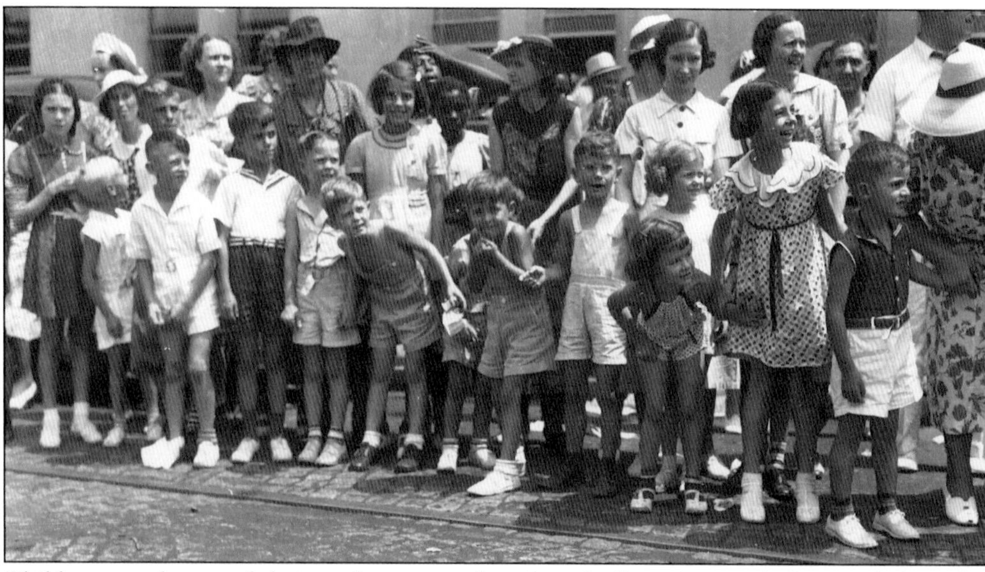

Children eagerly craned their necks to view their first thrilling glance of what was believed to be the last circus parade of its kind through Norfolk, particularly since circus parades were fast disappearing from the American scene. The date was August 10, 1938. The Robbins Brothers Circus was in town. The parade, which began at Twentieth Street that morning, proceeded east to Church Street; south on Church to Main Street; to Granby Street; and then north on Granby back to Twentieth and the show grounds. The circus big top for this show was two city blocks in length. Altogether, 22 tents covered about 12 acres of land. The Robbins Brothers Circus had upwards of 1,000 men, women, and horses in the parade, including trumpeting bands, calliopes, 20 elephants, and 2 caravans of camels from Asia and Siberia, in addition to cages, dens, and allegorical floats. The legendary Hoot Gibson, western star of the silver screen, headed a congress of rough riders, cowboys, cowgirls, Native Americans, and Cossacks in one of the Robbins Brothers' featured acts. (Charles S. Borjes, photographer.)

One

Nothing Is So Beautiful as Spring. . .

"Nothing is so beautiful as spring——
When weeds, in wheels, shoot long and lovely and lush;
Thrush's eggs look little low heavens, and thrush
Through the echoing timber does so rinse and wring
The ear, it strikes like lightnings to hear him sing;
The glassy peartree leaves and blooms, they brush
The descending blue; that blue is all in a rush
With richness; the racing lambs too have fair their fling."

—From *Spring*, 1918
Gerard Manley Hopkins, English poet (1844–1889)

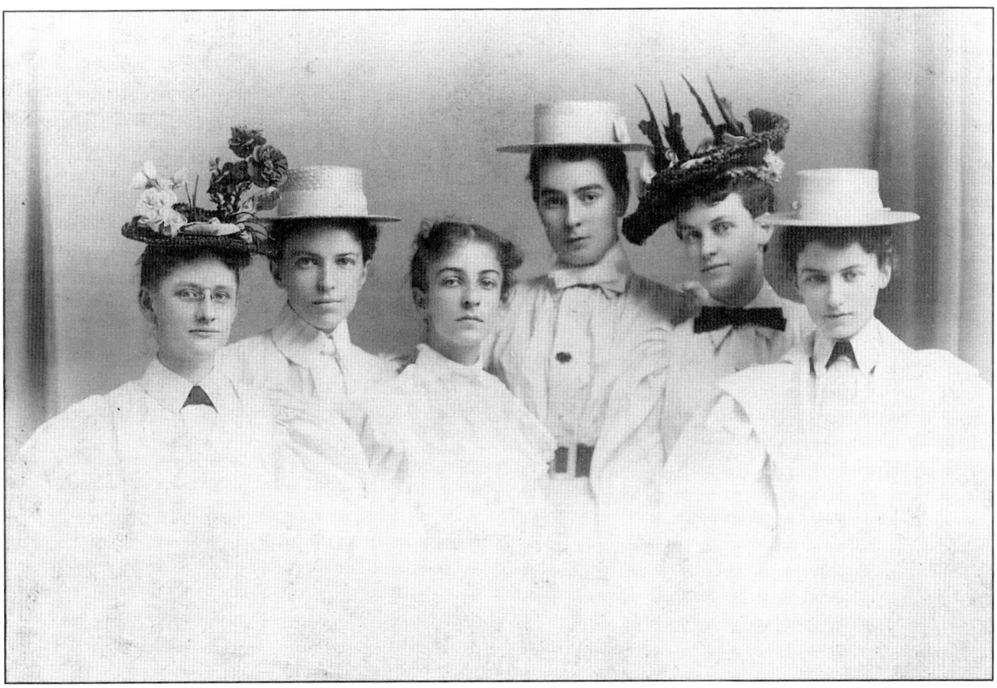

Dressed in their spring attire, these young ladies, members of the Weston family of Norfolk, posed for J.H. Faber about 1896. The style of their clothing was all the rage before the turn of the century. Leg-of-mutton sleeves, high-neck blouses, and hats decorated with extravagant arrays of flowers and feathers to those as simple as a man's Fedora or Homburg, plain or dressed with a simple feather were what the best-dressed young ladies were wearing.

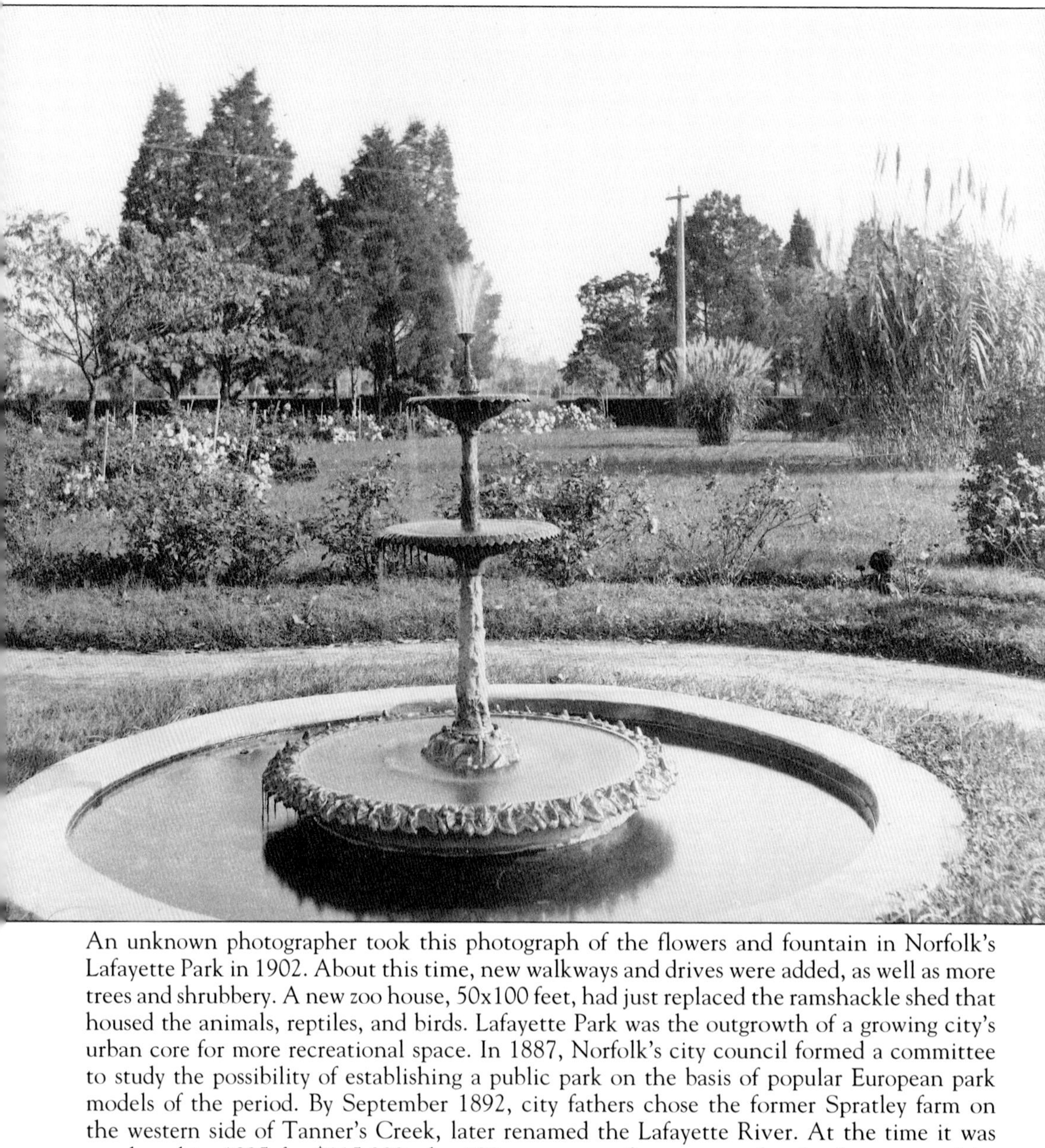

An unknown photographer took this photograph of the flowers and fountain in Norfolk's Lafayette Park in 1902. About this time, new walkways and drives were added, as well as more trees and shrubbery. A new zoo house, 50x100 feet, had just replaced the ramshackle shed that housed the animals, reptiles, and birds. Lafayette Park was the outgrowth of a growing city's urban core for more recreational space. In 1887, Norfolk's city council formed a committee to study the possibility of establishing a public park on the basis of popular European park models of the period. By September 1892, city fathers chose the former Spratley farm on the western side of Tanner's Creek, later renamed the Lafayette River. At the time it was purchased in 1895 for $115,000, the 120-acre tract of overgrown farmland was owned by three land companies. Popularly called "City Park" by residents of Norfolk, the park has been officially named Lafayette Park since 1899. Captain William Smith was the park and zoo keeper when this picture was taken.

This Easter postcard of chicks and violets, a divided back, was manufactured in the United States between 1907 and the First World War. The U.S. Postal Service approved divided back postcards on March 1, 1907, which allowed for a message on the left and an address on the right. Many of the more elaborate cards, such as this one, were made in England or Germany, but an unknown American maker achieved a high-quality postcard with this card that would rival those coming out of Europe during the same period. The symbolic use of chicks and violets to indicate new life and love at Easter are sweet reminders of spring. Violets, however, have played a tumultuous role in the peaks and valleys of human passion for centuries. When *Hamlet* was first performed in 1601, William Shakespeare (1564-1616) incorporated an eloquent passage on the famous flower, spoken by Laertes to his sister Ophelia, Hamlet's lover: "For Hamlet, and the trifling of his favour / Hold it a fashion, and a toy in blood; / A violet in the youth of primary nature / Forward, not permanent, sweet, not lasting, / The perfume and suppliance of a minute; / no more."

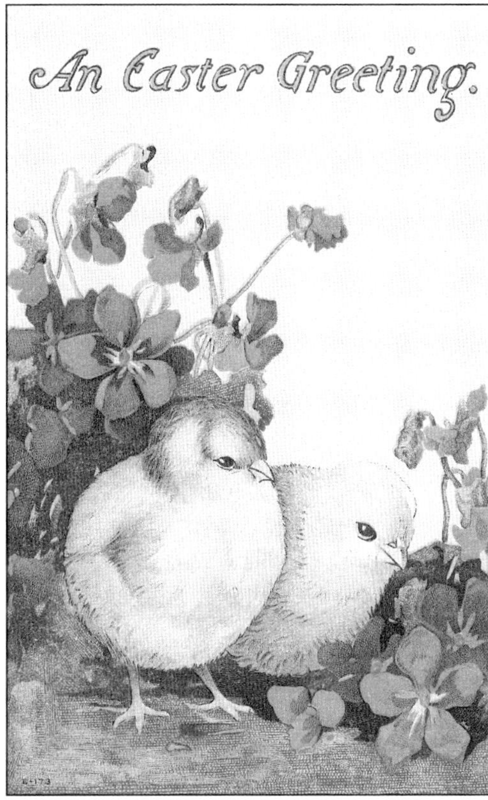

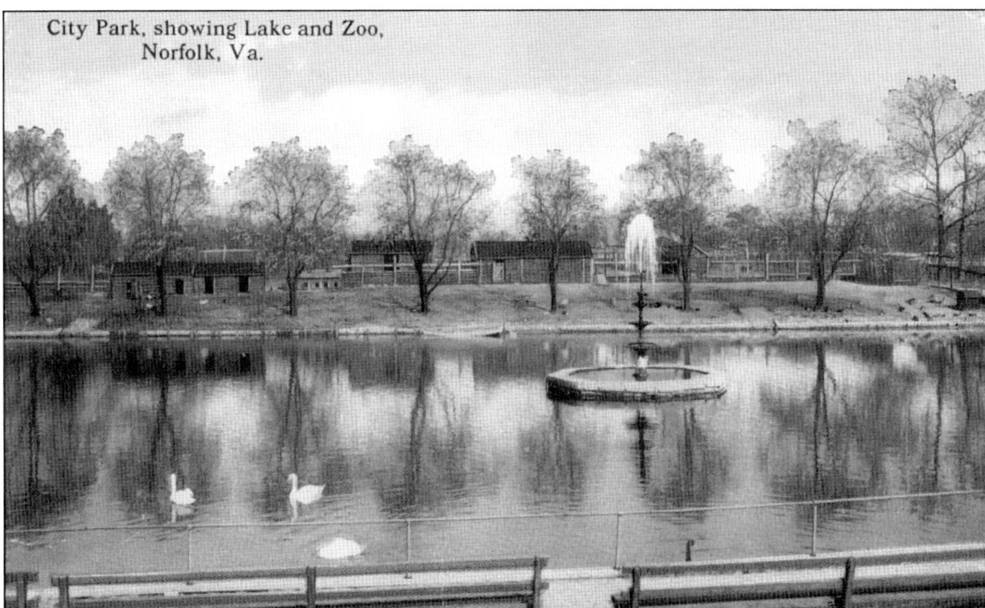

An image of Norfolk's Lafayette Park, showing the lake and zoo, was sent on this postcard from Portsmouth to Hickory, Virginia, now part of the city of Chesapeake, in 1916. The penny postcard, a divided back, was published by Louis Kaufmann & Sons of Baltimore, Maryland.

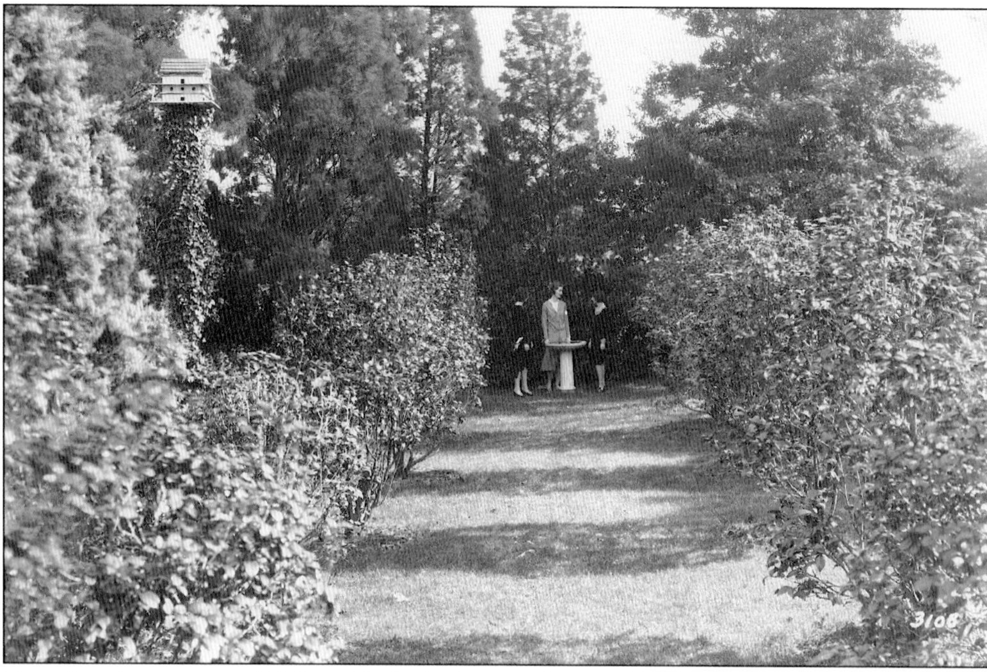

The Camellia Japonica Walk at Holly Lodge, residence of Harry Buchanan Goodridge, was photographed by an unknown photographer in April 1928.

"For the satisfaction of his soul . . ."

Holly Lodge, located on the north side of Tanner's Creek in Norfolk on a finger of land called North Shore Point, was a short distance east of the country club. Harry Buchanan Goodridge bought the entire peninsula, comprised of 42 acres and a small cottage, in 1906. Between 1906 and 1911, he divided the peninsula into three distinct tracts, selling one parcel to F.W. McCullough and another to Henry H. Little. Goodridge, a wealthy bachelor with only his Chow dogs, gray parrot John Silver (famous as the only bird in Norfolk who slept at night in a miniature canvas hammock), gold oriole, and Malayan mynah bird for company, spared neither time nor expense on his horticultural pursuits as he developed his property. Though he found gardening relaxing, Goodridge opted for the challenge of growing fine and rare plants. Goodridge planted Japanese persimmons, pomegranates, bay trees, osmanthus, and eventually, Camellia Japonicas. He also brought azaleas from the mountains of China and sacred olive trees from Palestine. The English boxwoods he planted around the main house and grounds were 150 to two hundred years old. Successful with his first camellias, Goodridge bought, through E.A. McIlhenny of Avery Island, Louisiana, carloads of large grown camellia specimens in a variety of colors cultivated from the old plantations of McIlhenny's home state. At the time this picture was taken, Holly Lodge had the largest collection of camellias in Virginia. Goodridge, born on Holt Street on October 7, 1870, to George K. and Ella Murphy Goodridge, attended the old Norfolk Academy. His business life was as varied as his political one. His first important business venture was a wholesale grocery and meat store at Commerce and Water Streets, which he had for 20 years, but his main business from 1920 on was as general sales agent and secretary-treasurer of the Cape Henry Syndicate, the group which in the early part of the century acquired all the property that is now Fort Story, First Landing/Seashore State Park, and Lynnhaven Inlet north along Long Creek and Crystal Lake to the Atlantic Ocean—about 5,000 acres total. The syndicate's efforts led to much of Virginia Beach's shoreline development. Goodridge never married. He died on July 30, 1952, at the age of 81.

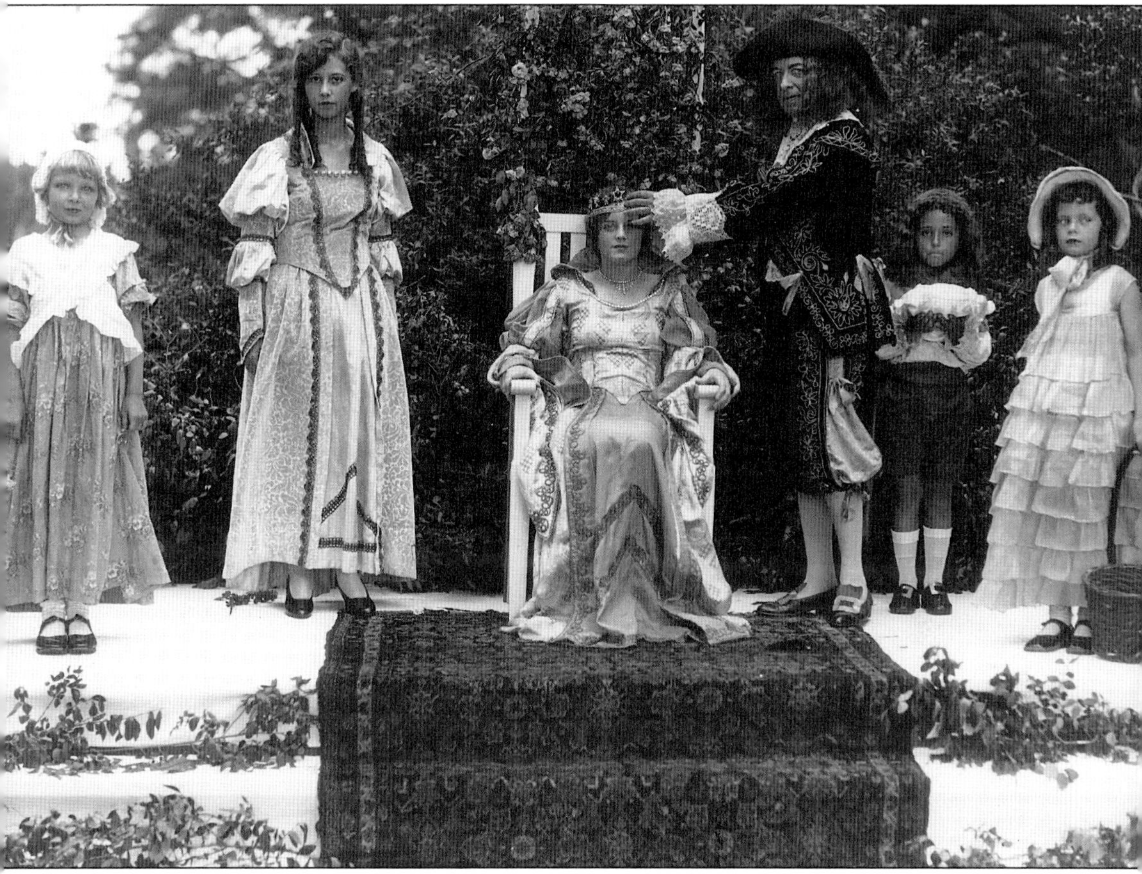

Jessie Smith of Kempsville is shown here being crowned Queen of the May by Rufus Parks of Princess Anne County, who played the part of Adam Thoroughgood at the pageant held at the Adam Thoroughgood House. Orpha Parks, the queen's maid of honor, is at the queen's right in this picture, taken in May 1930 by an unknown photographer. The tradition of May Day, also called Beltane, meaning bright fire, symbolizes the transition of spring to summer. In ancient agrarian societies, it was common for villagers to name a young, attractive couple as King and Queen of the May, May Day being the first day of the summer. References to this ritual abound in our literature, perhaps one of the finest examples of which originates with Alfred Lord Tennyson (1809-1892), English poet laureate, in his poem *The May Queen*: "You must wake and call me early, call / me early, mother dear; / To-morrow 'ill be the happiest time / of all the glad New-year; / Of all the glad New-year, mother, the / maddest merriest day; / For I'm to be Queen o' the May, mother, / I'm to be Queen o' the May." As for Adam Thoroughgood, he received his earliest land grants to property on the west side of the Lynnhaven River toward Little Creek on June 14, 1635, and on the east side of the river that December. Some writers believe the house to have been built between 1636 and 1640, assuming the structure now standing was a manor house. This is not clearly the case. The east or former front wall and both gables are English bond brick while the west wall is Flemish bond, pointing to a date around 1660, with remodeling or reconstruction of the west wall at a later date. A 1781 map of Princess Anne County showing Cape Henry to Little Creek is enlightening to this argument. In the area between Lynnhaven Inlet and Little Creek, north being at the bottom of the map as was customary of the period, "J. Torogood on Lynnhaven River" is designated as the house which stands today, with an unnamed house near a pond. A manor house plantation is mentioned in several descriptions as being near such a pond.

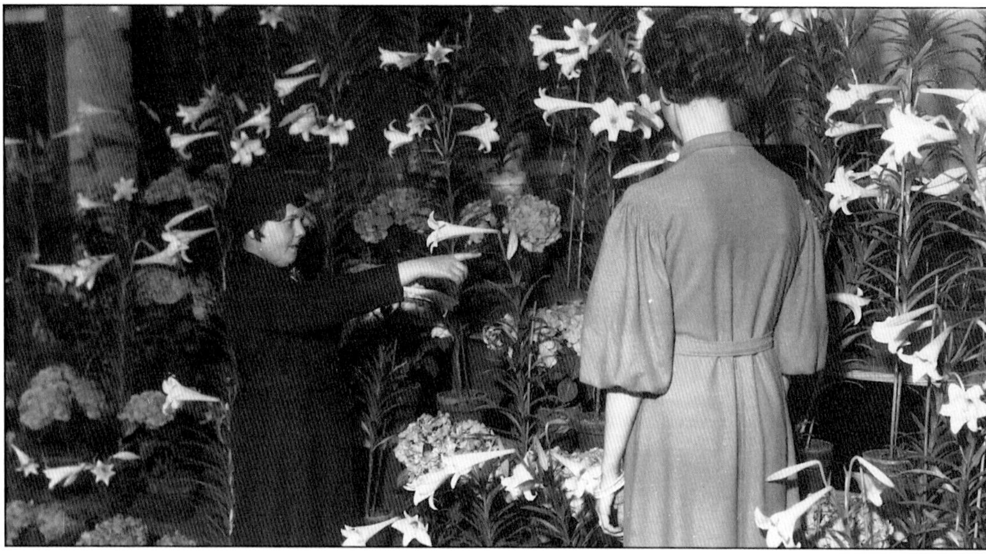

Taken on April 14, 1933, this photograph shows that the choice of full, white Easter lilies, traditionally a sign purity of purpose and perhaps the most ancient and religious of flowers, was a favorite with Norfolk shoppers as they prepared for Easter Sunday. Next to lilies, the pale blue hydrangeas visible in the photograph were the most popular, as were hundreds of azaleas and tulips being sold around the city. Corsages fashioned from red and yellow roses, lilies of the valley, violets, and sweet peas remained popular choices for the ladies. The City Market was thronged with purchasers and the sidewalks in and around downtown were choked with men and women carrying awkward bundles of spring blooms. An anonymous poet wrote of the Easter lily: "And the stately lilies stand / Fair in silvery light / Like saintly vestals, pale in prayer; / Their pure breath sanctifies the air, / As its fragrance fills the night." (Charles S. Borjes, photographer.)

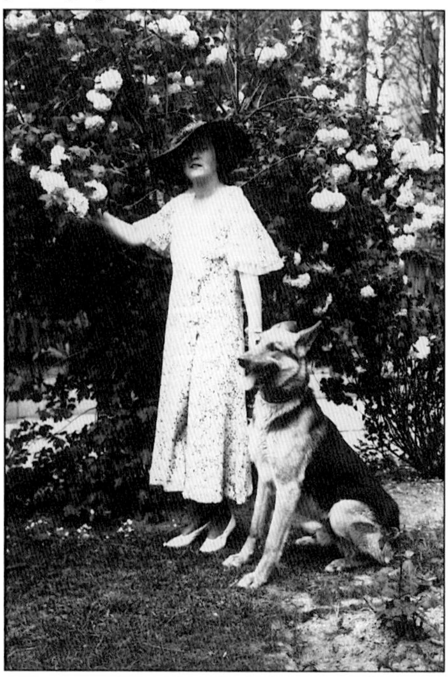

Grace Elizabeth Twohy, wife of John Twohy II, was photographed with her German shepherd in the garden of the couple's Ghent home on May 7, 1934. Grace, daughter of Frederick Chapman and Grace Elizabeth Merrick of Cleveland, Ohio, married John Twohy II on September 10, 1924. Upon moving to Norfolk, she took a constructive role in the community. An avid gardner, Grace was the founder of the Town and Country Garden Club, and had also served as president of the Garden Club of Norfolk and the Garden Club of America. Her husband, John II, a Norfolk native born June 11, 1900, to John and Katherine Dugan Twohy, had owned and operated a number of construction firms, but was best known for his interest in the Commonwealth Sand and Gravel Corporation, which he founded and which was headquartered in Richmond. The couple were the parents of three children: Patricia Ann, wife of Dr. George H.B. Rector; Edward Merrick; and John Twohy IV. (Charles S. Borjes, photographer.)

Back when marbles made kings of kids, Early Croft was the perennial favorite and a true champion. Early, photographed with his mother on May 12, 1934, as reigning Tidewater Marble Champion, was a student at the Ballentine School and a young man with great dink shooter abilities.

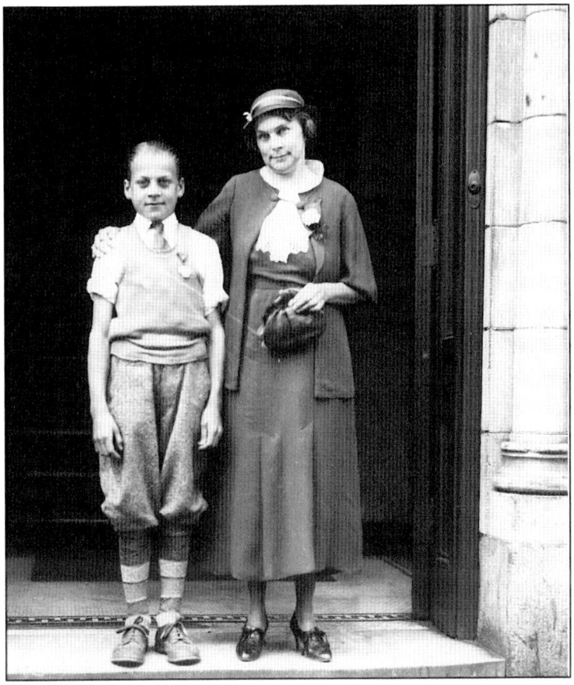

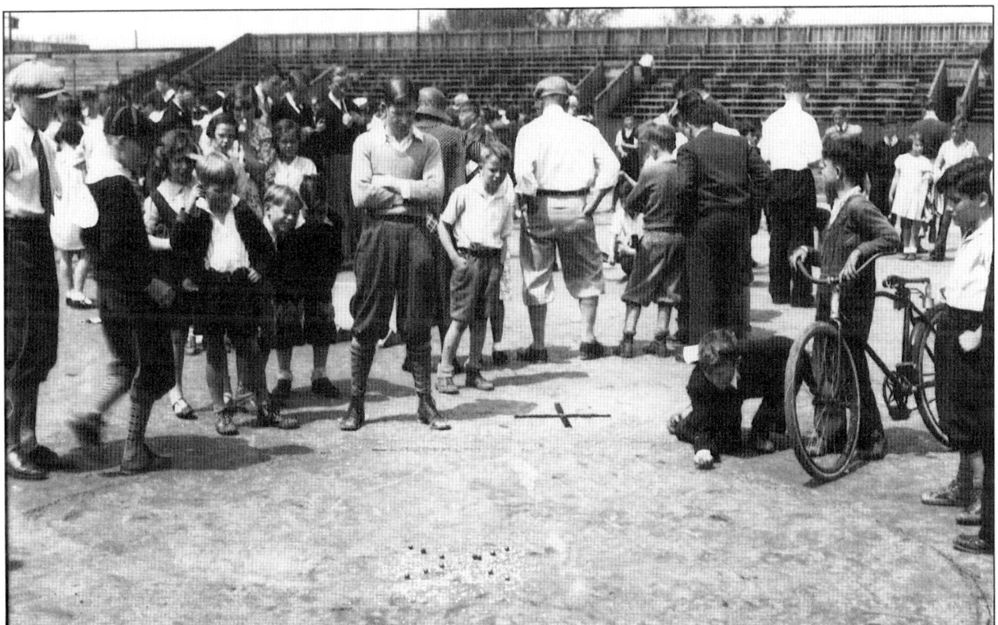

During the competition for top honors in the Tidewater tournament at Bain Field, Ernest Chaney, a Madison School sharpshooter, got hot and challenged him, but Early hung on and bettered his rival by five points. While Early Croft won an all-expenses paid trip to Ocean City, New Jersey, to compete in the national marble tournament, runners-up Chaney, Horace Culpepper of Norview, and William Gates of John Goode School won gold wristwatches. There were no losers of the 45 school champions who competed for the top title. Everyone walked away with a medal for his effort and a smile on his face. (Charles S. Borjes, photographer.)

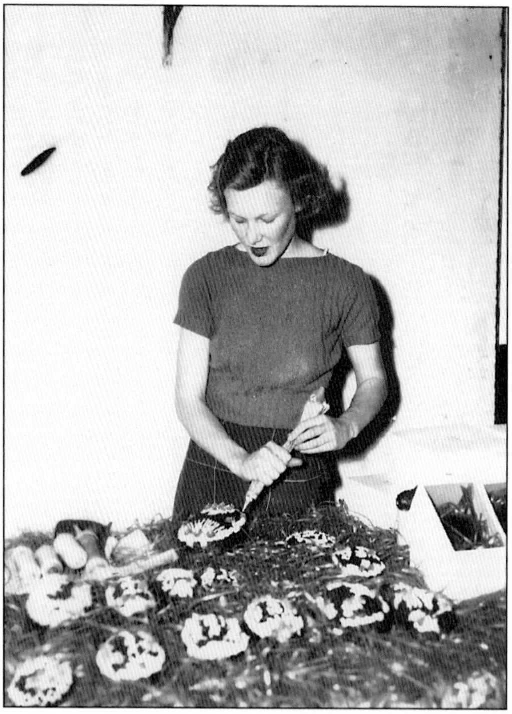

The Easter eggs being decorated in this photograph from 1938 are reminiscent of the rich chocolate confections given as gifts to family and friends on Easter morning. Though they have affixed themselves in our memory, chocolate Easter eggs, while certainly part of our tradition, are recent in origin. The real egg, either painted or decorated with bright colors or coated in metallics such as gold and silver, have been a symbol of new life and resurrection at spring festivals in cultures pre-dating Christian faith. And to early Christians, the egg came to symbolize new life through Jesus' resurrection, the shape of the egg resembling the stone rolled away from Jesus' tomb on the morning of his arisening from the dead. At churches in Norfolk, Ocean View, and Virginia Beach, churchgoers experienced the sonorous peals of organ music and choral singing accompanied by clergymen repeating the age-old story of how "He is risen." (Charles S. Borjes, photographer.)

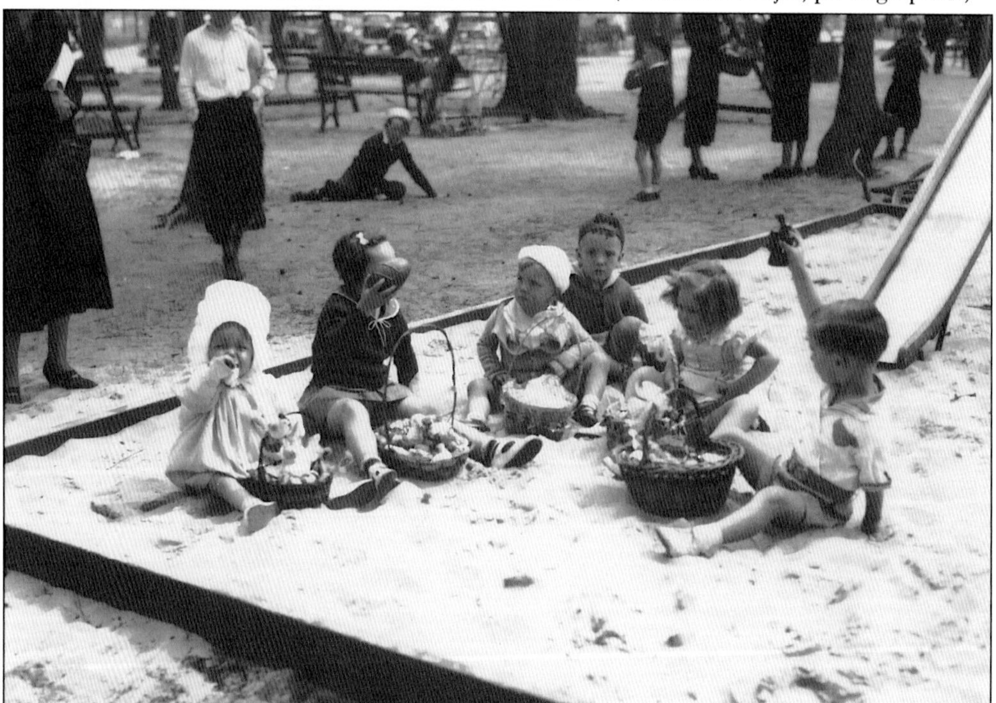

Children gathered at Norfolk's Lafayette Park on Easter Monday, April 18, 1938, for an informal and unofficial celebration of the holiday. School-aged children, out of school for the day, joined infants and toddlers in a day devoted to showing off what the Easter Bunny brought them. The children also participated in games. (H.D. Vollmer, photographer.)

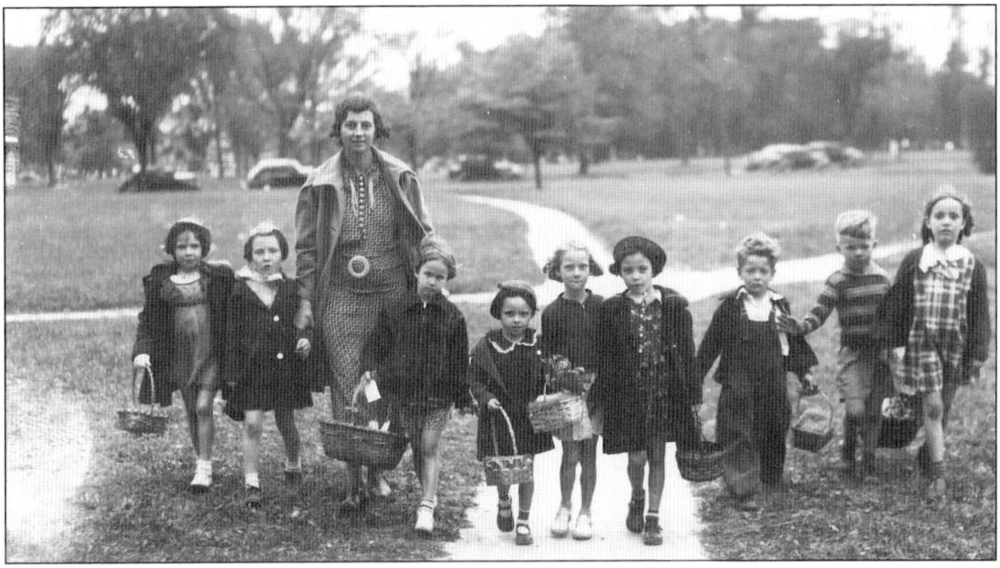

A good time was had by all the youngsters in this photograph, taken at the Easter egg-rolling contest at Lafayette Park on April 18, 1938, as part of the children's Easter Monday celebration. The only rule to an Easter egg-rolling is to see who can roll an egg the greatest distance or can make the egg roll without breaking it. The baskets of the children in this picture are filled to capacity not only from egg-rolling, but a strenuous afternoon of egg-hunting, which would account for the tired looks on the faces of this group. In the tradition of community Easter egg hunts, eggs were hidden throughout the park and children from Norfolk's neighborhoods were invited to find them. Prizes of candy were given to children finding the most eggs. (Charles S. Borjes, photographer.)

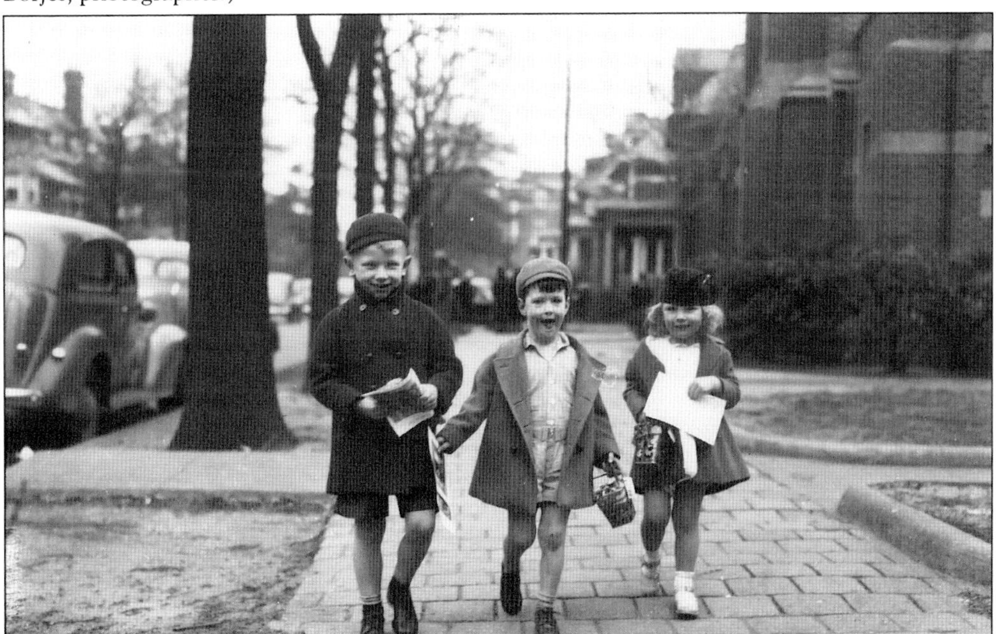

Photographer Charles S. Borjes snapped a picture of these children who obligingly mugged for his camera on Easter Sunday in 1940. The picture was taken in Norfolk's Ghent section.

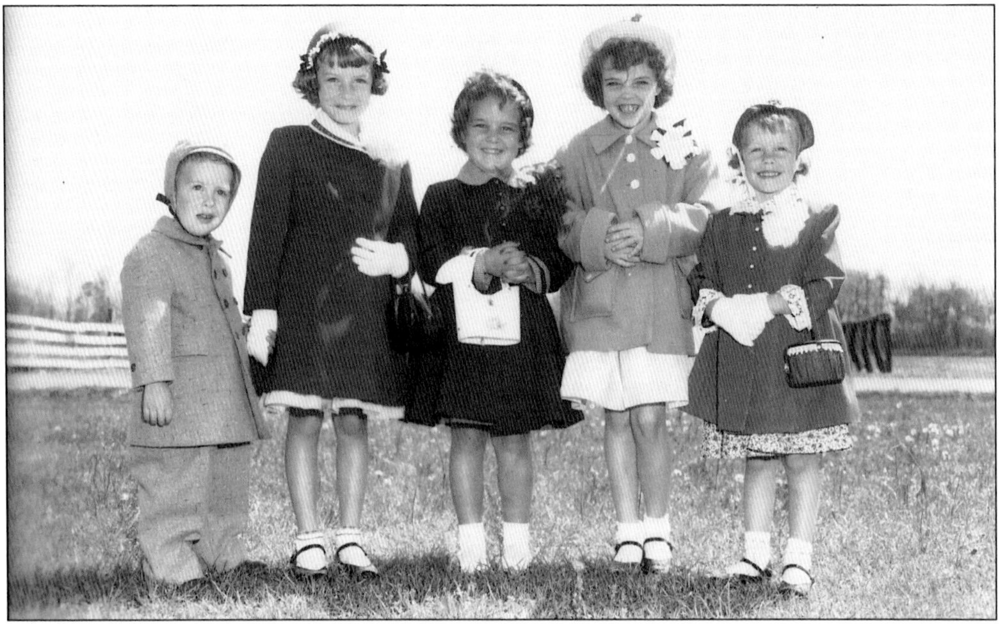

The children in this picture were photographed on Easter Sunday, April 16, 1955. Looking proper in their Easter finest and smiling broadly, these unidentified youngsters are clearly having a good time with photographer Jim Mays.

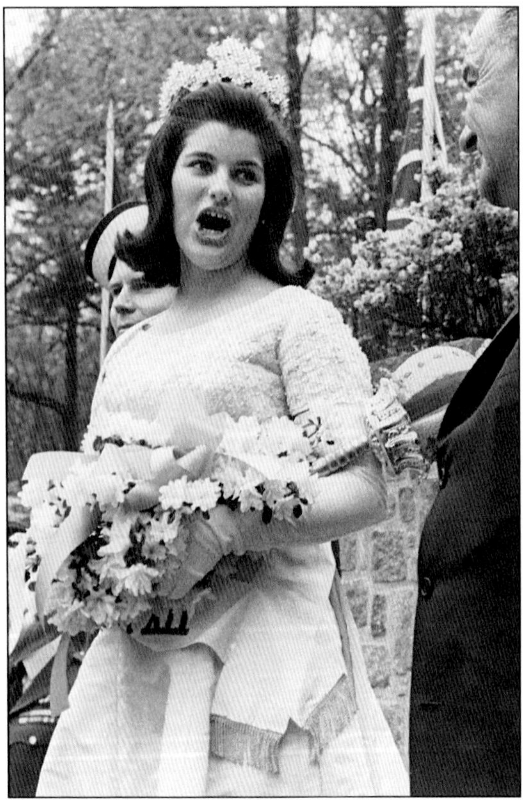

Luci Baines Johnson, 17-year-old daughter of President Lyndon Baines Johnson, was photographed on her coronation day as Queen Azalea XII in 1965. President Johnson, accompanied to Norfolk by the First Lady and daughter Lynda Bird, reportedly leaned over as the announcer prepared to introduce Luci and said, "The joyous moment is at hand—sweet Luci's coronation." The president's eldest daughter, Lynda, was crowned Queen Azalea VIII in 1961. The 48-degree temperature did little to dampen the spirits of 11,000 spectators at Luci's coronation. The large turnout to see the crowning of a new queen is indicative of the overall success or failure of the festival to draw people to its events over the years. The International Azalea Festival, launched in 1954 by the Norfolk Chamber of Commerce and the city as a salute to the North Atlantic Treaty Organization (NATO) established in Norfolk in April 1952, has seen the celebration's success flower and wane given the magnetism of the queen. (Photographer unknown.)

During the week preceding her coronation as Queen Azalea XVI, Tricia Nixon, daughter of President Richard M. Nixon, visited historic sites, military installations and ships, and the Children's Hospital of the King's Daughters. Jean Nagle, one of the hostesses of the Moses Myers House and shown here with the president's daughter in the dining room of the historic home, gave Tricia Nixon a tour on April 24, 1969.

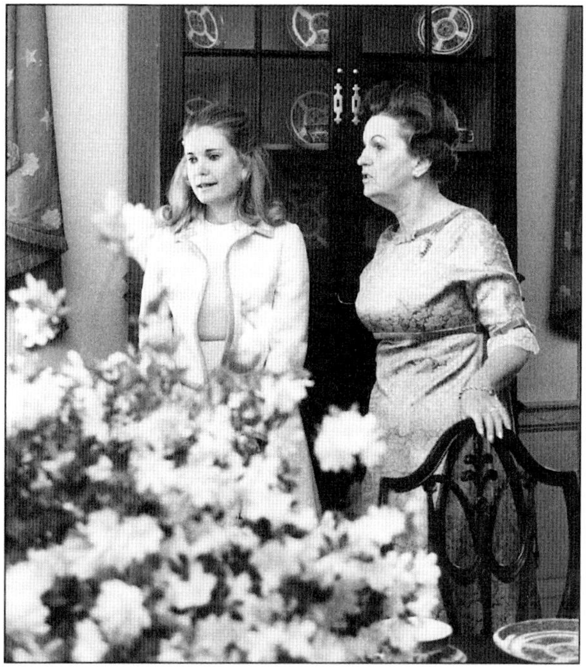

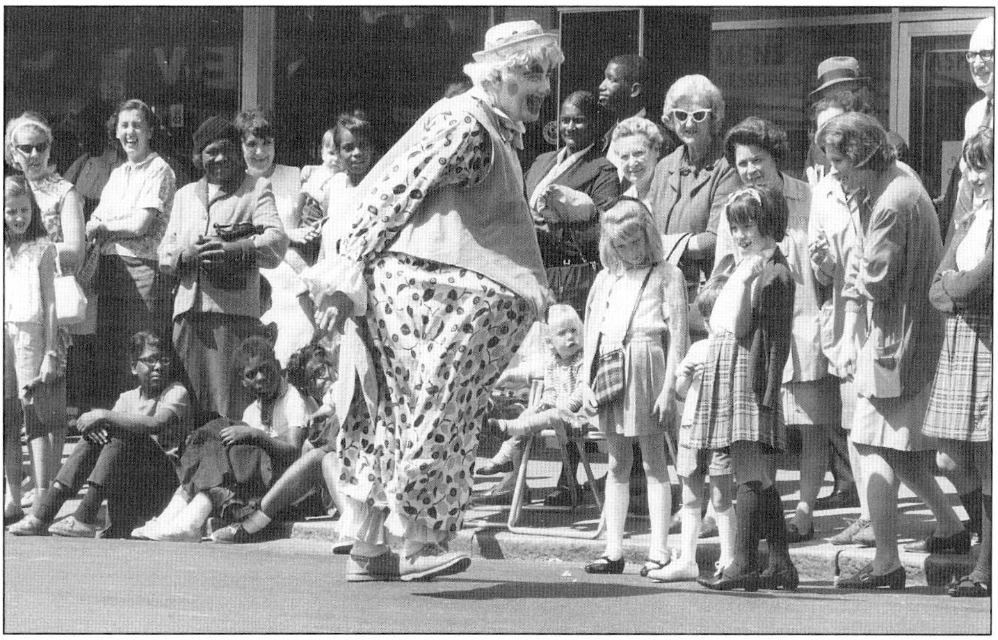

In years gone by and set apart from the pomp and pageantry of the International Azalea Festival, was the joy of the festival's parade and the fun children experienced as they were entertained by colorful floats, lively music, and creative clowns. This picture by Richard L. Dunston takes everyone back to the April 1969 Azalea Festival parade. There were 90 units in the parade that year, many of them elaborate representations of life in the NATO's member nations at that time: Belgium, Canada, Denmark, France, Germany, Greece, Ireland, Italy, Luxembourg, the Netherlands, Norway, Portugal, Turkey, the United Kingdom, and the United States.

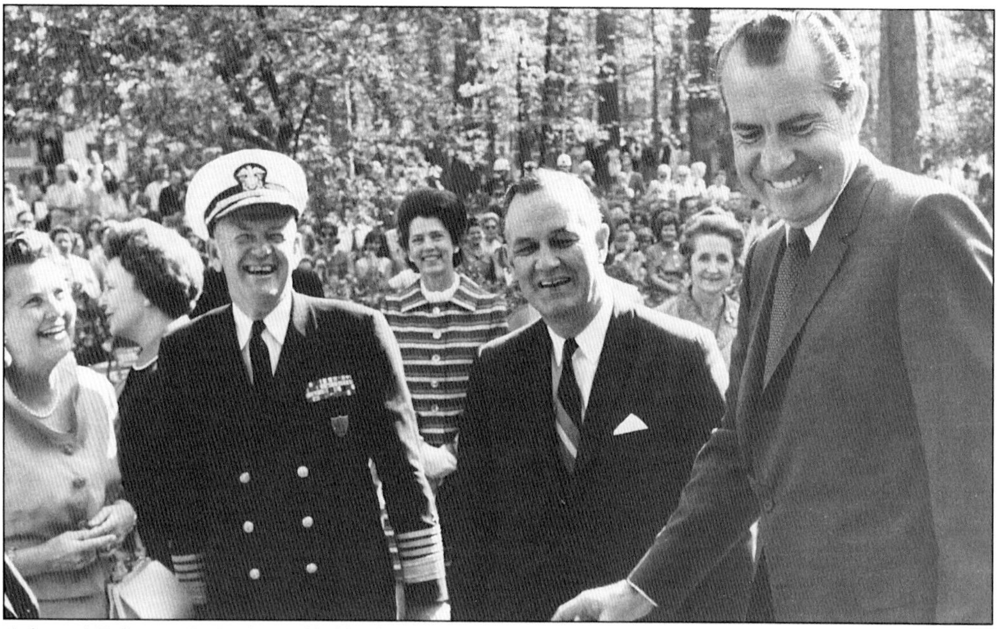

Admiral Ephraim P. Holmes (left), the NATO's Atlantic commander, Virginia Governor Mills E. Godwin Jr. (center), and President Richard M. Nixon share a happy moment at the coronation of Nixon's daughter Tricia, as Queen Azalea, April 26, 1969. (Clifton Guthrie, photographer.)

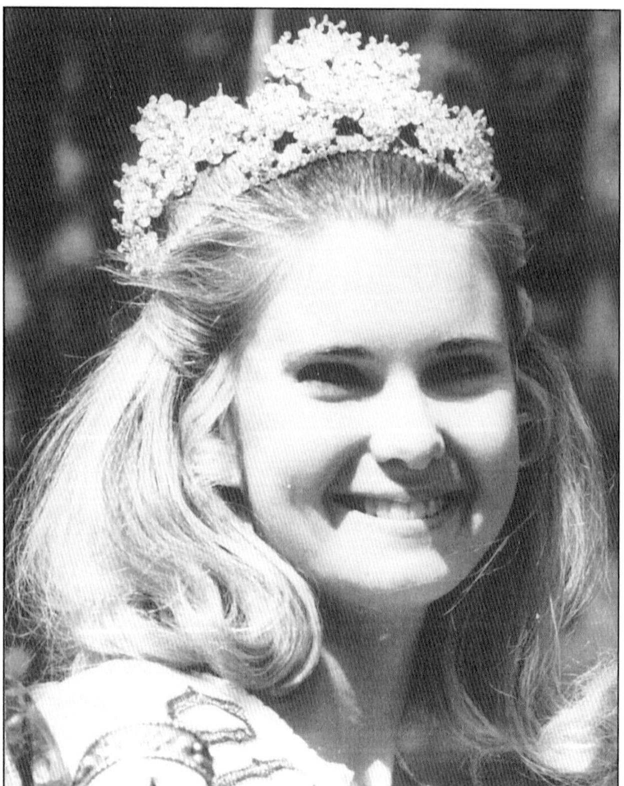

Tricia Nixon, 23-year-old daughter of President Richard M. Nixon, was all smiles shortly after being crowned Queen Azalea XVI by her father at the Norfolk Botanical Garden on April 26, 1969. The president was in Norfolk all of 80 minutes as he took time from affairs of state to bestow the crown of Queen Azalea upon his daughter. The ceremonies were held as part of the International Azalea Festival, an annual event in the city of Norfolk since 1954. Tricia graduated from Finch College in New York in 1968, where she majored in modern European history. (Photograph courtesy of the Associated Press.)

Two

Memorial Days and Wartime Memories

"The things that make a soldier great and send him out to die,
To face the flaming cannon's mouth nor ever question why,
Are lilacs by a little porch, the row of tulips red,
The peonies and pansies, too, the old petunia bed,
The grass plot where his children play, the roses on the wall:
'Tis these that make a soldier great. He's fighting for them all."

—From *The Things That Make a Soldier Great*, n.d.
Edgar Albert Guest, American journalist (1881–1959)

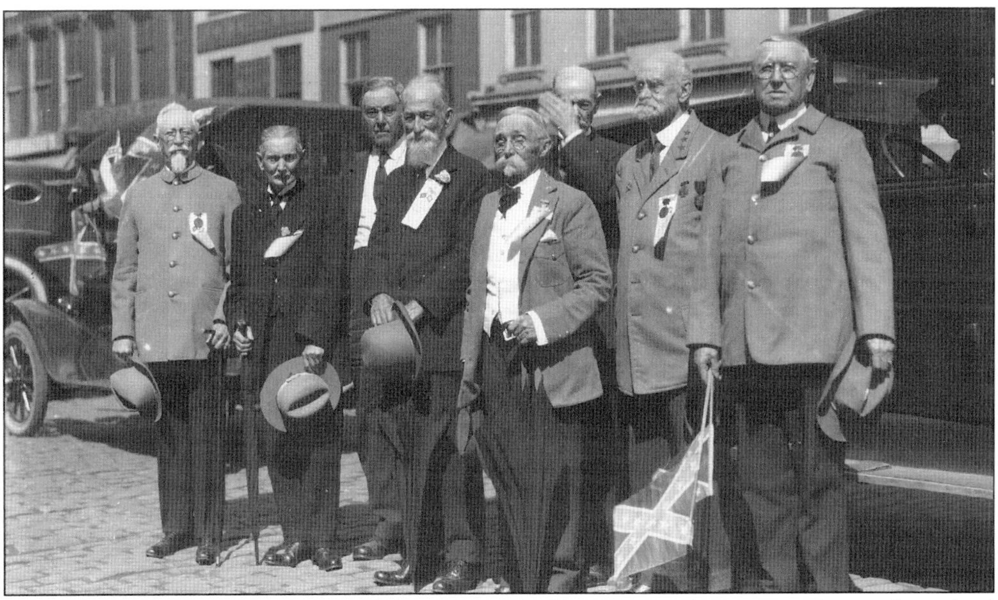

A few of the survivors of the Confederate army held a memorial service to honor their dead comrades on Memorial Day, May 18, 1922. A scant handful of gray-haired men, faltering with the passing years, but whose eyes still burned with the same bright fire that brought them glory in the war, stood tall as intermittent rain showers pelted them during ceremonies held at the Confederate monument in Commercial Place. This ceremony, part of the annual Memorial Day exercises once held by the Pickett-Buchanan Camp of the United Confederate Veterans, continued with a procession of automobiles to Elmwood Cemetery, where hundreds of people had scattered flowers upon the graves.

Memorial Day was first observed as a national holiday on May 30, 1868, on the order of General John A. Logan, commander of the Grand Army of the Republic, but its inspiration came from Petersburg, Virginia. On April 9, 1868, a party of Northerners, including General Logan's wife, Mary, toured the battlefields and historic towns of the commonwealth. The tour reached Petersburg, where its members visited the Crater and sites of interest around Petersburg. As their carriages drove in the gates of Old Blandford Cemetery, Mary Logan was amazed at the masses of faded flowers and decoration on all the graves. The whole place had come alive in her mind's eye with color and bloom, to which she reportedly exclaimed, "why . . . What is it all about?"

What it was all about went back to June 9, 1864, when Petersburg experienced a surprise attack up Jerusalem Plank Road by 1,300 men of a Federal cavalry division led by Brigadier General August V. Kautz. Jerusalem Plank Road, begun in 1853 and built with heartpine timber, was an important route of trade and travel in the antebellum period. The road served as a connection between Littleton and Hawkinsville in Sussex County, and Templeton in Prince George County. The route was strategically consequential in the Civil War, and Confederate forces, particularly toward the last year of the war, were spread thin in their ability to protect it. Old men and young boys who composed the home guard heard alarm bells sound at the first sight of Federal cavalry moving toward the city. They grabbed whatever they could to defend themselves and rushed to the breastworks around Petersburg while the call went out to the nearest Confederate regulars. Armed with shotguns, scythe blades, pistols, pick axes, Bowie knives, and squirrel rifles, a thin line of old men and boys—scarcely 125 in all—spread out and waited for Kautz's cavalry. When the cavalry came, the home guard repulsed them. Thinking the resistance would be heavy, the cavalry fell back and waited for artillery. The home guard came under intense fire from the flank and rear while continuing to battle the Federals in front of them. Though certainly overwhelmed, they held their ground until Confederate artillery and cavalry clattered through town and forced Federal troops to retire under the cover of Major General Benjamin Butler's gunboats to City Point and Bermuda Hundred Peninsula between the James and Appomattox Rivers. The efforts of a courageous few saved Petersburg.

The gallantry of old men and boys won the admiration of friend and foe. General William B. Wise, Confederate commander of the city, issued an order thanking them and their commanding officer, Colonel Fletcher H. Archer. Of the 125 reserves and second class militia, 11 were killed and nearly all the rest wounded or captured. The women of Petersburg nursed the wounded and helped bury the dead. The experience of these grim tasks moved schoolteacher Nora Fontaine Maury Davidson (1836-1929) and her students to start their own Memorial Day observance on April 26, 1866. Their care in decorating the graves started a ground swell of support for a larger and more organized effort to remember the fallen. While the fields around the city still wore the marks of battle, the ladies of Petersburg formed an association, the Ladies' Memorial Association, on May 6, 1866, to care for the graves of their soldier dead and to commemorate June 9 as Memorial Day. It was the remnants of Petersburg's previous year's celebration that Mary Logan saw on her visit to the city. The beauty and sentiment attached to Petersburg's day of remembrance made such an indelible impression on her, she returned home and persuaded her husband to set aside a day each year when everyone might honor their dead heroes. General Logan set aside a general Memorial Day on May 30 by General Order No. 11 (issued May 5, 1868) as the annual date for decorating the graves of Union soldiers, sailors, and marines; however, the day was first known as Decoration Day and largely observed in the North. The idea spread from state to state, and gradually state legislatures enacted it into law. Memorial Day was not enacted as a legal holiday in Virginia until 1902. The day first appeared in statutes of the United States in 1887 as a legal holiday in the District of Columbia and for federal employees. It is wholly appropriate that Petersburg, around which 13 pitched battles of the Civil War were fought and where President Abraham Lincoln met General Ulysses S. Grant to dictate the terms of surrender to be presented to Confederate General Robert E. Lee, was the city that inspired a nation's Memorial Day, a day of tender memory.

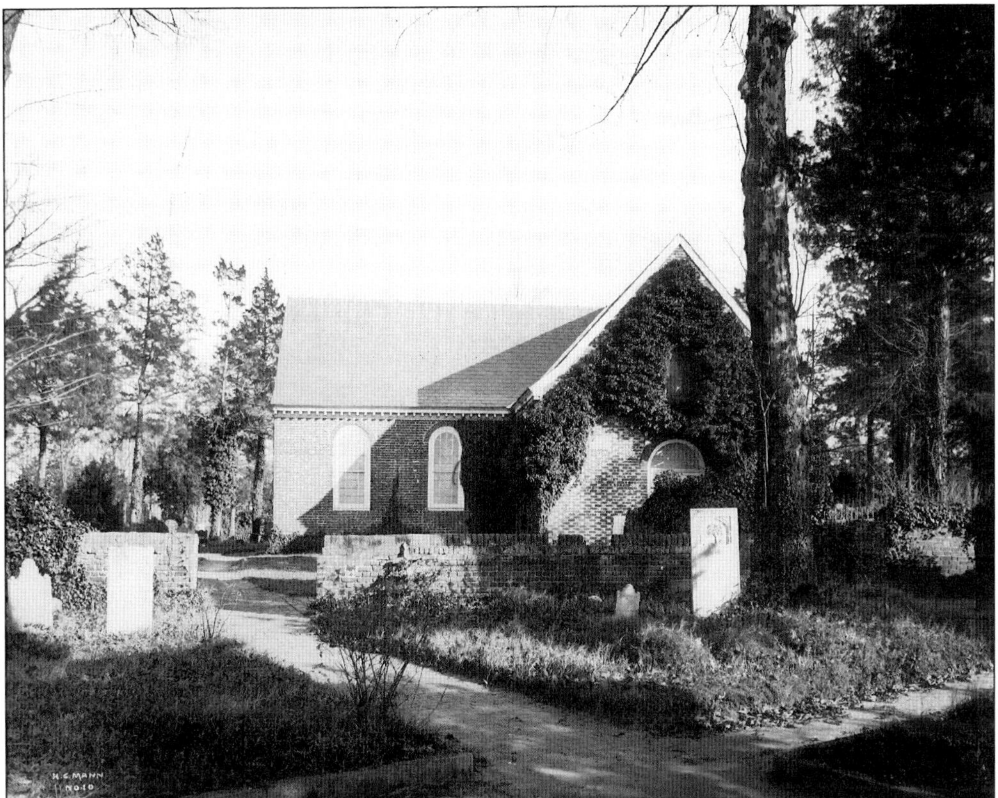

Old Blandford Church, site of the cemetery which Mary Logan observed on her visit, was built in 1737 as the third church of Bristol Parish. The church was eventually abandoned after its disestablishment, and fell into ruins, though its walls still stood. Blandford Cemetery developed around the ruins of the church. At the time of Logan's visit, thousands of Confederate graves had been decorated in remembrance. The Petersburg city council authorized the Ladies' Memorial Association to restore the church in 1901, which they did. The church was being used as a Confederate memorial chapel at the time Harry C. Mann photographed it in 1908. The chapel has memorial windows, designed by Louis Comfort Tiffany, representing each of the Confederate states in addition to one special window Tiffany donated to the ladies' association. John Randolph (1773-1833), of Roanoke, and one of Virginia's ardent statesmen and politicians, once worshipped at Old Blandford Church. Mann, who died in Lynchburg, Virginia, on December 12, 1926, after a prolonged illness, is buried in Blandford Cemetery.

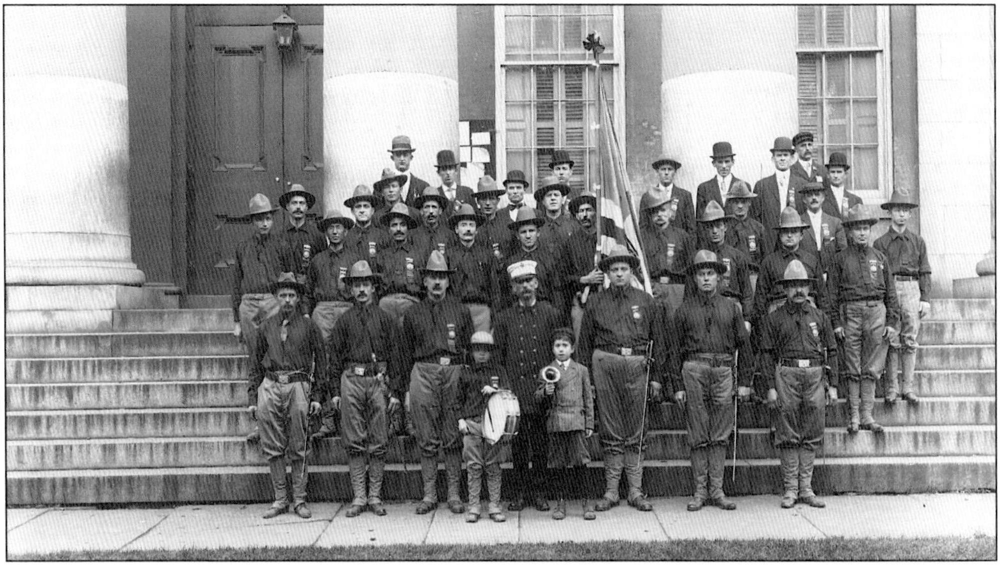

Veterans of the Spanish-American War marched in the Memorial Day parade through downtown Norfolk in 1908 and then posed on the steps of the old city hall, located at the corner of Bank Street and City Hall Avenue. (Harry C. Mann, photographer.)

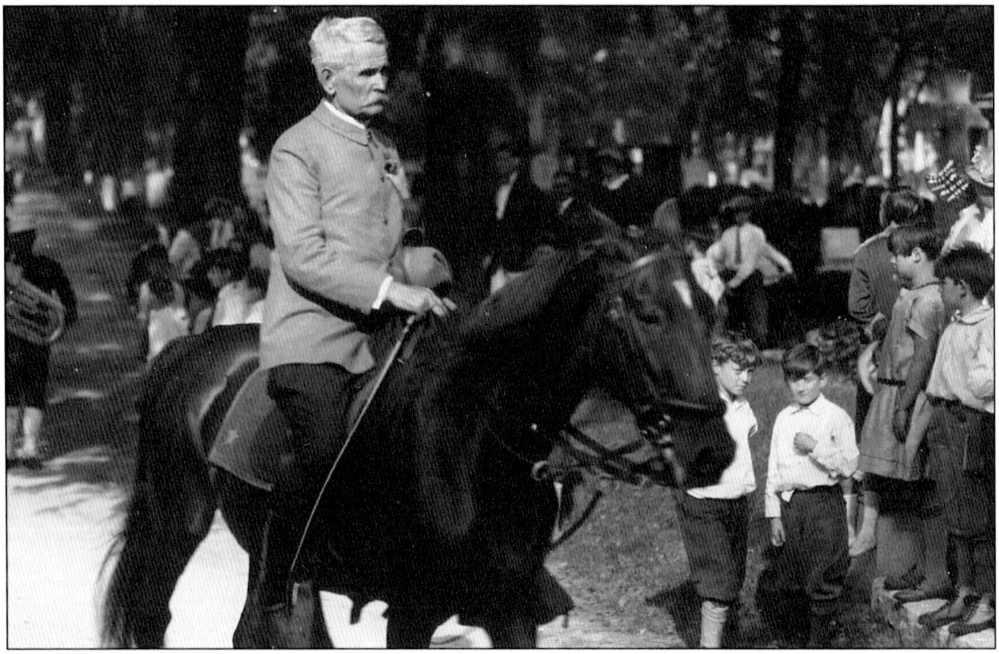

A Confederate veteran, identified as Sergeant James "Cocky" Tatem, rides through Elmwood Cemetery during Memorial Day ceremonies held in 1929. Tatem was a mainstay of many such Memorial Day parades through the cemetery. Tatem, cock-eyed, was never a good shot during his Civil War days. Following the bead on the enemy with one eye, he often fired in the direction of the other eye, missing his target by a mile. It is believed that Tatem actually expired in the cemetery during one of his Memorial Day rides. After not being noticed for awhile, one of the celebrants went to locate Tatem only to find him leaning against one of the headstones where he had quietly passed away. (Charles S. Borjes, photographer.)

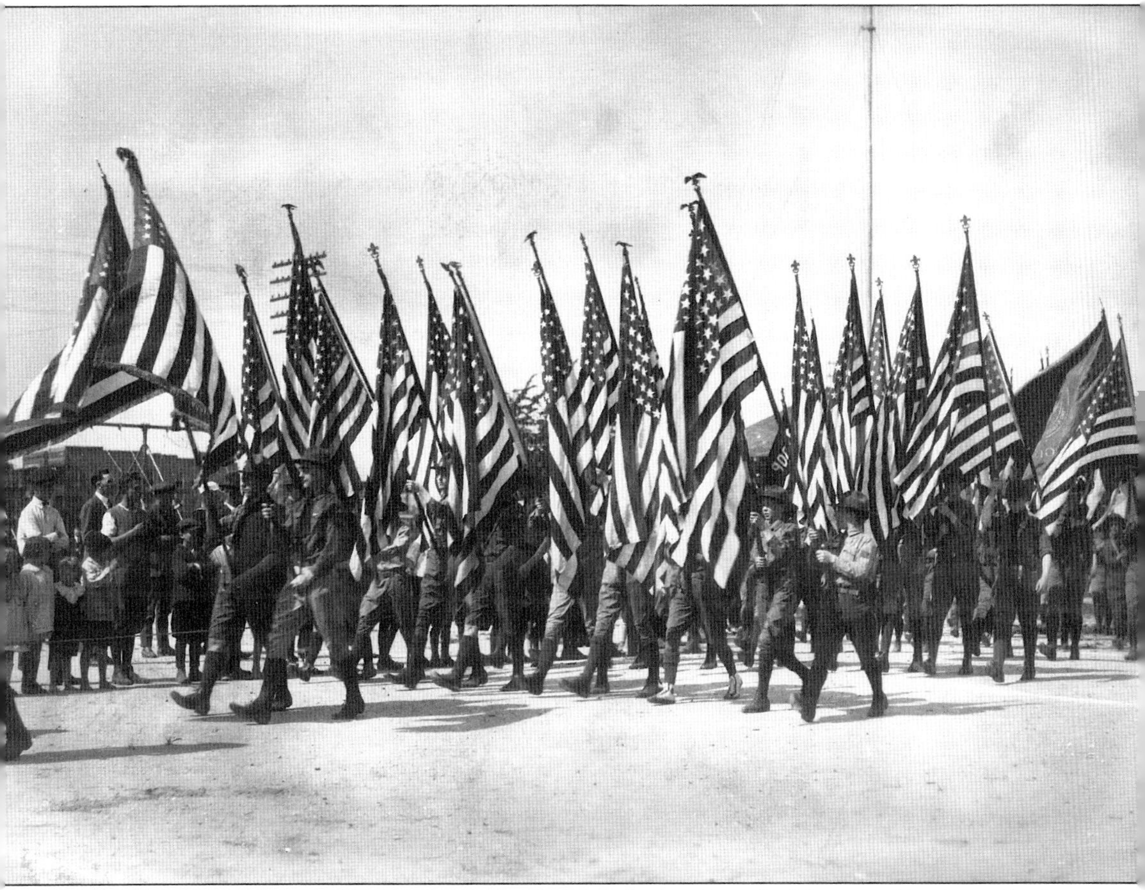

A parade of Boy Scouts held on May 23, 1923, brought scouts from the Hampton Roads southside together in Norfolk. The scouts would play an important role in ceremonies held a few months later on August 28 to dedicate the Westover Oak as a living memorial to the Norfolk boys who died in service during WW I. The program was opened that day by Colonel Clifford D. Davidson, national encampment chairman of the Veterans of Foreign Wars (VFW), who said that there were solemn sides to the lives of all citizens and remembering those who paid the ultimate price in war was one of them. While men of the 80th, or "Virginia's Own," Division of the American Expeditionary Forces stood at attention, Boy Scouts Templar Licklider and Minetree Payne unveiled the bronze tablet bearing the inscription of dedication and telling its purpose. As the flag was lifted from the tablet, the Boy Scouts snapped to attention alongside members of the 80th. Captain Robert Woodside of Pittsburgh, former head of the national VFW, in his reminiscences of the war that day, told the story of a soldier from the South who served and died under his command on July 22, 1918. As he lay dying, the young man clasped Woodside's hand and said, "I have fought my last fight, Captain. I wish I could go through with it, but its over now." As the soldier breathed his last, he smiled with a contentment that transcended his agony. Woodside observed that, "You can kill a Southerner or a Virginian, but you can't conquer him." (Charles S. Borjes, photographer.)

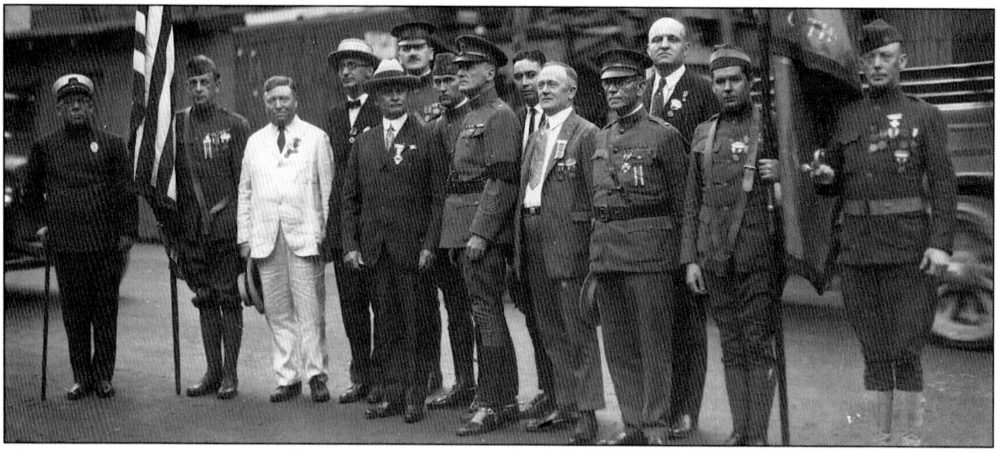

Veterans gathered in Norfolk for the 24th annual encampment of the VFW, the fourth annual reunion of the 80th, or "Virginia's Own," Division, and affiliated organizations from August 28-31, 1923. This photograph, taken behind the Norfolk Armory on August 31, shows a group of new VFW national officers. Sergeant Steffens, the national color bearer, is second from the left. The gentleman standing in the front row, fourth from the left, is General Lloyd M. Brett, commander-in-chief of the national VFW. Dan B. Shertle, junior vice commander, is sixth from the left in the first row, and Lieutenant Colonel Samuel J. Smith (retired), national VFW chaplain, is standing between Shertle and Ernest J. Boughey, the color bearer on the right. Standing directly behind Smith and Boughey is Captain F.A. Tabor, surgeon general. (Charles S. Borjes, photographer.)

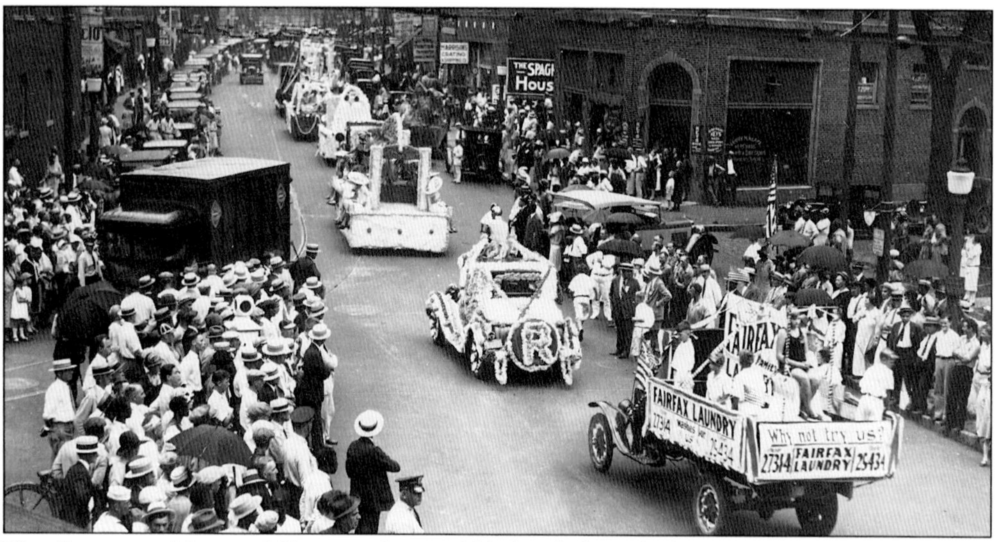

The floats in a Memorial Day parade, c. 1930, headed north down Bank Street as admiring crowds gathered to catch a glimpse of friends and neighbors and remember those who fought in America's wars. The cross-street in the foreground is Market Street. The Pender Building anchored the northeast corner of the intersection of Bank and Market. The building was named for David Pender of the David Pender Grocery Company, and housed the company's offices. Pender opened his first grocery store on the southwest corner of Market Street and Monticello Avenue in 1905, but by 1919, this store could not keep up with customer demand and Pender opened his first branch. By January 1, 1926, Pender had 244 stores in his grocery chain. (Photographer unknown.)

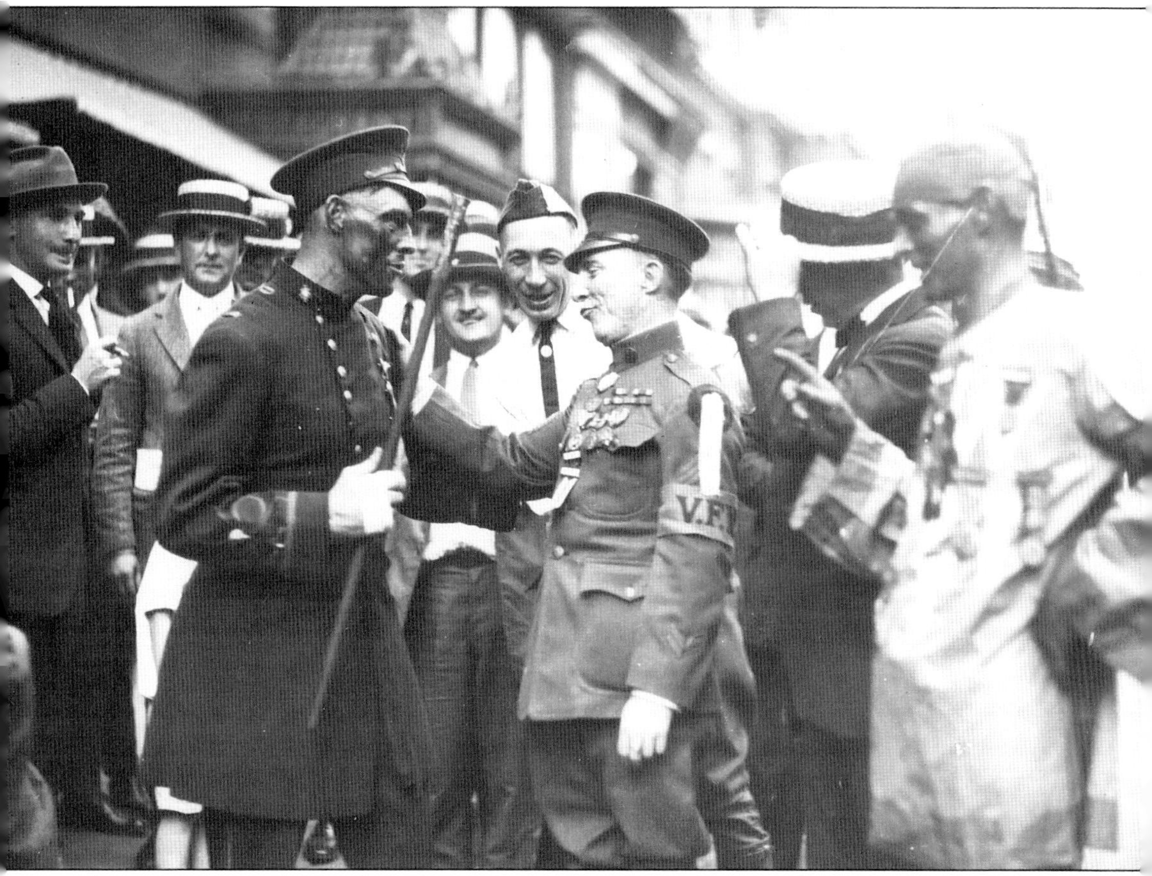

The Cooties, a rollicking branch organization of the VFW, cast dignity to the winds and disported themselves around downtown Norfolk on August 29, 1923, during the VFW national convention. Thousands came out at nine o'clock in the evening to participate in the widely-heralded Cootie snake dance on City Hall Avenue. With the burst of a red flare, the Cooties arrived on cue to get the dance going. Down City Hall Avenue they marched, several hundred of them strong, lady Cooties as well as men, in a sinuous, cheering, shouting, singing line. Bands played and aerial bombs burst with staccato cracks high overhead. The fun being had in the streets of downtown included some interesting stunts. As soon as the leader of the Cooties darted into the Monticello Arcade, his cohorts followed, and the snake dance was over, but the evening's mischief was just beginning. One particularly well-remembered event was the initiation that involved placing members of the group, blindfolded and gloved, on a trapeze, and permitting them to box until one had been knocked from their swinging perch. The match ended without a decision, in this case, because the trapeze ropes broke and pitched both boxers headlong into a blanket being held underneath. The photograph shown here was taken during one of the Cooties raucous afternoon high jinks. (Charles S. Borjes, photographer.)

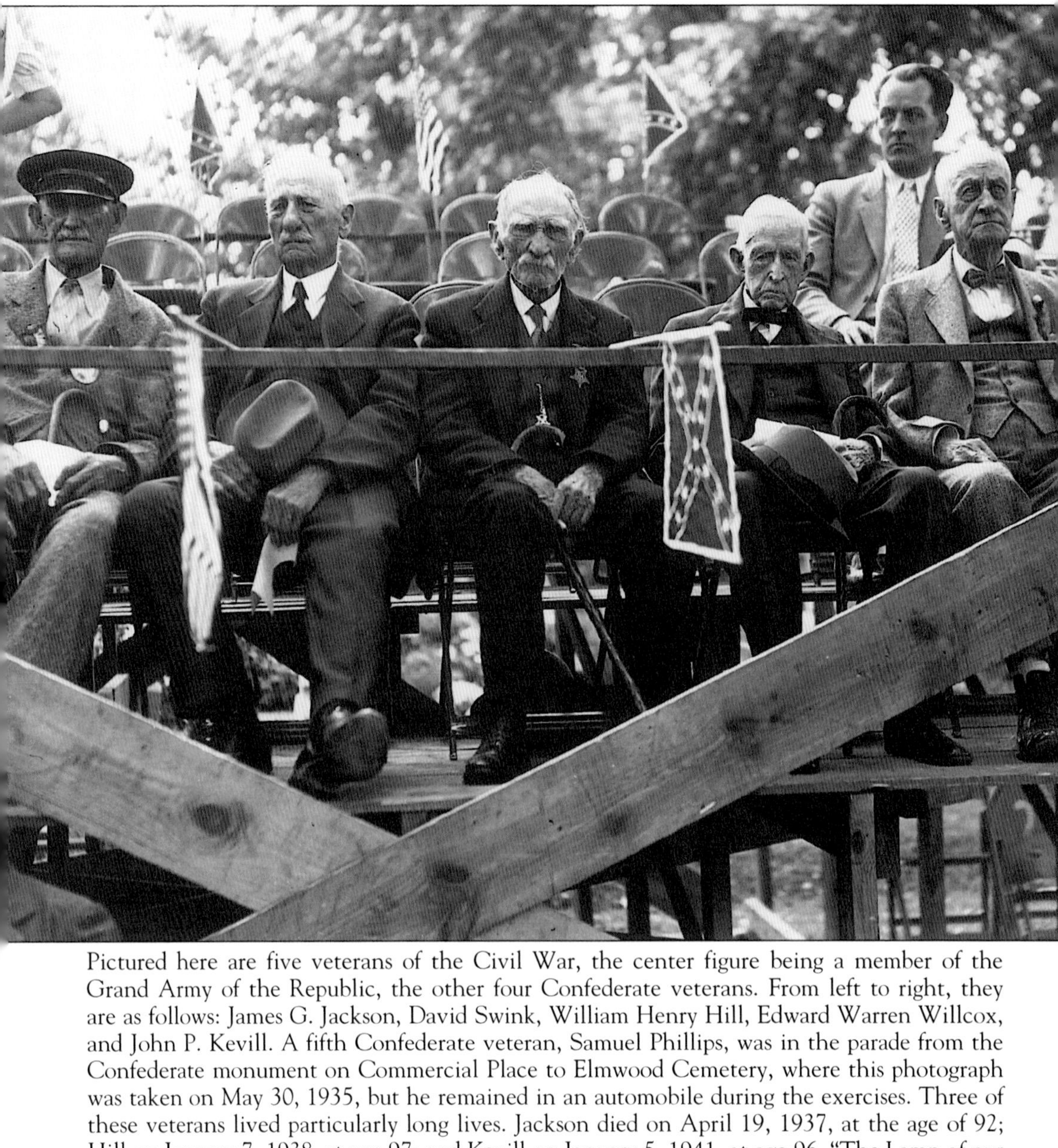

Pictured here are five veterans of the Civil War, the center figure being a member of the Grand Army of the Republic, the other four Confederate veterans. From left to right, they are as follows: James G. Jackson, David Swink, William Henry Hill, Edward Warren Willcox, and John P. Kevill. A fifth Confederate veteran, Samuel Phillips, was in the parade from the Confederate monument on Commercial Place to Elmwood Cemetery, where this photograph was taken on May 30, 1935, but he remained in an automobile during the exercises. Three of these veterans lived particularly long lives. Jackson died on April 19, 1937, at the age of 92; Hill on January 7, 1938, at age 97; and Kevill on January 5, 1941, at age 96. "The Lamp of our Youth will be utterly out, but we shall / subsist on the smell of it; / And whatever we do, we shall fold our hands and suck our / gums and think well of it. / Yes, we shall be perfectly pleased with our work, and that / is the Perfectest Hell of it!" [From *The Old Men*, 1902; Rudyard Kipling, English poet (1865-1936).] (Charles S. Borjes, photographer.)

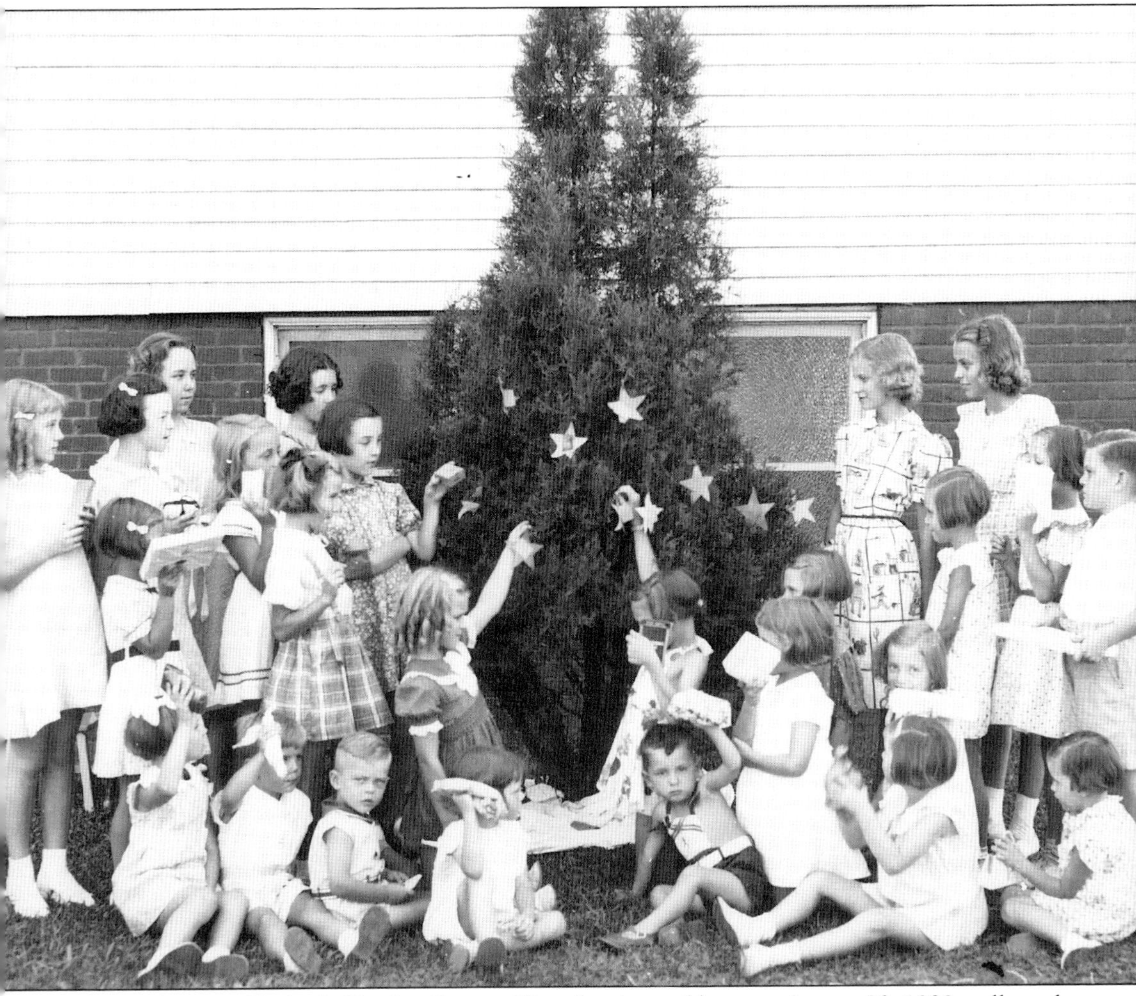

The Sunbeams of Raleigh Heights Baptist Church, pictured here on August 23, 1938, collected gifts for Chinese children. Efforts by American school-aged children to appease the suffering of children in China were not isolated to Norfolk. With newspaper headlines across the United States decrying Japanese atrocities in what the Western world dubbed the Sino-Japanese War, children were aware of the needs of their Chinese counterparts. Though Japan had invaded the Chinese province of Manchuria as early as September 1931, the conflict between the two Eastern nations which broke out in July 1937 became the start of what the Chinese referred to as *k'ang-Jih chan-cheng*, or the "War of Resistance Against Japan." The *k'ang-Jih chan-cheng* lasted until Japan was defeated by Allied forces in 1945. At the time this picture was taken, the Sunbeams were probably most conscious of Japanese-inflicted horrors in the incident known to the world as the "the rape of Nanking," which started on December 13, 1937, and continued through early January 1938. (H.D. Vollmer, photographer.)

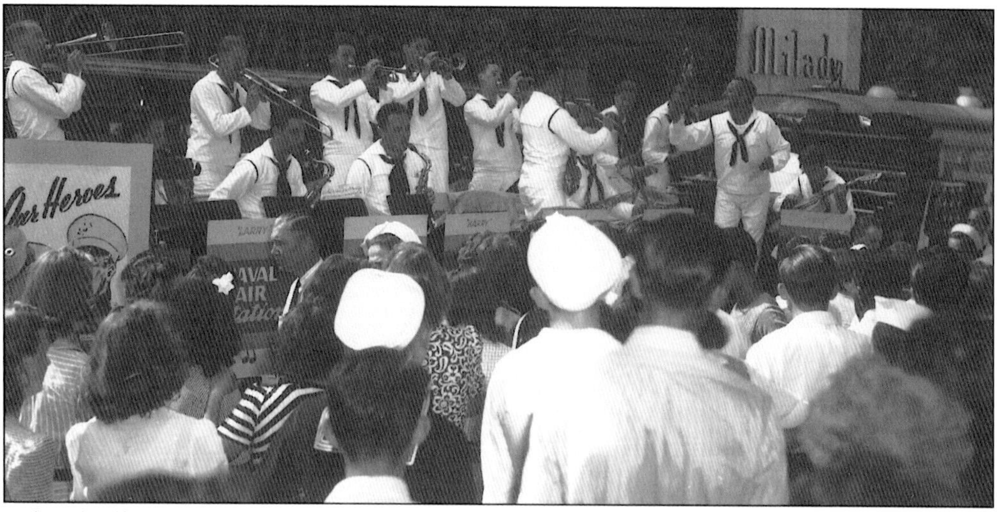

A bond rally was held on Granby Street, July 17, 1942. Members of the Naval Air Station Norfolk swing band entertained the crowd which thronged to listen, despite the intense temperatures of mid-July. (Charles S. Borjes, photographer.)

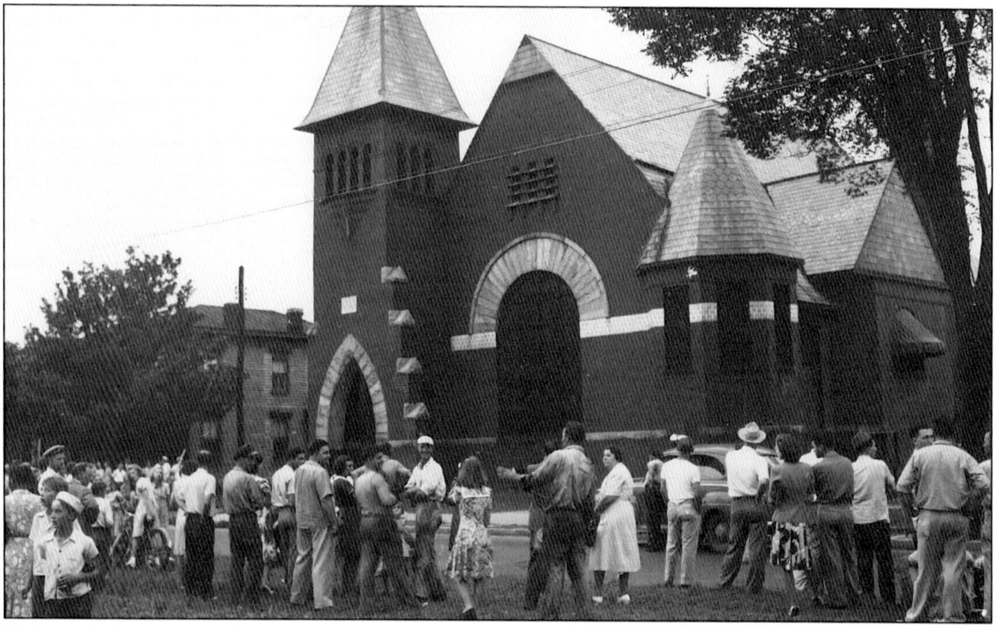

Tales of German and Japanese spies and saboteurs in Norfolk and the vicinity were not uncommon during WW II. Most spy chases, clouded in rumor and innuendo, were unfounded, but some got out of hand and crowds turned more menacing—and dangerous—than anyone cares to remember. One such incident occurred on August 7, 1942, at LeKies Memorial Methodist Church in Norfolk's Atlantic City section. A mob, armed with pistols, rifles, and even a submachine gun, went on a frantic hunt for a German saboteur reported in the area. Though the report proved untrue, the crowd, which thought they had cornered a spy, acted out their pursuit of the enemy in New England witch-hunt fashion. LeKies Memorial Methodist Church was located at the corner of Camp Avenue and Fort Street. Reverend Laxton C. Smart was pastor at the time this picture was taken. (Charles S. Borjes, photographer.)

Watching for enemy aircraft from a U.S. Army Air Corps aircraft warning observation tower at Ocean View was serious business. Residents of Virginia's coastal areas were given constant warnings of the threat of German U-boats and aircraft. The ladies and gentleman in this picture, taken September 4, 1942, kept a vigil on the tower during their shift, which typically lasted two hours at a time, scanning the skies for an enemy air raid. (Charles S. Borjes, photographer.)

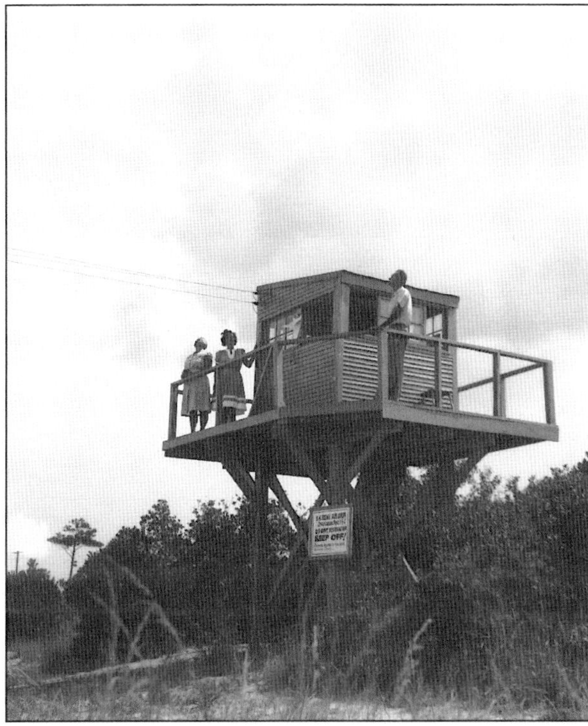

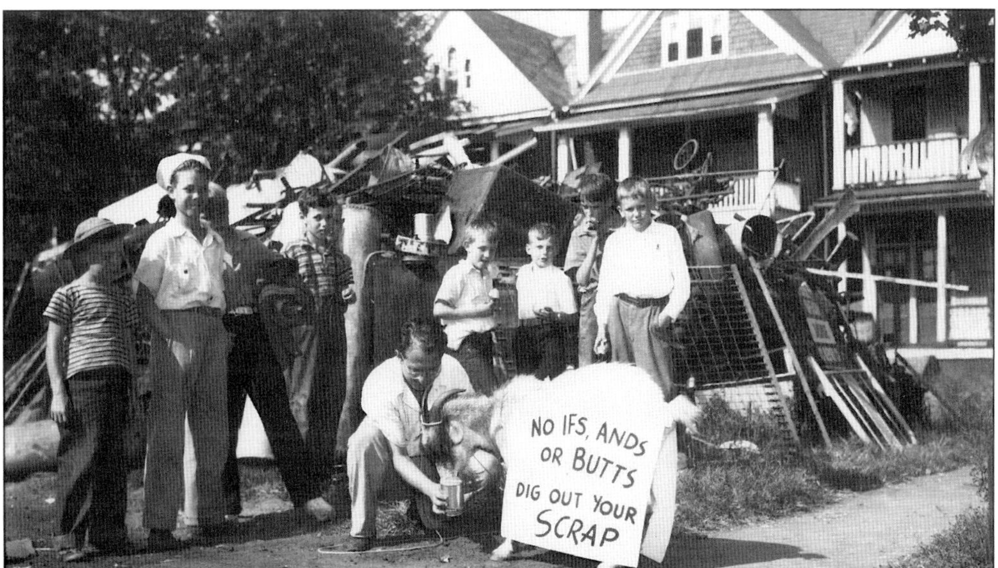

Billy, the goat, took his last sniff of a tin can before going vegetarian for the duration of WW II. Shown with Billy in this picture, taken September 23, 1942, is Leon Odessky (holding the cup), his owner, on Duke Street in front of a scrap metal pile. Tin cans were actually not being collected in the scrap drive being advertised by Billy and sponsored by the Norfolk newspapers. Metal scrap drives were conducted in aggressive phases in Norfolk and its surrounding cities and counties throughout the war. As soon as one drive ended, another began. Area Boy Scouts had just completed a scrap drive in which they exceeded 350,000 pounds of metal materials collected and hauled away by the United States Army. (Charles S. Borjes, photographer.)

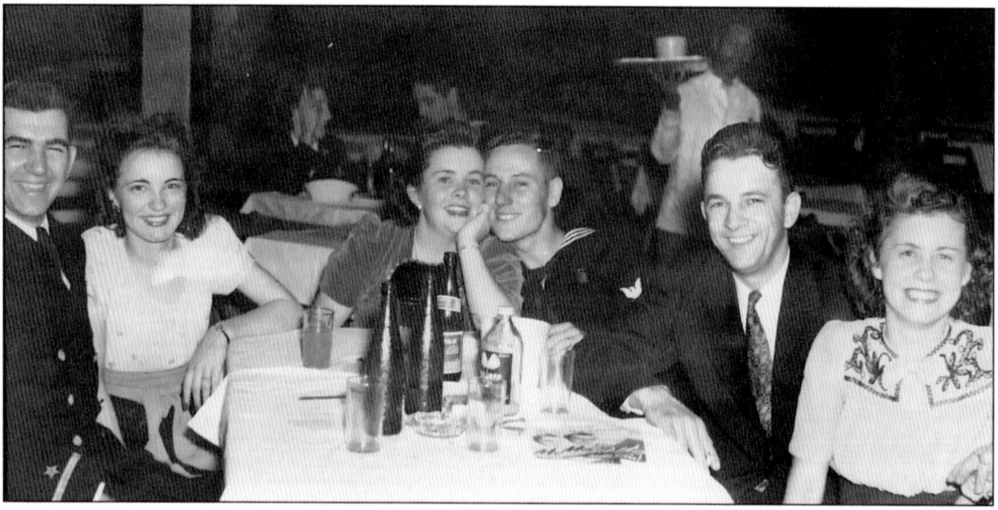

One of the most popular dance halls for servicemen opened at 2000 Monticello Avenue in Norfolk in 1942. The Palomar Club, shown here in 1944, was managed by Walter Buster. The three couples in this picture, from left to right are: Ensign Falvey McKee Sandidge, a naval aviator, and his wife, Mildred; Seaman James A. Claverie and his wife, Margaret; and Herbert Maitland Fentress and his wife, Helen. The ladies are sisters. (Photographer unknown.)

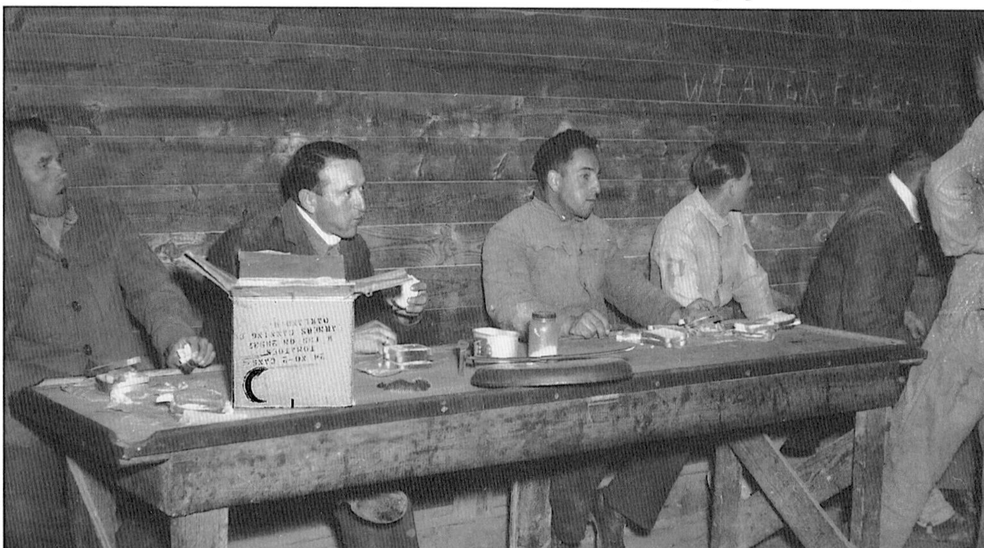

German prisoners-of-war, as shown in this April 6, 1944 photograph by H.D. Vollmer, were put to work at the Weaver Fertilizer Company plant as part of the War Manpower Commission's effort to use them to supplant serious labor shortages in ten fertilizer plants around the area. The establishment of a holding facility for several hundred German POWs at Camp Ashby, officially called Prisoner of War Side-Camp 1326, Service Unit, in Virginia Beach during the spring of 1944, enabled the detainees to keep Weaver's production at peak levels through the end of the war. The camp, commanded by U.S. Army Captain John Polhemus, was in the woods at Thalia, close to Virginia Beach Boulevard. It is interesting to note that the Germans detained at Camp Ashby had been members of Field Marshal Irwin Rommel's North Afrika Corps and included air and ground forces as well as enlisted, non-commissioned, and commissioned officers of Rommel's elite unit.

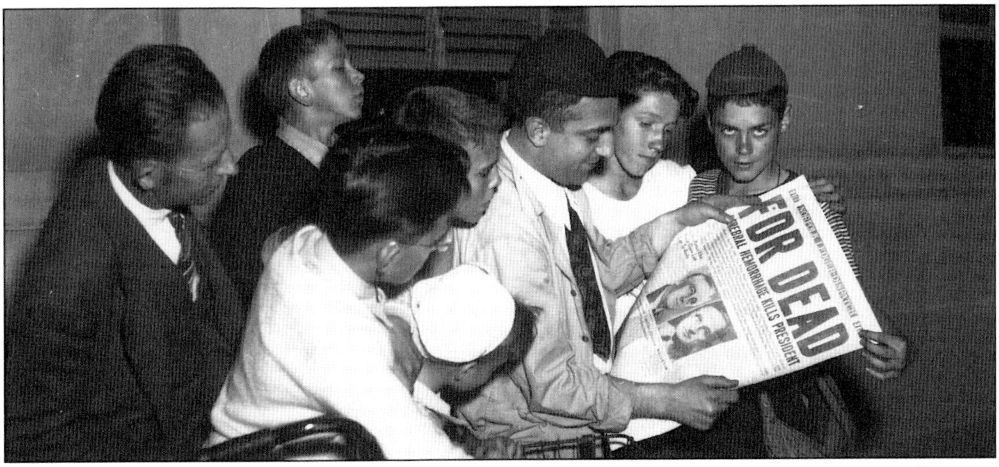

The sudden death of President Franklin Delano Roosevelt on April 12, 1945, at Warm Springs, Georgia, shocked the nation. Paperboys for the *Ledger-Dispatch* could not distribute the day's newspaper announcing Roosevelt's death fast enough for patrons, as seen in this picture taken that afternoon. Roosevelt's last words were reportedly to his Navy physician, Commander Harold Bruenn: "I have a terrific headache." The President, 63 years old, collapsed a few moments later as the result of a massive cerebral hemorrhage. Roosevelt was in the third month of his fourth term as president and had traveled to Warm Springs to relax. Vice President Harry S. Truman took the oath of office as the nation's 33rd chief executive the evening of April 12. (Charles S. Borjes, photographer.)

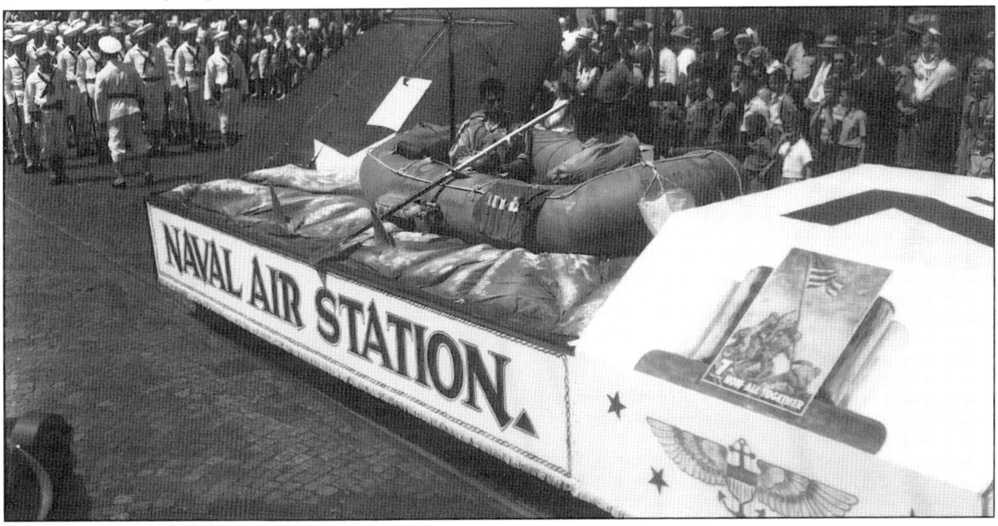

With the ruffle of drums and the martial of music coming from at least half a dozen brass bands, one of the largest parades in Norfolk history started up West Main to Granby Street the morning of May 30, 1945, in celebration of Memorial Day. The two naval aviators aboard the Naval Air Station Norfolk float, shown here, participated with 4,000 persons either marching or riding in the parade. In addition to the float, the Navy contributed three bands, a company from the Naval Training Station, units of the Shore Patrol, WAVES (Women Accepted for Voluntary Emergency Service), Marine Corps Women's Reserve, and motorized equipment. As with all the city's Memorial Day parades in days gone by, participants snaked their way down Granby Street, turning on Princess Anne Road past the Twelfth Street Armory to Elmwood Cemetery. (Charles S. Borjes, photographer.)

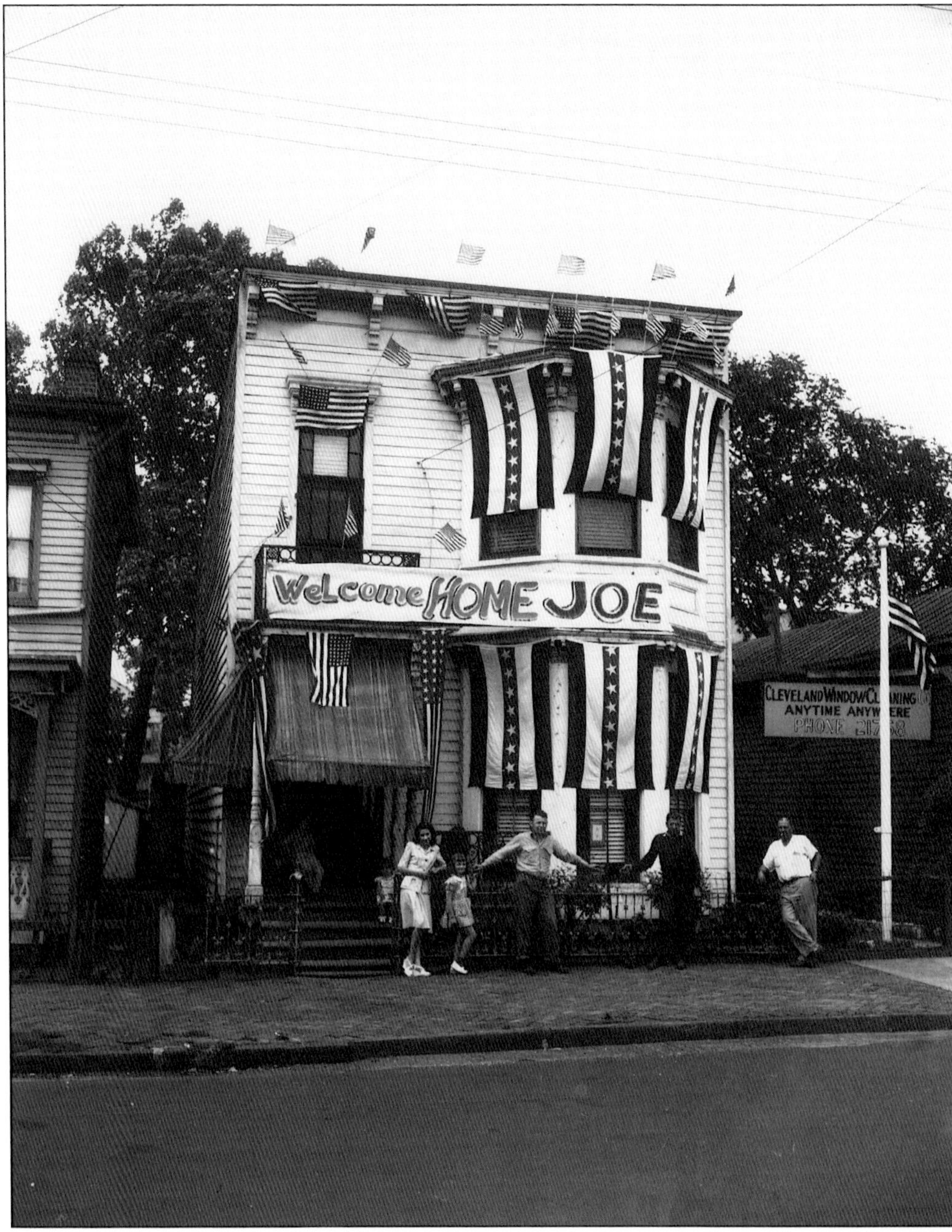

The Bipere family of 1504 Brambleton Avenue waited to welcome home their soldier, Staff Sergeant Joseph Bipere, on May 19, 1945. The Biperes, from left to right, are as follows: Camilla Bipere Daley, Dora Lee Murden (Pat's granddaughter), C.C. Murden (Pat's son-in-law), Dominick Bipere, and Pat Bipere. Staff Sergeant Bipere had joined the United States Army in 1940 at the age of 23. During his three years in the Pacific theater of the war, Bipere saw service in Australia, New Guinea, the East Indies, and the Philippines. Pat, Dominick, and Johnny Bipere, Joseph's brothers, operated the Cleveland Window Cleaning Company, located next door to the house. Before entering the Army, Joseph was also a partner in the business. (Charles S. Borjes, photographer.)

Three

Summer Solstice and Dog Days

"There came a Day at Summer's full,
Entirely for me—
I thought that such were for the Saints,
Where Resurrections—be—

The Sun, as common, went abroad,
The flowers, accustomed, blew,
As if no soul the solstice passed
That maketh all things new—"

—From *There Came a Day at Summer's Full*, 1890
Emily Dickinson, American poet (1830–1886)

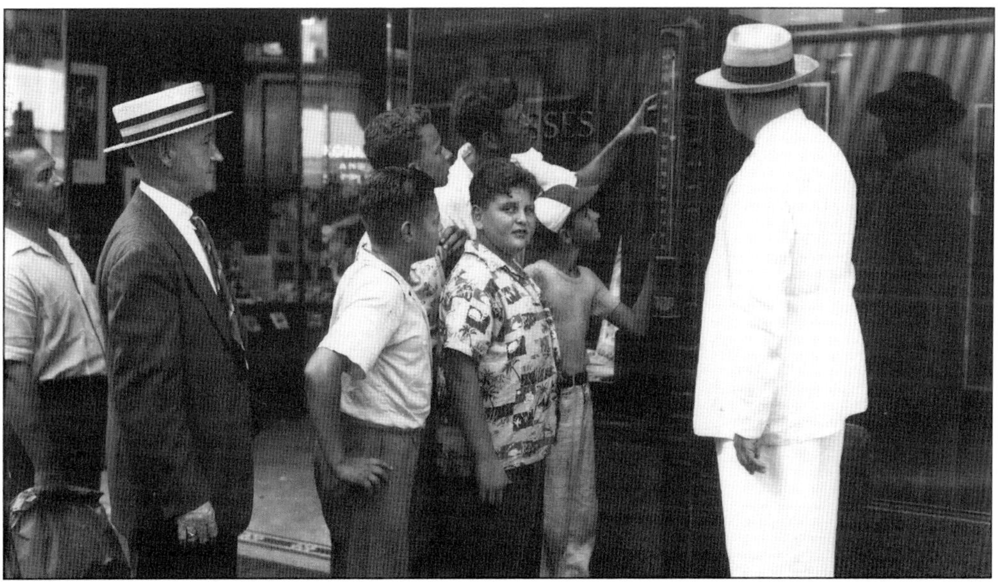

It might have been officially a mere 100 degrees, but on July 26, 1940, on Granby Street, it was 103 degrees. That figure was registered on the thermometer outside the G.L. Hall Optical Company between 12:20 p.m. and 2 p.m. When the picture was taken, it was 3:30 p.m. and 102.5 degrees in the shade. Norfolk and the vicinity were experiencing a six-day intensive heat wave which cast a wilting pall over the entire population, but particularly those working in the downtown Norfolk area. R.L. Johnson, clerk of the New Virginia Hotel on Plume Street, placed a high-priced thermometer on the sidewalk in front of the hotel at 1 p.m., and it soon registered 122 degrees. (Charles S. Borjes, photographer.)

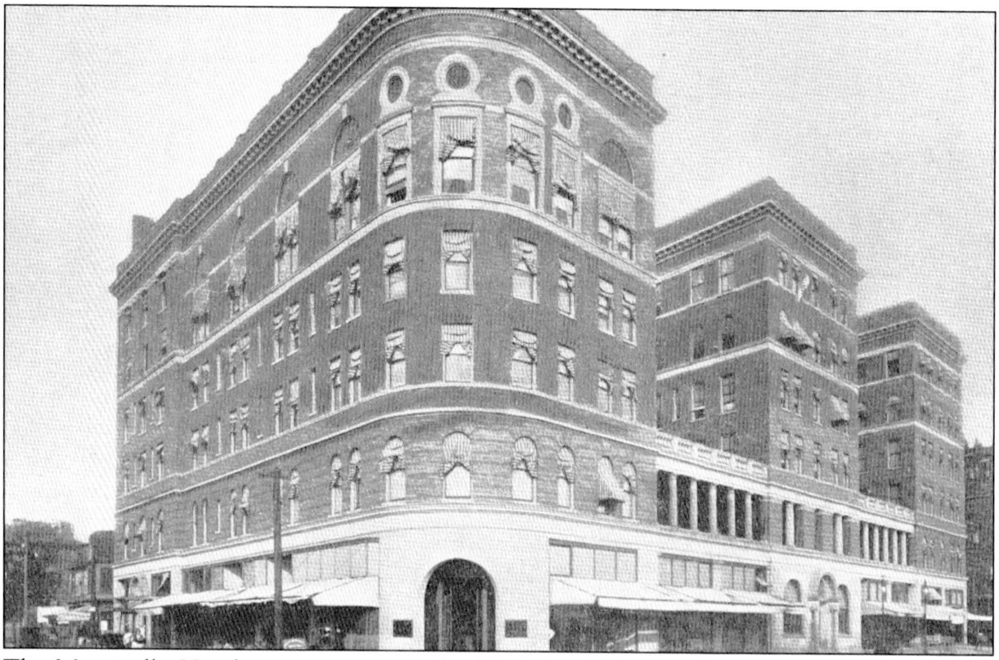

The Monticello Hotel, once occupying the block between the corner of Granby Street and Monticello Avenue facing City Hall Avenue, opened September 27, 1898. This picture was taken by an unknown photographer during a hot summer day in 1899. Patrons of the hotel had their awnings out and windows open seeking relief from the intense heat. Note that north of the hotel stood homes and stately, tree-lined streets. When the hotel came, it took virtually no time at all for these homes to be replaced by storefronts. The Monticello Hotel was sold in 1970. When the federal government was looking for property to locate a building in Norfolk, city officials offered the site of the hotel. On January 26, 1976, the Loiseaux Company, a professional demolition outfit, imploded the grand old landmark.

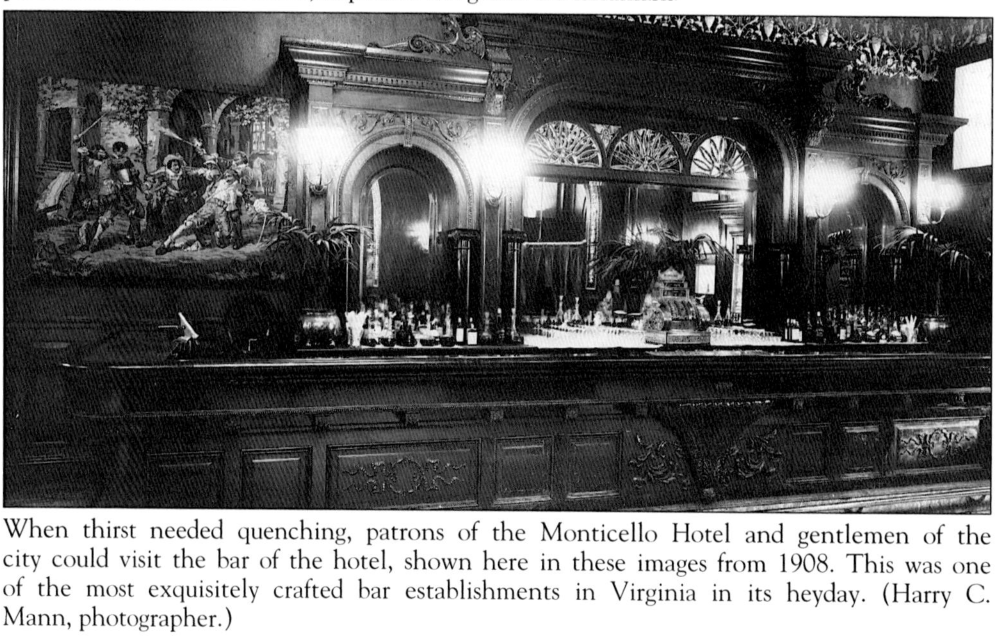

When thirst needed quenching, patrons of the Monticello Hotel and gentlemen of the city could visit the bar of the hotel, shown here in these images from 1908. This was one of the most exquisitely crafted bar establishments in Virginia in its heyday. (Harry C. Mann, photographer.)

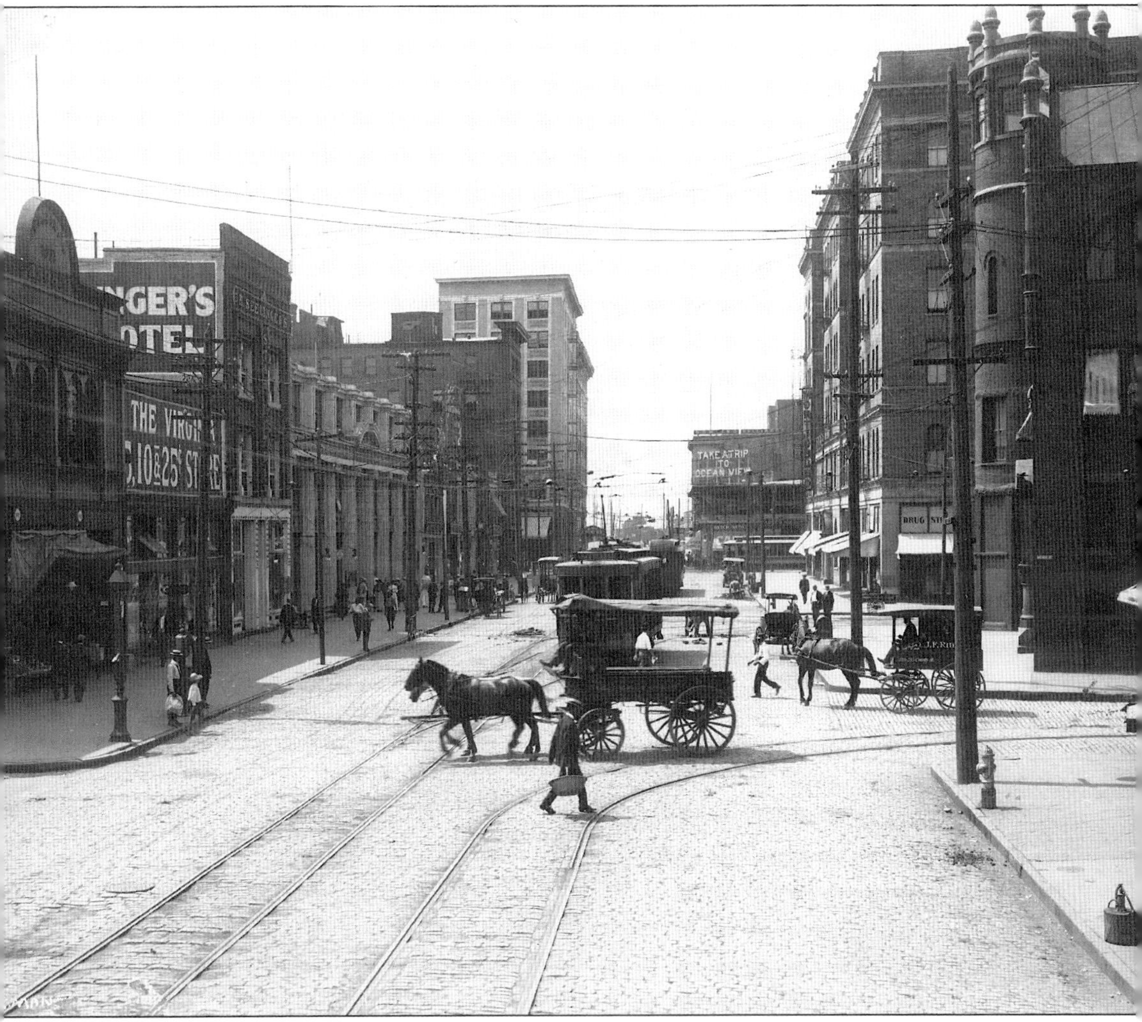

Taken from the intersection of Atlantic Street and City Hall Avenue, looking west, during the peak of summer 1907, this Harry C. Mann photograph is bustling with activity and important buildings. Starting with the right foreground is the foot of old Brewer Street. The Armory sits on the corner, and beyond the Armory is the Monticello Hotel. Granby Street runs between the hotel and the café building with the sign that reads, "Take A Trip To Ocean View." The café structure would be replaced in 1912 with the old Royster Building. Along the left side of City Hall Avenue are equally interesting buildings. In the foreground sits the Terminal Arcade, built in 1901. Next to the Terminal Arcade was the Virginia 5, 10 & 25¢ Store, Henry Seelinger's Star Hotel, opened at 39-41 City Hall Avenue in 1906, and the Monticello Arcade. Next to the Monticello Arcade is Michael McKevitt's Saloon, a fine sample room and cigar store opened in 1903 at 23 City Hall Avenue and strategically located across from the Monticello Hotel. The electric cars coming down the avenue were part of the Norfolk Southern Railway's electric division. The cars ran to Virginia Beach and Cape Henry as well as Ocean View.

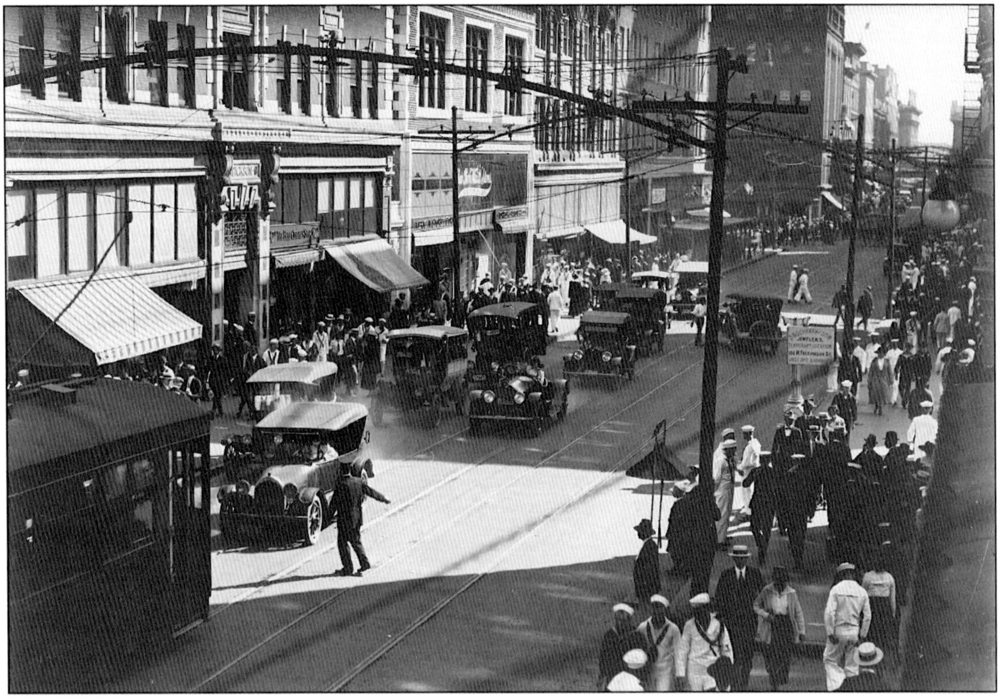

This image was taken by Harry C. Mann looking south on Granby Street from Tazewell Street in 1918. With the United States embroiled in WW I, the number of U.S. Navy sailors in the city peaked. Sailors make up the majority of people on the street in Mann's picture. It is interesting to note that 8 of the 11 automobiles in the picture have signs posted on their windshields indicating their point of destination. These vehicles were popularly called "jitney buses" because it cost 5¢, or a "jitney," for a ride in one of them. The Dickson Building is in the left foreground.

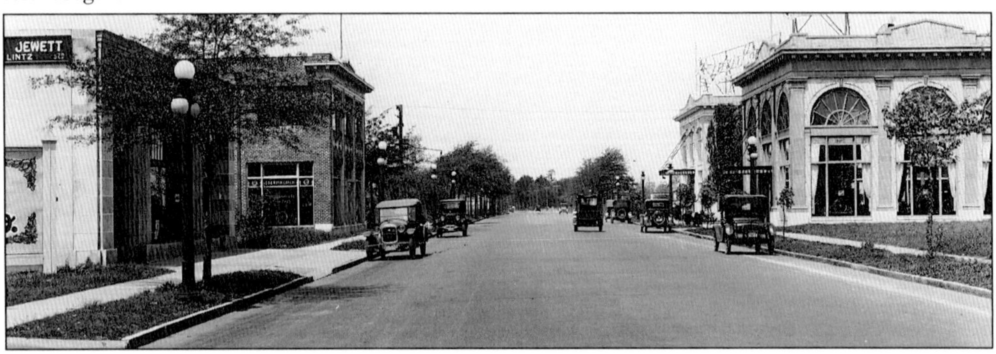

Norfolk's Twenty-first Street was known as "Auto Row" at the time this picture was taken by Acme Photo Company founder Henry W. Gillen in 1925. The Dixie Motor Car Company is the second building on the left, located closest to the street's intersection with Manteo Street. Overland Buick occupies the two large buildings on the right. The view in this photograph is looking toward Colley Avenue down Twenty-first Street. As for Gillen, he was an important figure in the commercial photography business and had a national reputation as one of the pioneer motion picture camera operators. He had also worked for the largest pictorial news syndicates in New York and Chicago, before coming to Norfolk in 1912 as the first cameraman for the Pathe Company, and later Paramount and Artcraft and other studios around the city. Gillen started his own studio, Acme, in 1918.

Edwin Way Teale (1899-1980), the great American naturalist and author, wrote in his piece *A Walk through the Year*, that "Before dawn this morning, in a flick of time, the summer solstice came and slipped by. Season slid into season; spring ended and summer began. Now, in the warm and humid night, the lowland fields spread across us ablaze with tiny aerial lights. We are wandering in the midst of one of the great firefly displays of the year." He refers, of course, to the day the sun is at its highest path through the sky and the day is longest. Because the day, June 21, is so long, the sun does not exactly rise in the east, but rises north of east and sets north of west, giving the impression that the sun has hardly changed position from the time it rises to the time it sets. Summer solstice marks the longest day and shortest night of the year. The day has been marked by mankind since Cro-Magnon man, or modern man, appeared about 35,000 B.C. Conscious of time and celestial phenomenon, Cro-Magnon man of the Old Stone Age was known to have scratched tally marks in ivory or bone to track the moon and the passage of seasons. By the time his successors came along during the New Stone Age (6,000 to 8,000 years ago), seasonal celebrations were readily apparent in mankind's community life, including the inception of Midsummer's Eve, now June 20 of the year. Midsummer's Eve was celebrated by the use of fire rituals and bonfires, begun out of fear that the sun, which burned so brightly for so long, would burn out, never to return again. The celebration of Midsummer's Eve spread to Europe and the Christian calendar as the feast of St. John the Baptist, the saint born six months prior to the announcement of the birth of Jesus Christ. Midsummer's Eve and summer solstice became symbolic as a time of rejuvenation and healing in commemoration of the work of John the Baptist. William Shakespeare took the celebration a bit further and spun one of his happiest comedies, *A Midsummer Night's Dream* (1594), a play full of absurd dreams and midsummer madness brought upon lovers destined for marriage. Europeans believed the midsummer bride bodied forth the fertility and sexuality of people, again, a link to rejuvenation and new life. June is the most popular month, even today, for weddings.

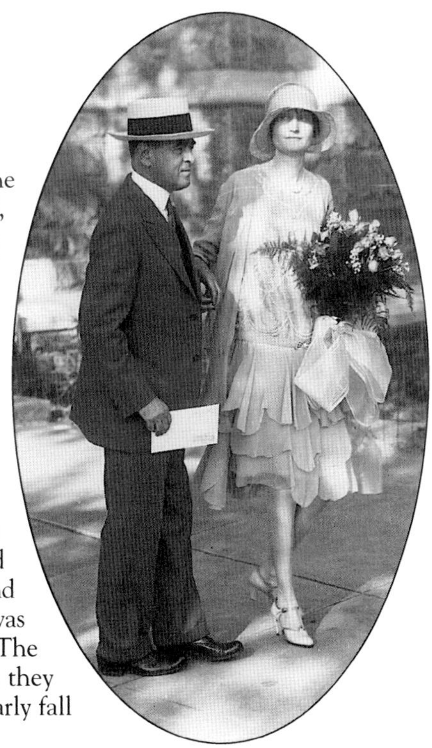

The marriage of Selena Grace Jones, daughter of the late Mr. and Mrs. Norvell Paul Jones, of Smithfield, Virginia, to William Boswell Selden Grandy, son of the late Mr. and Mrs. Cyrus Wiley Grandy, of Norfolk, took place the afternoon of June 29, 1929, in the Selden Chapel of Christ and St. Luke's Church. The church's rector, the Very Reverend H. Dobson-Peacock, performed the ceremony. The chapel was decorated with palms and the altar adorned with adritum lilies. The bride was given in marriage by her brother, James J. Jones. She wore an ensemble suit of beige chiffon with a blouse of Breton lace. Her hat was natural-colored straw, trimmed with inserts of lace, and her flowers were a shower of roses and lilies-of-the-valley. Her only jewelry was a diamond bracelet, a gift of the bridegroom. Though the bride was unattended, Selden Grandy was his uncle's best man. The newlyweds left the ceremony for New York, where they sailed on the SS *Homeric* to spend the summer and early fall in Europe. (Charles S. Borjes, photographer.)

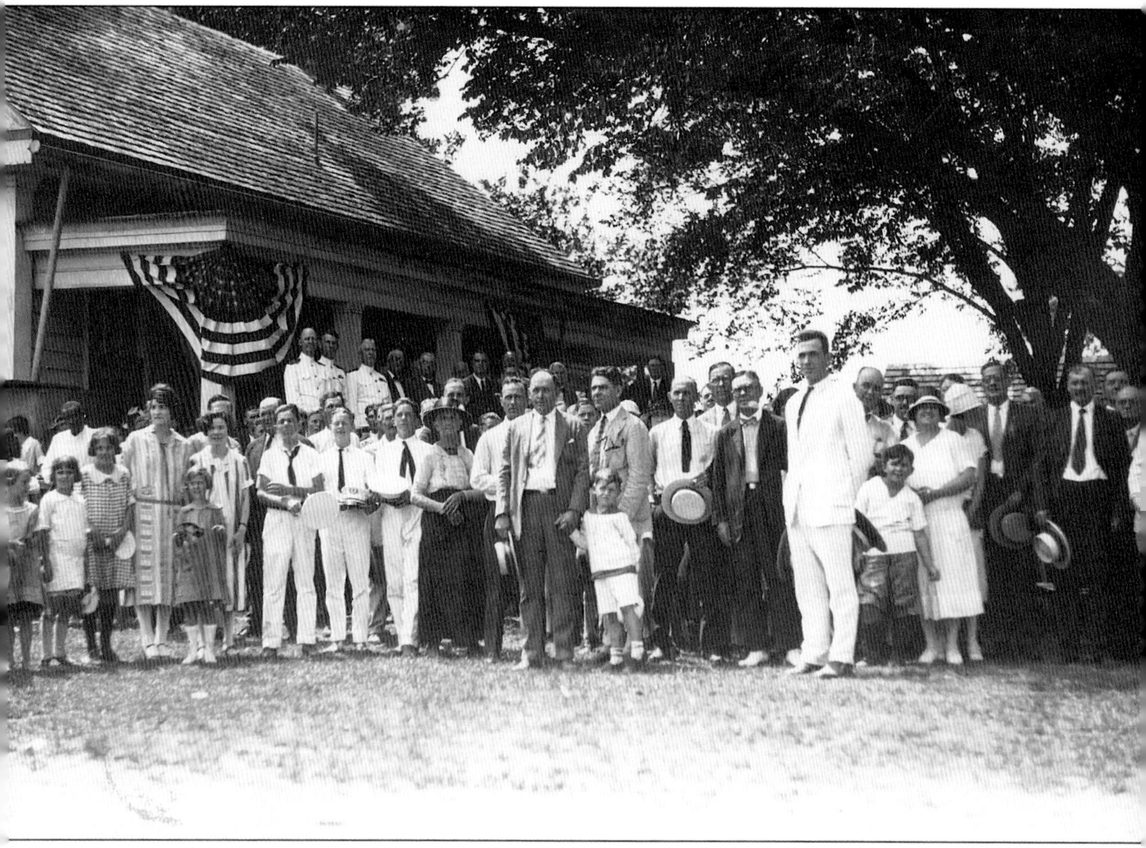

Five thousand Virginians and North Carolinians celebrated the formal opening of the George Washington Highway at Wallaceton, 4 miles from the North Carolina line, on July 17, 1925. This was the first hard-surfaced road to the North Carolina border through Virginia. As originally constructed, the highway extended along the historic banks of the Dismal Swamp Canal through the swamp for 15 miles to the state border after leaving the village of Deep Creek. Prominent speakers at the festivities were Virginia Governor E. Lee Trinkle, the commonwealth's chief executive from 1922 to 1926; General J.P. Jervey, city manager of Portsmouth; Hugh Johnston, commissioner of Norfolk County who presided over the ceremony; Colonel George C. Cabell; W.A. Hart, North Carolina district road commissioner; H.G. Shirley, chairman of the Virginia State Highway Commission; and R.J. Job, secretary of the Elizabeth City Chamber of Commerce. Among the distinguished visitors on the speakers' platform, erected on the verandah of the historic Wallace plantation, were Senator Harry Flood Byrd, a candidate for governor of Virginia; Rear Admiral Roger Welles and several other high-ranking naval officers; Lieutenant Governor Junius E. West, of Virginia; and I. Walke Truxtun. Governor Trinkle is sixth from the left standing on the verandah in the picture above. (Charles S. Borjes, photographer.)

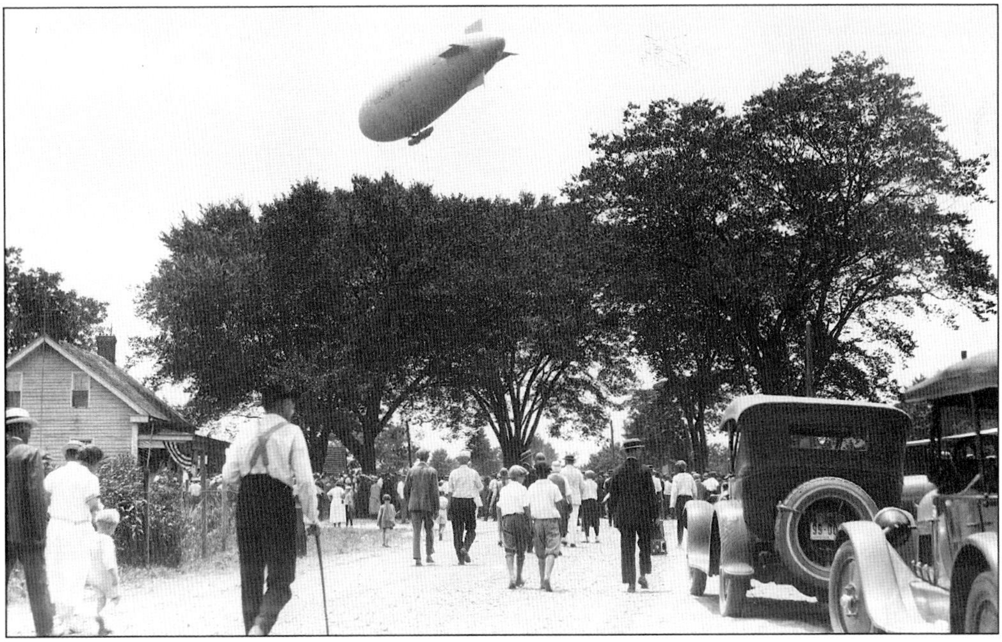

The U.S. Army sent the blimp, *TC-4*, from Langley Field to take part in the George Washington Highway celebration. (Charles S. Borjes, photographer.)

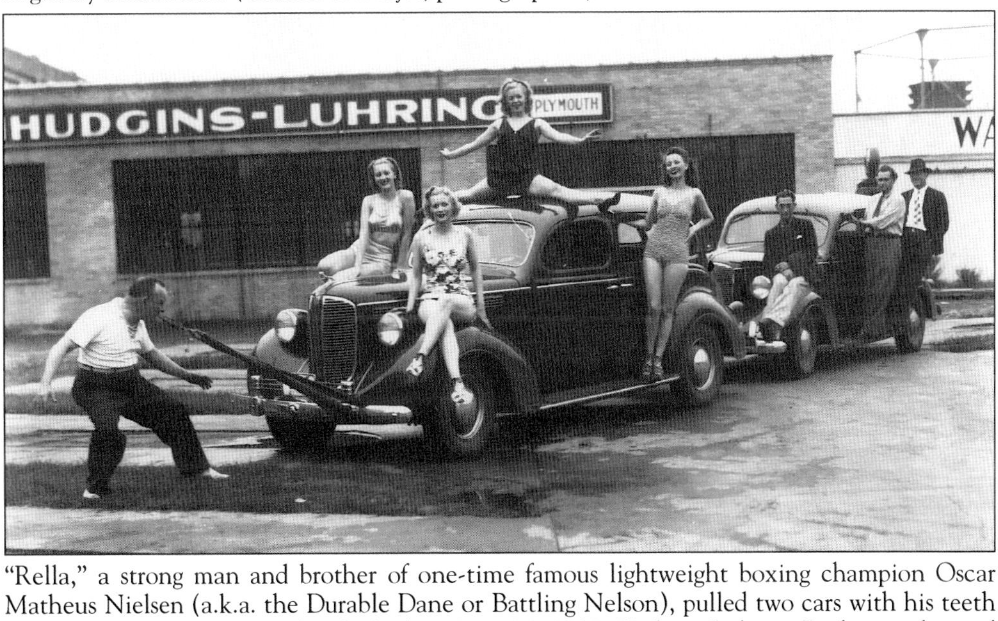

"Rella," a strong man and brother of one-time famous lightweight boxing champion Oscar Matheus Nielsen (a.k.a. the Durable Dane or Battling Nelson), pulled two cars with his teeth at the Hudgins-Luhring Dodge dealership, June 22, 1938. Hudgins-Luhring Dodge was located on the corner of Twenty-first and Manteo Streets in Norfolk. "Rella" had been brought to the city by the management of the Sears store on Freemason Street to advertise the Sears Economy Tractor, which he pulled with his teeth across the stage of the Colonial Theatre four times a day for a week. The Nielsen brothers, both born in Copenhagen, Denmark, were known for their brute strength and scrappy lifestyle. Fight watchers used to swear that Matheus's skull was three times thicker than a normal man's because he had sustained such a beating in the ring during his professional career, which lasted from 1896 to 1923. (H.D. Vollmer, photographer.)

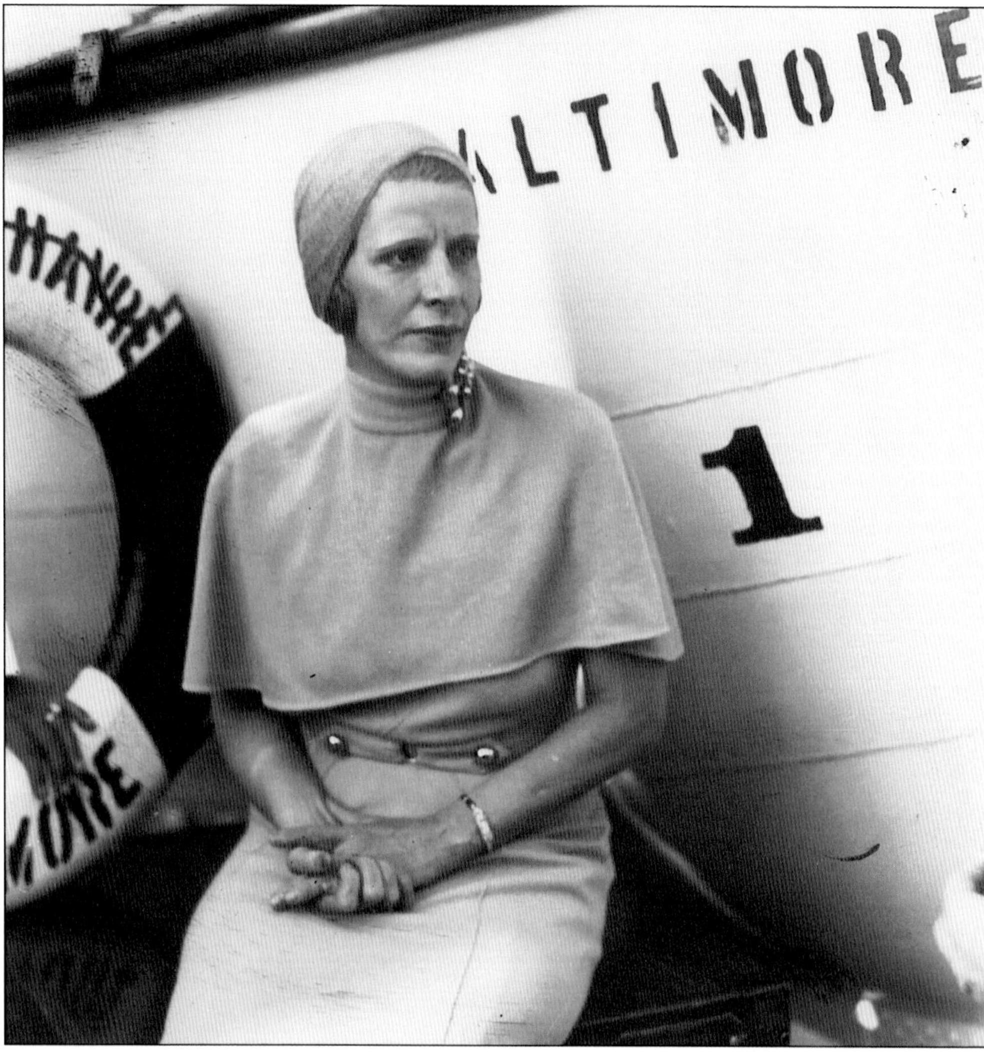

Evangelist Aimee Semple McPherson passed through Norfolk in July 1933 on one of her revival tours. The founder of the Foursquare Gospel, a Pentecostal mission in Los Angeles, in 1922, and the immense circular church, the Angelus Temple, the following year, Sister Aimee was renowned for her magnetic personality and lively revival meetings. Her publicity was positive and her reputation unscathed until her purported kidnapping on May 18, 1926, near Venice Beach, California. The kidnappers, calling themselves "the Avengers," demanded a half-million-dollar ransom, but nothing ever came of leads into the kidnapping and there was no sign of Sister Aimee—until she stumbled out of the desert near Douglas, Arizona, 32 days later. Though she claimed to have been legitimately kidnapped, tortured, drugged, and held against her will, there was no proof nor logical explanation of her disappearance found. The district attorney of Los Angeles, Asa Keys, eventually charged her with perjury, but she was cleared of the charges. A cloud of doubt and scandal followed Sister Aimee as a result of the kidnapping incident, and the American press, which had so loved her, now pursued the evangelical phenomenon with negative headlines wherever she went. Sister Aimee's troubled countenance, evident in this picture by Charles S. Borjes, reflected troubled times for the princess of the pulpit. She had married a third time in 1931, but by 1934 had divorced. She died on September 27, 1944, of an accidental overdose of barbiturates.

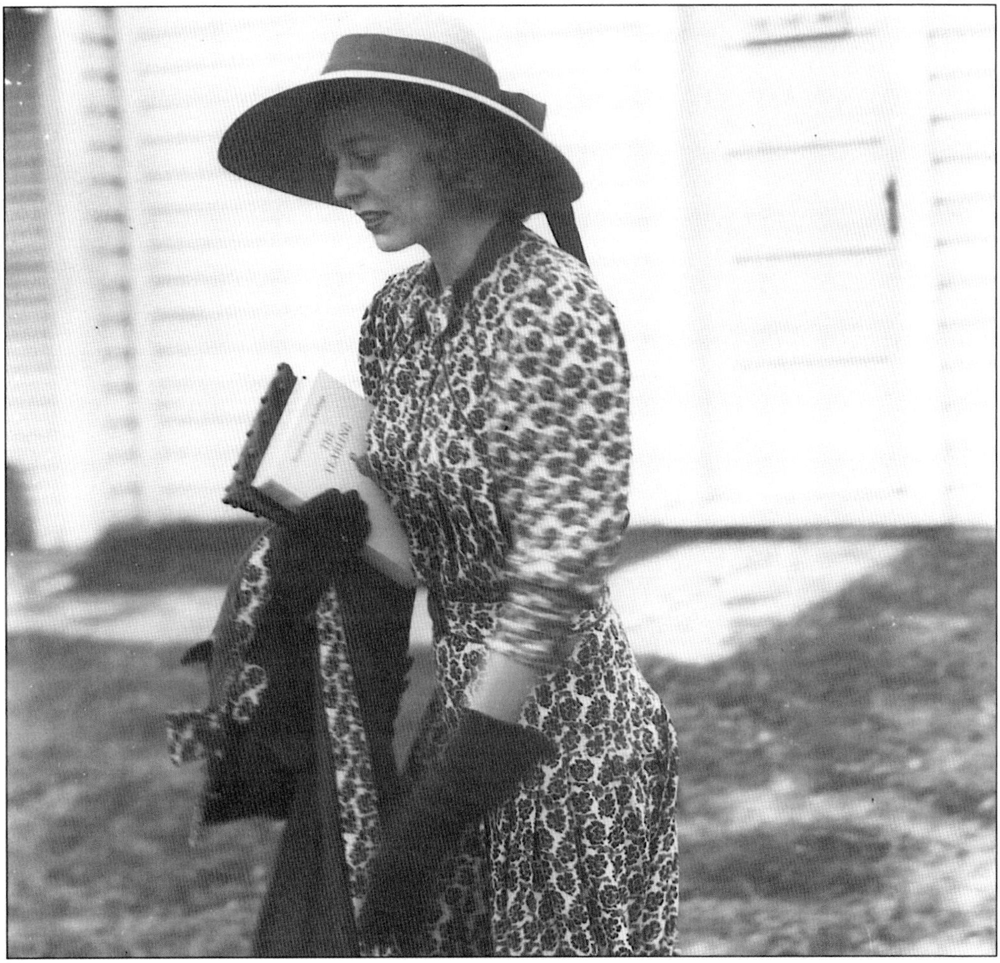

The vivacious Margaret Sullavan, star of stage and screen and a native of Norfolk, came home for a surprise visit to see her parents on July 25, 1938—her first trip to the area in three years. Arriving at the Norfolk Municipal Airport on a flight from Washington, D.C., Sullavan was met by friends and taken directly to her parents' house at 728 Westover Avenue. She had spent most of the flight reading Marjorie Kinnan Rawlings's bestseller, *The Yearling*, shown here clutched in her arm. Born Margaret Brooke Sullavan on May 16, 1911, to a wealthy stockbroker, Cornelius Hancock Sullavan, and his wife, heiress Garland Council Sullavan, young Margaret lived the life of privilege and private schools. She performed with the University Players at Harvard and made her Broadway debut in *A Modern Virgin* in 1931. Her Christmas Day, 1931 marriage to Hollywood film legend Henry Fonda lasted only two months, and her subsequent marriages to director William Wyler and agent Leland Hayward, to whom she was married from 1936 to 1947, were tempestuous at best. She had three children with Hayward, two of whom spent time in mental institutions. Between troubled courtships and children, Sullavan found little emotional peace and her health declined. She died of an accidental overdose of barbiturates on January 1, 1960, and is buried in St. Mary's Whitechapel Trinity Episcopal Churchyard in Lancaster, Virginia. At the time this picture was taken of the extraordinarily talented Sullavan, she had just starred in *Three Comrades* (1938), *The Shining Hour* (1938), and *Shopworn Angel* (1938) for Metro-Goldwyn-Mayer, to whom she was under contract. Sullavan was nominated for a 1939 Best Actress Academy Award for her role in *Three Comrades*. She lost to Bette Davis. (Charles S. Borjes, photographer.)

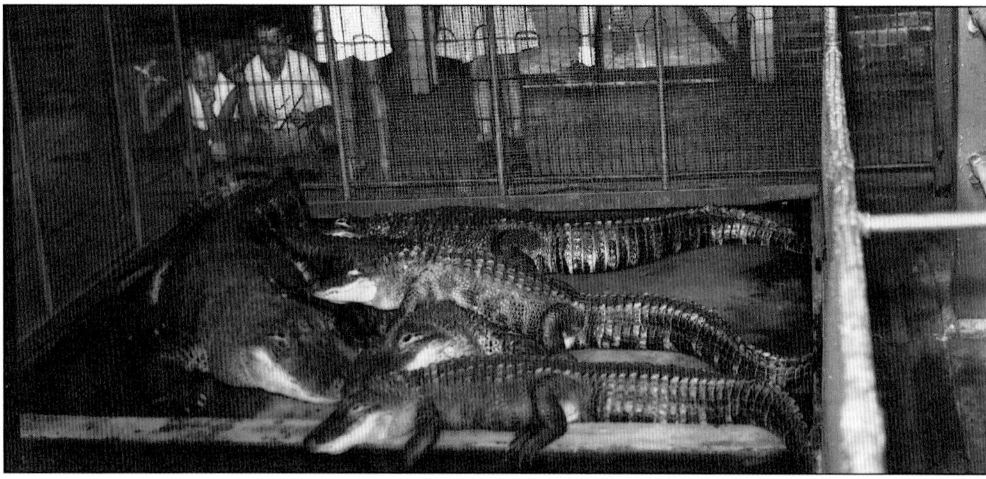

Alligators were star attractions at Norfolk's Lafayette Park and Zoo. Though this image was taken on August 29, 1938, alligators had been kept at the zoo since the turn of the century, at which time they were housed in an octagon-shaped pool area surrounded by a pretty green lawn and concrete verandah. None of the animals, reptiles, or birds lived too far apart from one another, according to the original layout of the zoo. "Old Bruin," a black bear, was housed near wildcats, a trio of pearl gray doves, white bunnies with pink eyes, Guinea pigs, squirrels, a half-dozen long-eared Belgian hares, and a family of opossums. Behind them, in a large caged area was a slate-colored African eagle who shared his area with an American bald eagle. Long-tailed monkeys and owls squawked and screeched next door. Thousands of people used to come out to the park and zoo every Sunday. (Charles S. Borjes, photographer.)

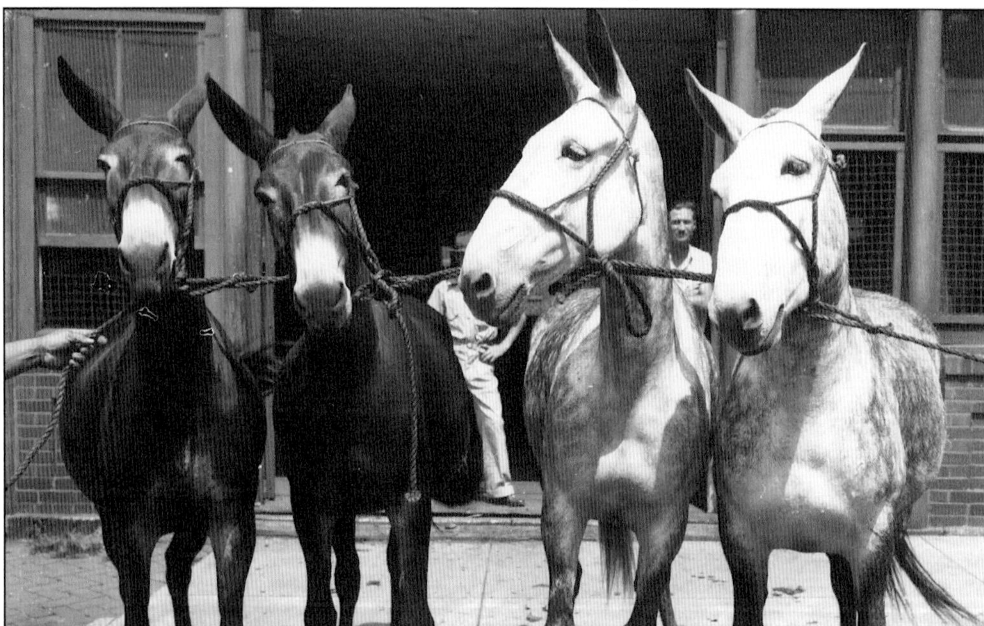

These fine mules belonged to J.R. Dodson's Sales & Exchange Stables, located on Church Street near Union Street. Dodson ran the last of Norfolk's stables trading in horses and mules. He went out-of-business about 1948. The picture was taken on July 13, 1942. (H.D. Vollmer, photographer.)

Four

June Bugs and Dragonflies

"The green-swathed grasshopper, on treble pipe,
Sings there, and dances, in mad-hearted pranks;
There bees go courting every flower that's ripe,
On baulks and sunny banks;
And droning dragon-fly, on rude bassoon,
Attempts to give God thanks
In no discordant tune . . .

The pranking bat its flighty circlet makes;
The glow-worm burnishes its lamp anew;
O'er meadows dew-besprent, the beetle wakes
Inquiries ever new,
Teazing each passing ear with murmurs vain,
As wanting to pursue
His homeward path again."

—From *Summer Images*, 1835
John Clare, English poet (1793–1864)

There is nothing that quite compares to the wonder of the great aerial bug show that comes every summer courtesy of the June bugs, dragonflies, and fireflies who grace us with their flights of fancy. We are inevitably drawn to the outdoors by the warm air, filled with the sweet breath of fragrant flowers. All of it is made all the sweeter by the sound of children's laughter at play and our own experiences and memories of secret places of beauty and serenity.

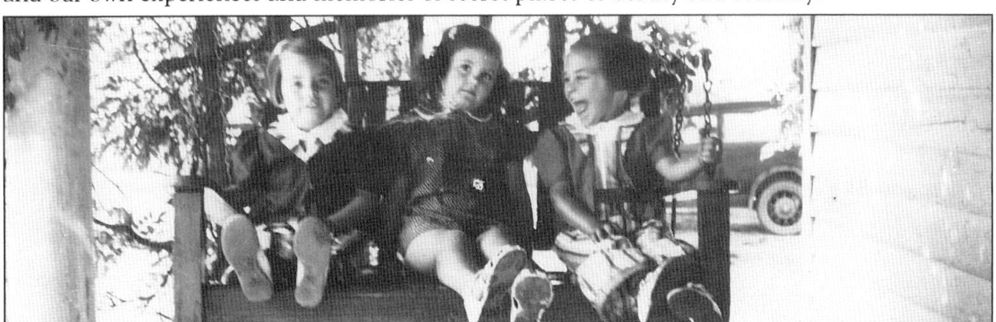

Ann O'Reilly (left), an unidentified child (center), and Ann's sister Kay, play on the porch swing of a house in the Brambleton section of Norfolk during the summer of 1942. "How do you like to go up in a swing, / Up in the air so blue? / Oh, I do think it the pleastantest thing / Ever a child can do!" [From "The Swing," *A Child's Garden of Verses*, 1885; Robert Louis Stevenson, Scottish poet (1850-1894).] (Photographer unknown.)

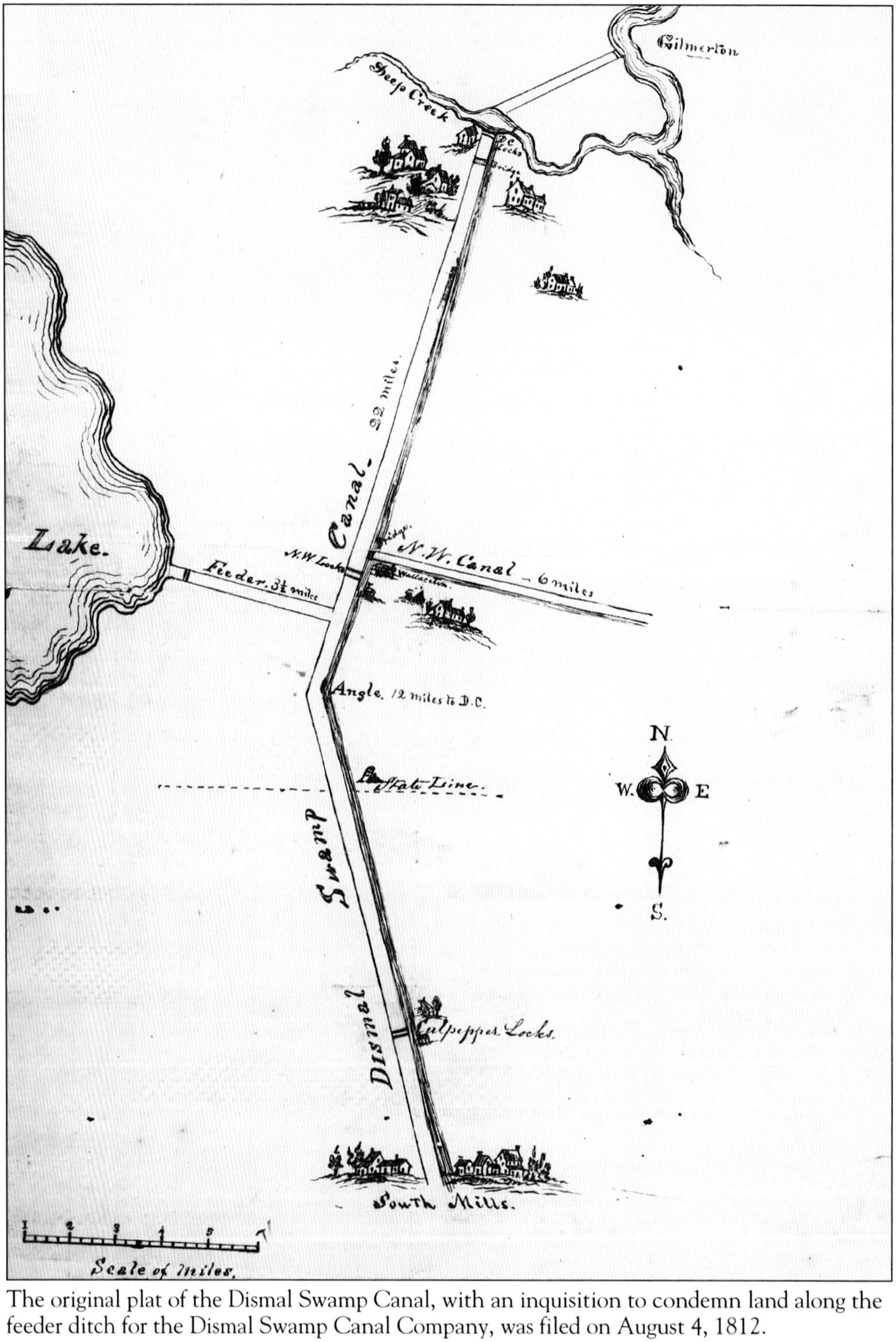

The original plat of the Dismal Swamp Canal, with an inquisition to condemn land along the feeder ditch for the Dismal Swamp Canal Company, was filed on August 4, 1812.

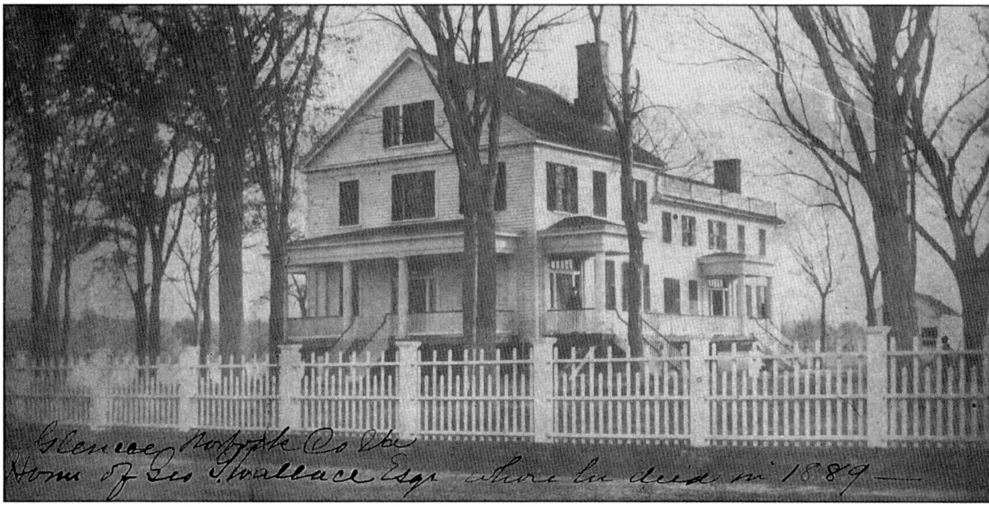

Historic Glencoe, built in 1841 by George T. Wallace, Esq., was constructed along the Dismal Swamp Canal in close proximity to the Northwest Canal Locks. Wallace's property was located in Norfolk County on land now incorporated into the city of Chesapeake. He died in this home in 1889. The picture was taken in 1890. Glencoe was tragically consumed by fire in the early morning hours of Thanksgiving Day in 1977 and not rebuilt to its former grandeur. The settlement of Wallaceton, situated a short distance from the house, derived its name from George T. Wallace's family, which settled in the southern part of Norfolk County in the early 1700s. William Wallace, an antecedent of George T., served as a seaman aboard the *Caswell* in the Virginia State Navy during the American Revolutionary War. (Photographer unknown.)

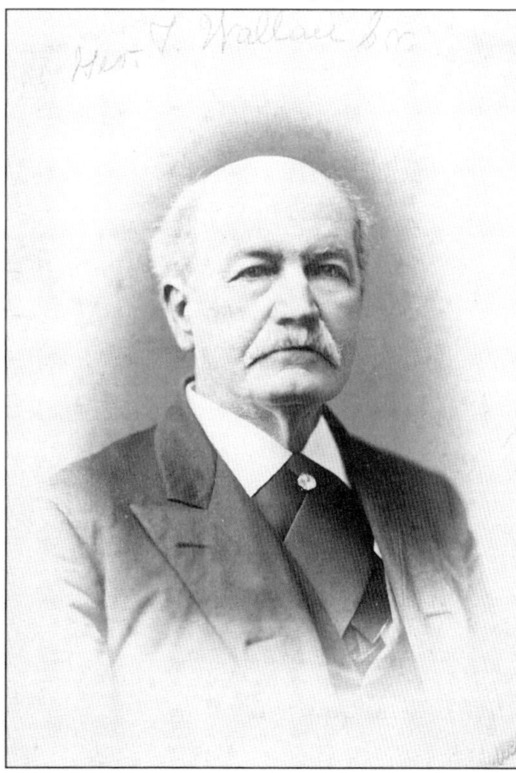

George T. Wallace, Esq., of Glencoe, was photographed near the end of his life, c. 1887, by Walter Studios of Norfolk.

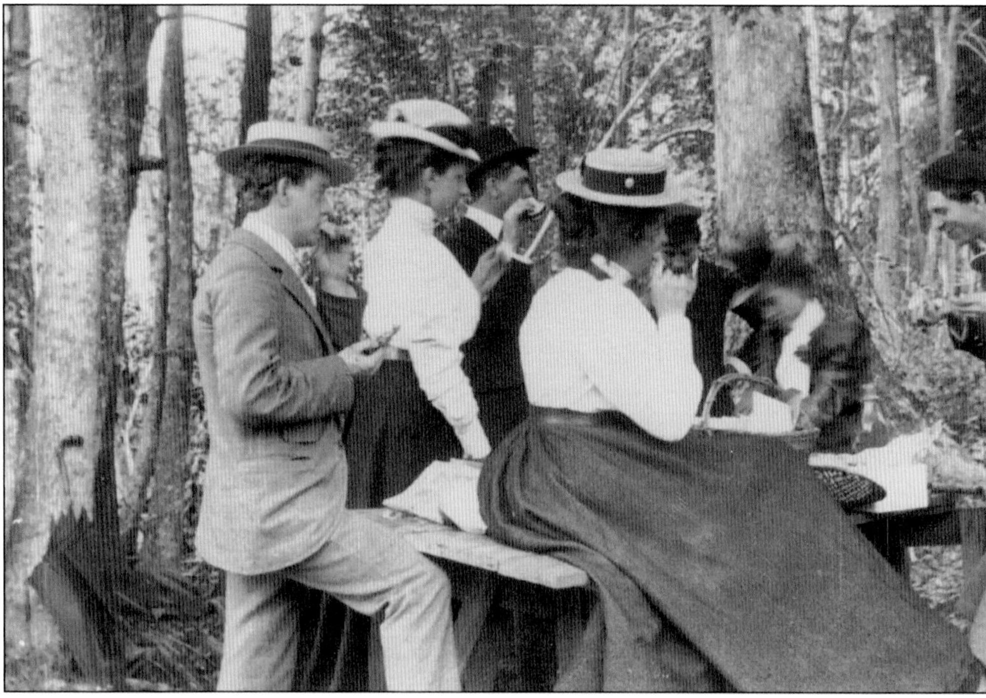

About 1900, a group of adventuresome young people took a summer's day excursion into the Great Dismal Swamp. Their picnic, captured on film by an unknown photographer, as well as their hike along the Dismal Swamp Canal, are priceless remembrances of the past. (Courtesy of the Museum of the Albemarle.)

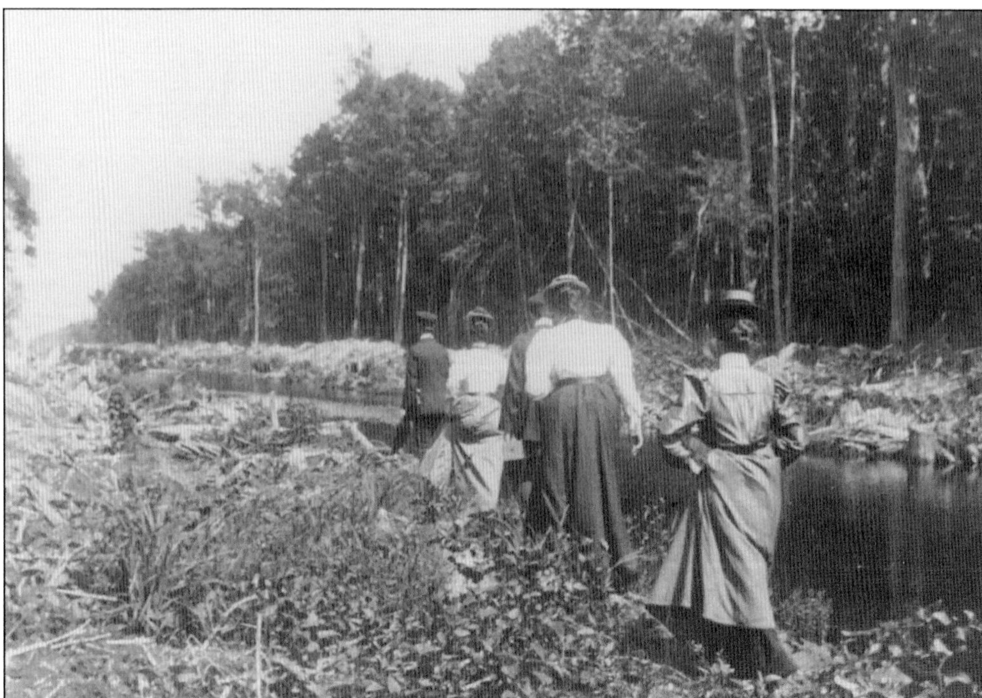

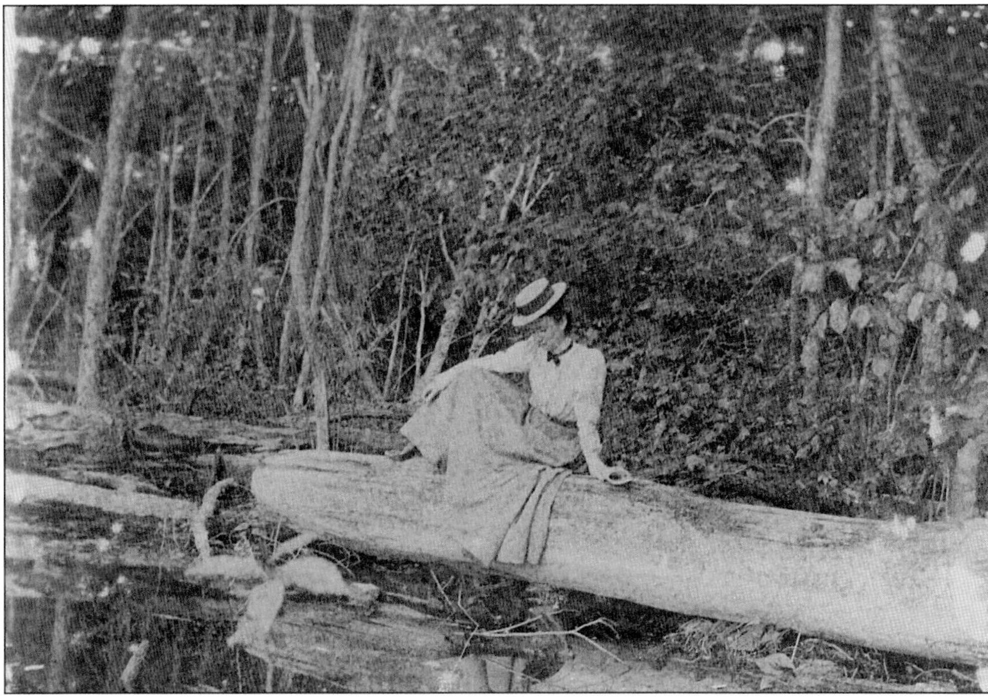

Perched on a fallen tree along the bank of the Dismal Swamp Canal, this young woman, part of the same group (opposite page), has nature's canvas of vibrant green foliage as her backdrop. "Amid the leafy wood; and ye have seen, / By a brook-side or solitary turn, / How she her station doth adorn: the pool / Glows at her feet, and all the gloomy rocks / Are brightened round her. In his native vale." [From *The Excursion*; William Wordsworth, English poet laureate (1770-1850).] (Courtesy of the Museum of the Albemarle.)

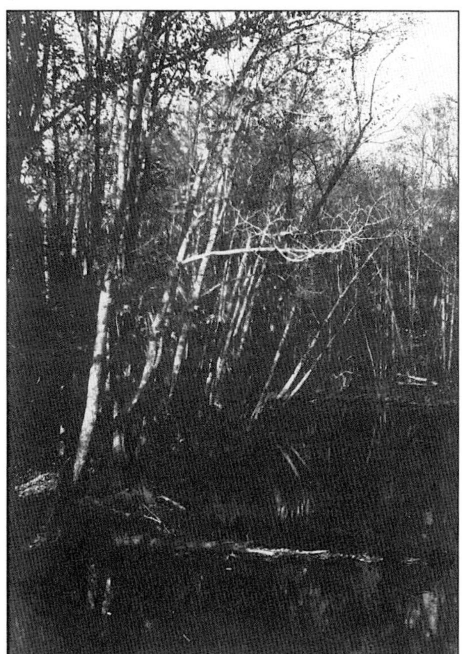

A trip through the Great Dismal Swamp's canals and low-lying waterways is a wondrous summer's day excursion. Going to such a place is also an experience which leaves an indelible impression on its visitors, just as Henry David Thoreau penned in *Walden* (1854): "I went to the woods because I wished to live deliberately, to front only the essential facts of life, and see if I could not learn what it had to teach, and not, when I came to die, discover that I had not lived." The overhanging black gum, red maple, and cypress branches are intertwined in such a way that cast imaginative shadows on the water below. By the turning of leaves in the fall, the fanciful array of autumn colors is spectacular. An unknown photographer snapped this postcard picture in 1907.

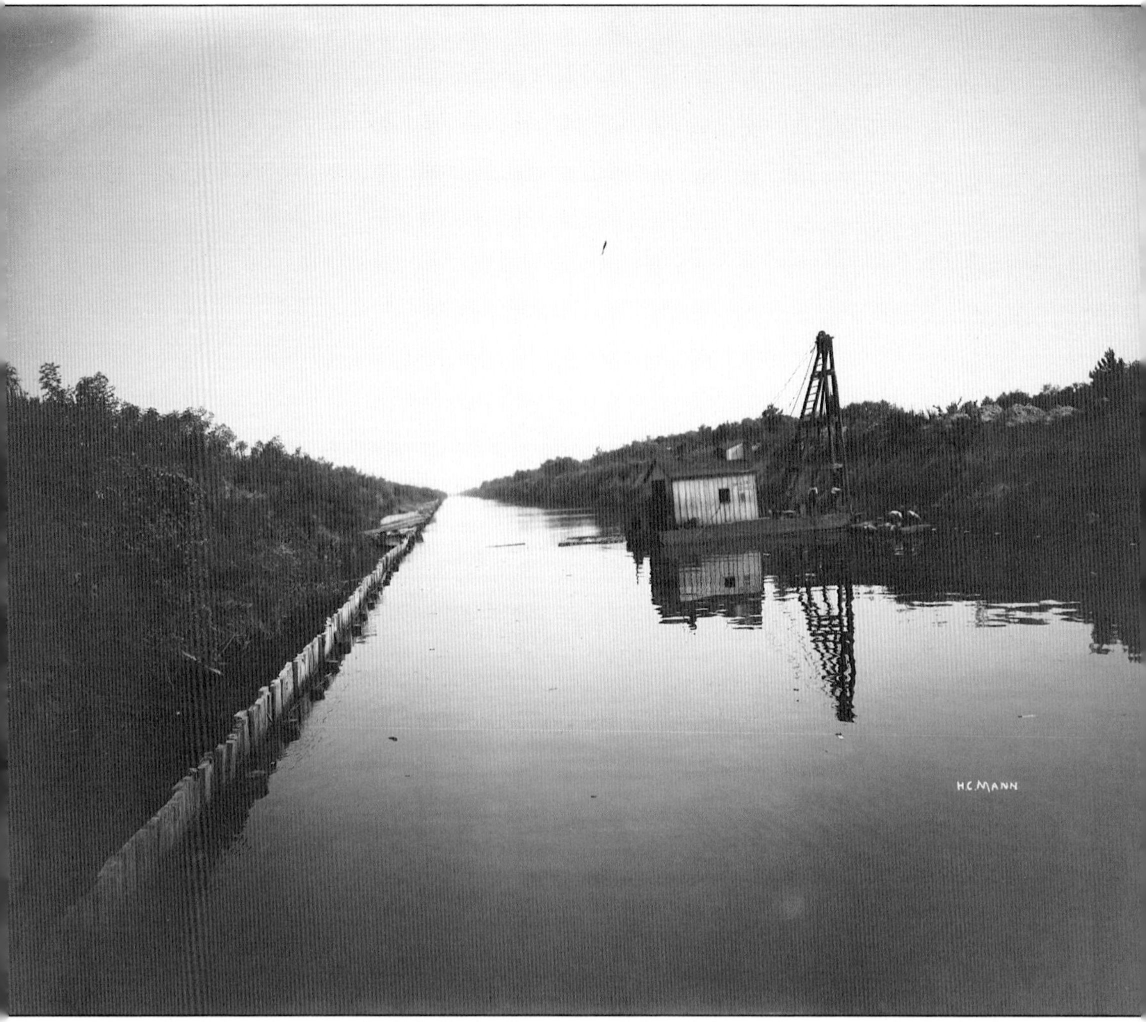

Harry C. Mann photographed the Lake Drummond Canal, better known as the Dismal Swamp Canal, about 1908. Workers began digging the Lake Drummond Canal in 1793, but progress was slow and the canal did not open for traffic until 1814. The canal extends from Deep Creek, an arm of the Elizabeth River in Virginia, to the Pasquotank River in North Carolina. It is approximately 22.5 miles long. The original canal was narrow and only 5 feet deep, but it was a useful means of transportation between the waters of North Carolina and the Chesapeake Bay. Shortly after the Civil War, a competitive canal, the Albemarle & Chesapeake, connecting the same waters was constructed, also with private capital. Since the new canal had larger dimensions, it soon attracted the bulk of the traffic and practically put its rival out of business until 1892 when its owners—the Lake Drummond Canal & Water Company—purchased and enlarged the Dismal Swamp Canal and took the competitive advantage over the Albemarle & Chesapeake Canal. This was short-lived prosperity. By 1912, the United States government planned, under the auspices of the U.S. Army Corps of Engineers, to take over the Albemarle & Chesapeake Canal, providing free access to the waterway to commercial traffic. This literally put the owners of the Dismal Swamp Canal, a toll-access waterway, out-of-business.

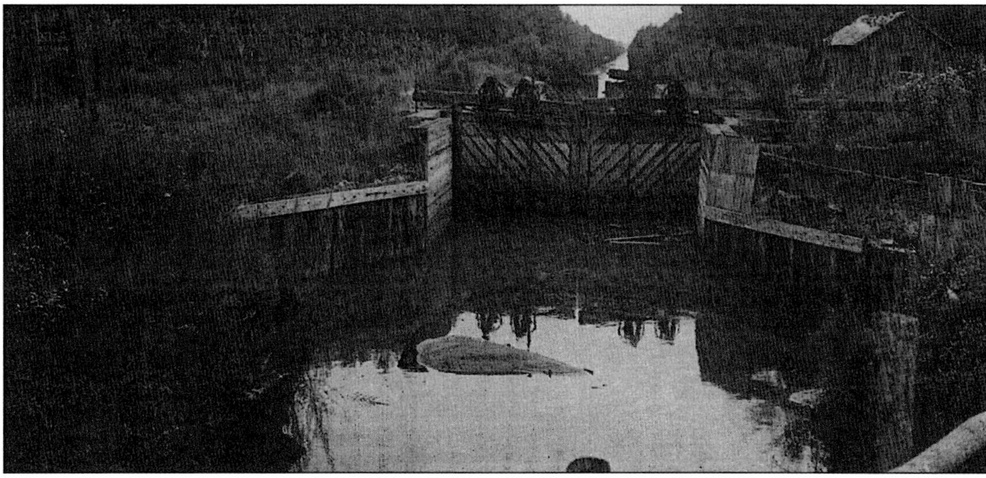

The Lake Drummond Lock had become no more than the overgrown entrance to a leafy tunnel on the way to the lake by 1896. The old barn on the right in this Harry C. Mann photograph, taken about 1910, had been on the property since the mid-1800s, where it once sat alongside a keeper's house. Lake Drummond was purportedly discovered by William Drummond, the first governor of North Carolina (he held that office from 1663 to 1667), while he was on a hunting trip. Drummond did not have the opportunity to profit from his "discovery"—or notoriety—as he was hanged in 1677 for his role in Bacon's Rebellion.

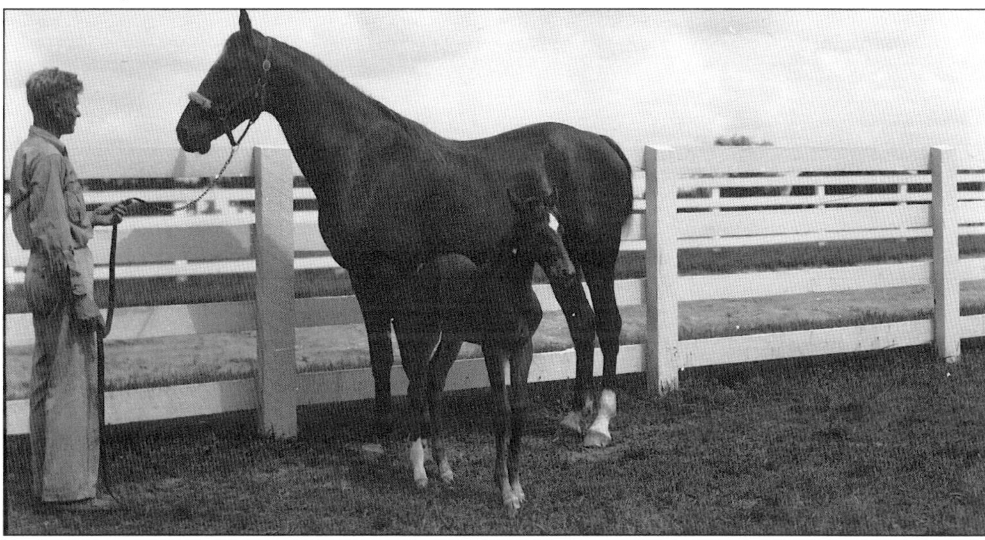

A mare, named Edna Newman, and her new foal were photographed at Carolanne Farms in the Kempsville section of Princess Anne County (now the city of Virginia Beach), July 6, 1937. Carolanne Farms was once home to some of the great race horses born and bred in Virginia. The 330-acre farm had been the property of Oscar Frommel Smith, a Norfolk philanthropist and industrialist, from the mid-1930s until the time of his death on May 1, 1950. He housed and trained show horses, race horses, and Shetland ponies on the property as a hobby. A few months after his passing, in September 1950, the horses were sold at auction. The top price for one of Smith's prize stallions was $12,600. The ponies were sold in June 1952. The investment-building firm of Buxbaum & Waranch bought the Smith parcel for a residential subdivision in September 1956, and started building in 1959. Most of the streets in the subdivision, also called Carolanne Farms, are named for Smith's champions. (H.D. Vollmer, photographer.)

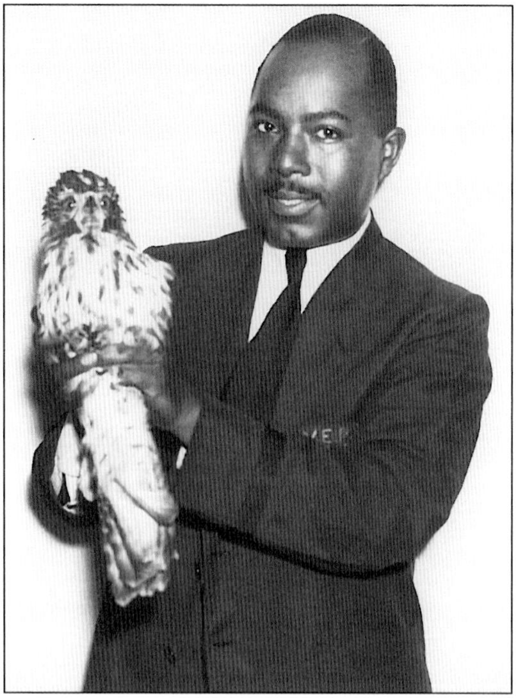

Thomas Jones posed with this eaglet on July 9, 1937. There is no way of knowing where Jones came upon the eaglet, a baby American bald eagle. The symbol of the nation, the American bald eagle is protected by federal law. The last poem that Southern-born John Thomas Watson (1822-1905) penned before the American Civil War, *The American Eagle*, appeared in his journal dated 1860. "The Stars and Stripes, with fluttering to the breeze, / He'll fix his bright eye on the dazzling sun, / And, rising proudly, like some huge balloon, / He'll stretch his long neck, spread his ponderous wings, / And plume his pinions for an upward flight. / Ascending like a rocket in the sky." Watson resumed writing shortly after the war came to an end in the spring of 1865. (H.D. Vollmer, photographer.)

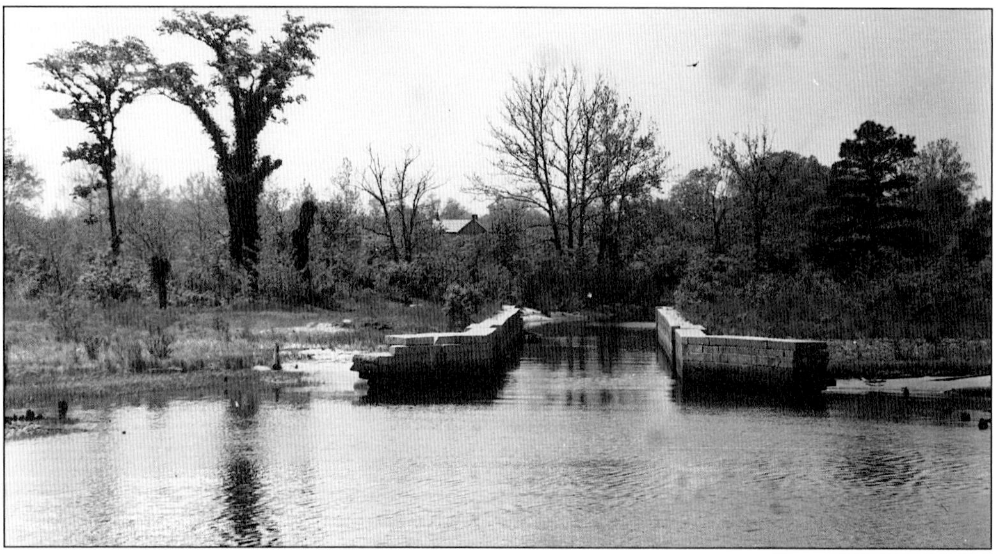

The Dismal Swamp Canal, pictured here May 7, 1940, was the product of a proposal by Virginia Governor Patrick Henry to build a canal between Norfolk's harbor, rich in trade, and North Carolina's Albemarle Sound. The General Assembly of Virginia approved the project in a 1787 compact providing for the cutting of a navigable canal from the Elizabeth River to the Pasquotank River in North Carolina. The compact also provided for the formation of the Dismal Swamp Canal Company. Work was begun on the canal in 1793, but it was not opened for waterborne traffic until June 1814. The first vessel to make its passage down the 22.5-mile-long Dismal Swamp Canal was a 20-ton decked boat owned by James Smith, which contained a consignment of goods, consisting mostly of bacon and brandy, from Scotland Neck, North Carolina, bound for Norfolk. (Charles S. Borjes, photographer.)

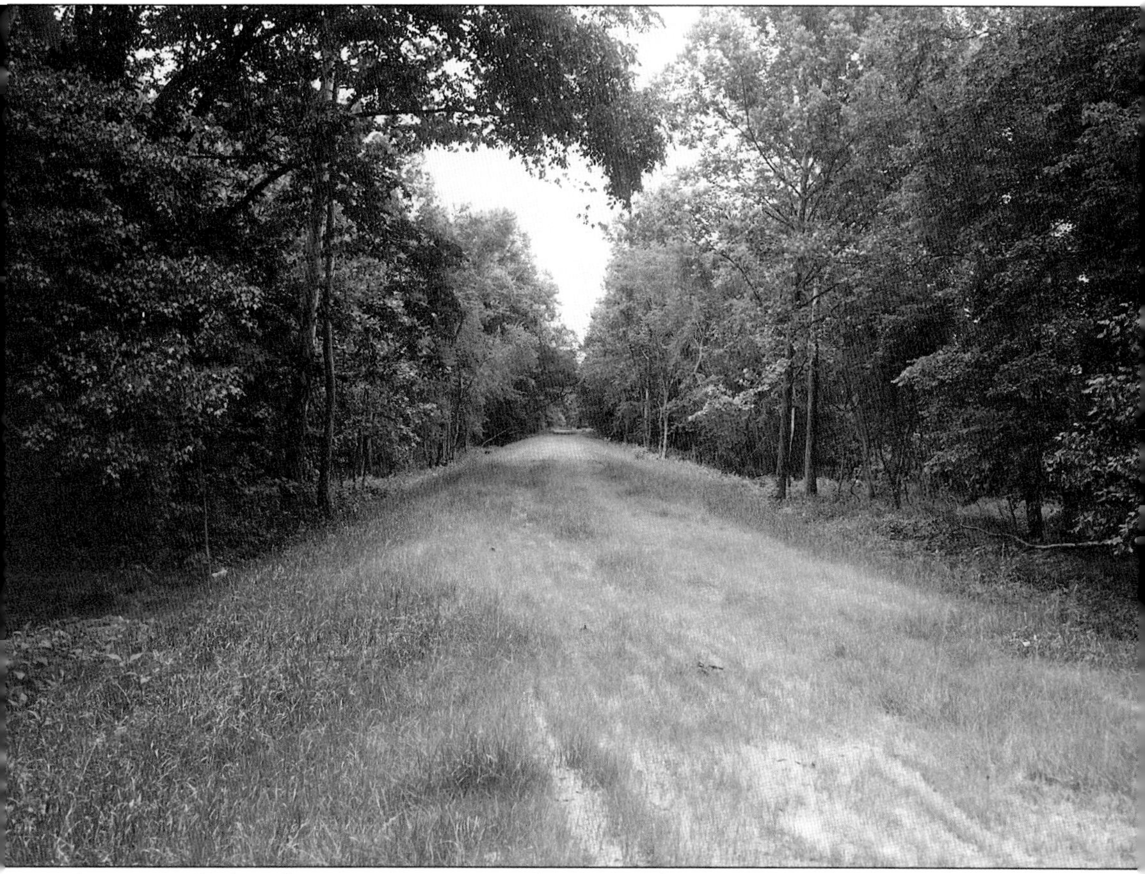

A snippet of John Thomas Watson's remembrances of the majesty of May titled *May Day and The Seasons* was composed at Petersburg, Virginia, in 1873. His portrayals of a bright and balmy day in Petersburg in the year 1860 so aptly describes the scene many years later at the Pocahontas Levee. The levee, also located in Petersburg along the Appomattox River, was photographed by the U.S. Army Corps of Engineers on June 24, 1947. The tranquillity and "beautiful grove of native forest trees" in the photograph certainly marry to Watson's descriptions. Watson, a native North Carolinian, was born in 1822 and died in Petersburg in 1905. Though a physician by profession, Watson was a gifted poet and observer of life. On one of the scraps of paper he saved from his college days at the University of North Carolina at Chapel Hill, it says the following: "The study of history, which is a study of human nature on a broad scale, gives the very training required in real life." Watson wrote:

> It was a bright and balmy day in April, 1860. The air was sweet with the perfume of flowers, and vocal with the songs of birds and the humming of insects. A few paces from the public road, and embowered in a beautiful grove of native forest trees stood a little country school house—one of those nurseries of youthful minds. The contemplation of which can never cease to be pleasing to minds of maturer growth. On this bright April morning, in response to the ringing of a bell, groups of merry girls came from various directions, many of them carrying sprigs and flowers which they had gathered in their early rambels. One little fairy had her head adorned with wreaths of the graceful yellow jasmine, another with the blooms of the wild crab, dogwood or fragrant honeysuckle.

(Photograph courtesy of the U.S. Army Corps of Engineers, Norfolk District.)

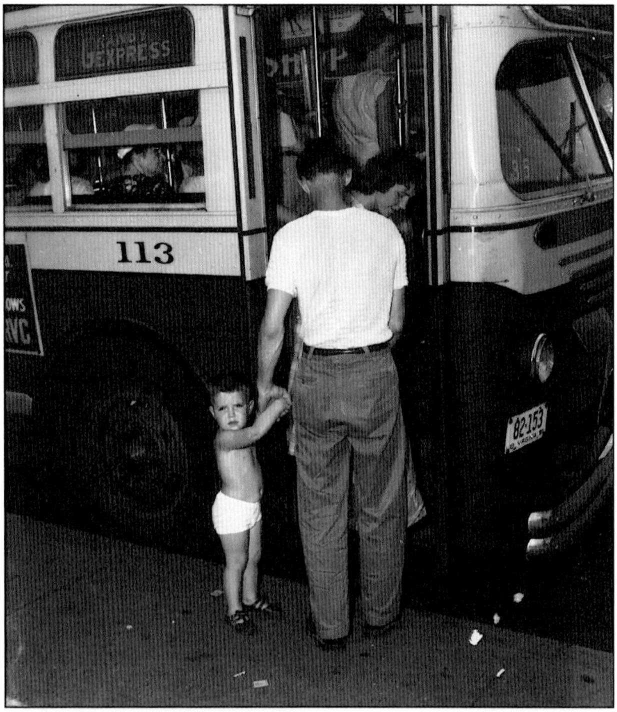

There was no relief in sight as Norfolk's heat wave settled in for a long summer's stay. The little boy boarding the bus with his parents on July 22, 1952, is beating the heat as best he can—donning only his shorts and sandals. Temperatures remained above 100 degrees. (Charles S. Borjes, photographer.)

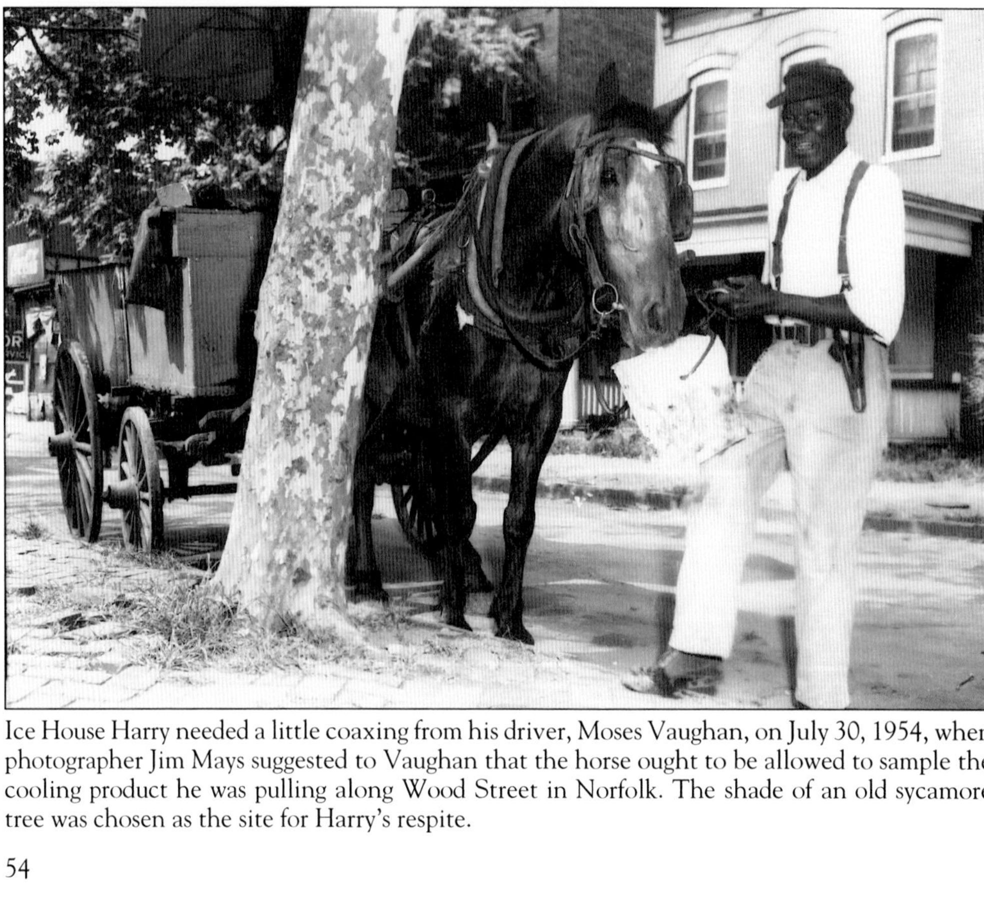

Ice House Harry needed a little coaxing from his driver, Moses Vaughan, on July 30, 1954, when photographer Jim Mays suggested to Vaughan that the horse ought to be allowed to sample the cooling product he was pulling along Wood Street in Norfolk. The shade of an old sycamore tree was chosen as the site for Harry's respite.

Five

The Boys of Summer

"The outlook wasn't brilliant for the Mudville nine that day;
The score stood four to two, with but one inning more to play,
And then when Cooney died at first, and Barrows did the same,
A pall-like silence fell upon the patrons of the game.

A straggling few got up to go in deep despair. The rest
Clung to that hope which springs eternal in the human breast;
They thought, 'If only Casey could but get a whack at that—
We'd put up even money now, with Casey at the bat.' "

—From *Casey at the Bat*, 1888
Ernest Laurence Thayer, American humorist (1863–1940)

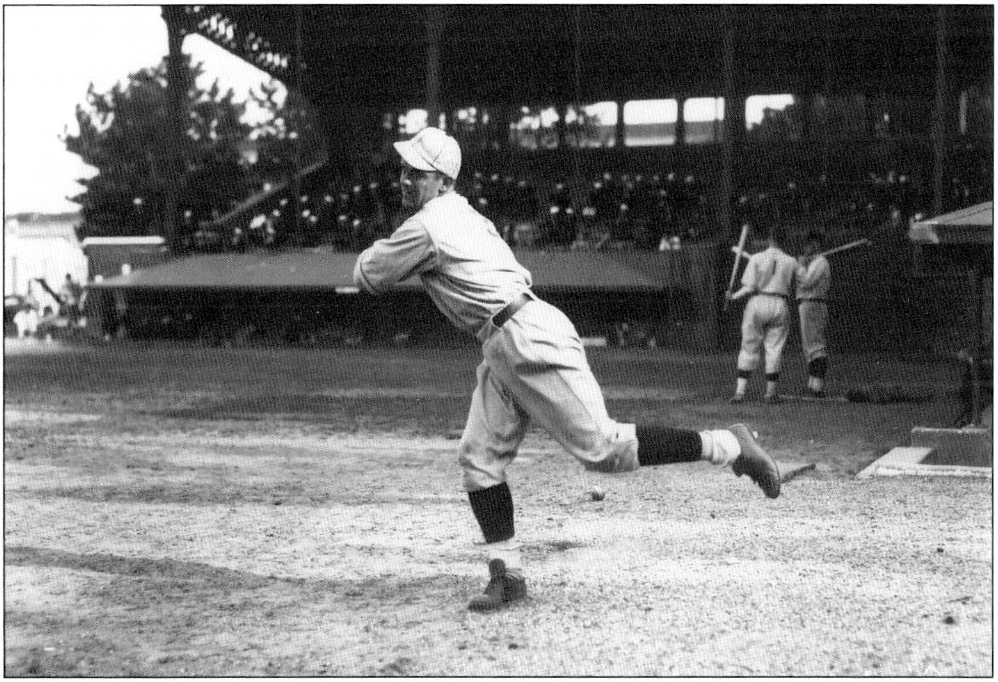

Jack Homer Harris, the famed one-arm pitcher of the College of William & Mary, Norfolk Extension, drew a sizable crowd to Bain Field to watch him work his fast pitches over the plate on May 11, 1938. Born in Waverly, Virginia, to Harvey and Mabel Harris, young Jack lost his right arm in an accident at the age of nine. He graduated from Oceana High School and spent the better part of his life in Virginia Beach. This extraordinary young man, despite his handicap, became a star pitcher and football back for the college's Norfolk extension during the 1938-1939 season. His teammates dubbed Harris the "One-Armed Brave." Jack died on May 13, 1998, at the age of 80. (Jim Mays, photographer.)

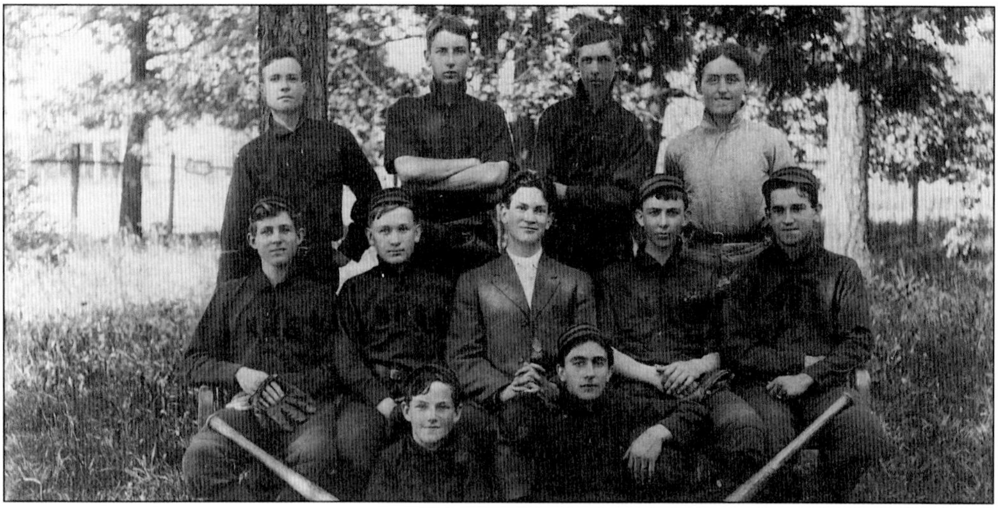

The Norfolk High School baseball team was a small, but scrappy, club when this picture was taken about 1905. From left to right, the players are as follows: (front row) little John Cahill and an unidentified friend; (middle row) Coach Ferebee, Aubrey Eggleston, team manager Walter Taylor, an unidentified boy, and Harry Evans Billups; (back row) three unidentified boys and Willis Sylvester. (Photographer unknown.)

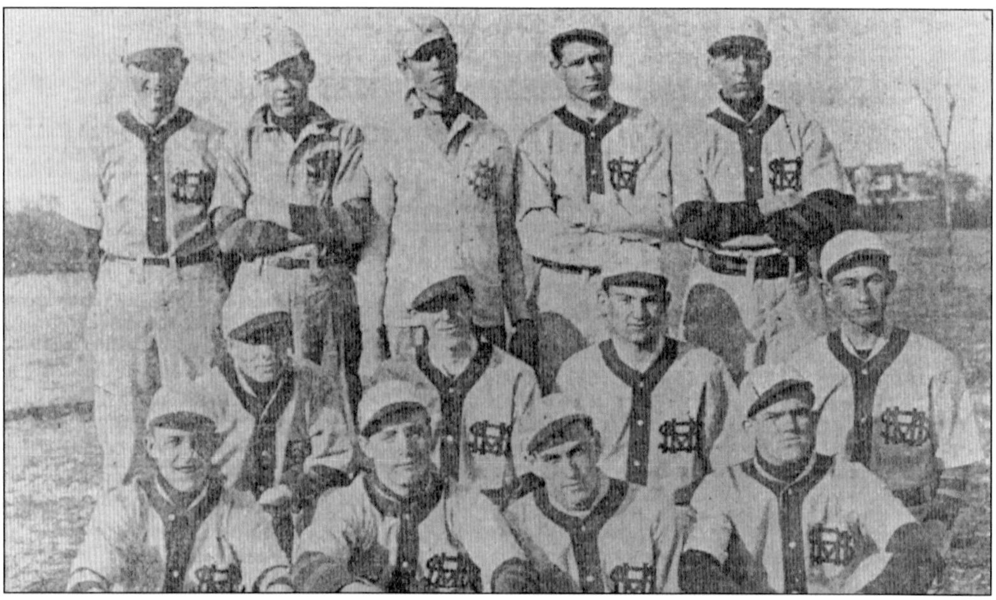

Maury High School's first baseball team was photographed by an unknown photographer on March 29, 1911, on the school grounds. The students were, from left to right, as follows: (front row) Wilfred Ferguson (second base), Charles J. Moore (right field), James Banks (pitcher), and Robert C. Jacobs (left field); (center row) Elton Seeley (shortstop), Robert or Young Gayle (catcher), Herman or William White (substitute), and J. Moore (pitcher); (back row) Luther Dear (team captain and first base), Sterling Palmer Potts (substitute), Benjamin Carter (centerfield), William Pierce (pitcher), and ? Gardner (third base). Pierce was a new pitcher on the 1911 Maury team, a group of boys who had made the transition from the old Norfolk High School.

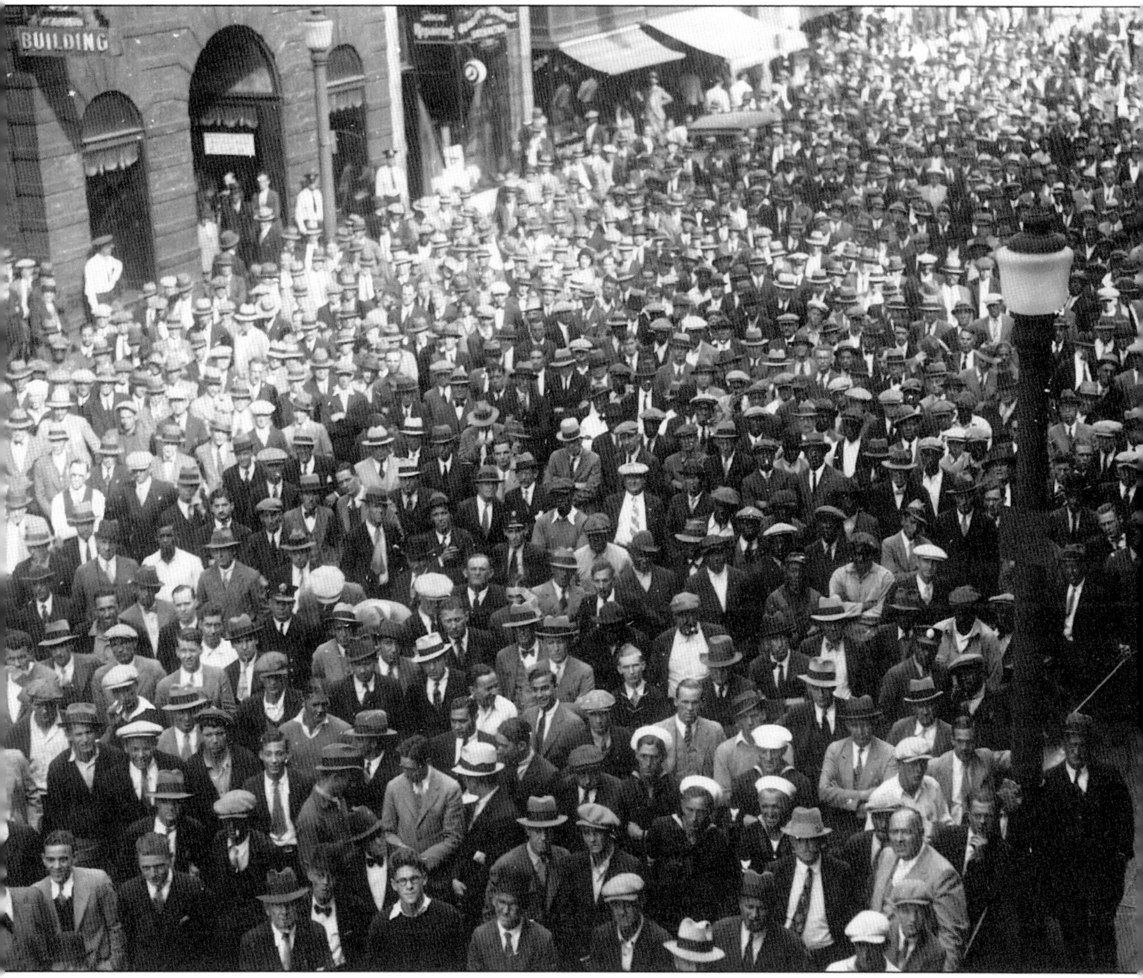

An attentive crowd gathered on Plume Street watched the *Ledger-Dispatch's* scoreboard and listened to the radio broadcast of a game of the World Series, played between the St. Louis Cardinals and the Philadelphia Athletics in October of 1931. The American League Philadelphia A's, managed by the great Connie Mack, lost the World Series four games to three to the National League St. Louis Cardinals, then under the tutelage of manager Gabby Street. The series was hard fought and the Cardinals were not all that sure they would win. The A's had won the American League pennant three consecutive years. It was not a wonder that the streets of Norfolk, and those around America, were packed with listeners on October 1-2, 5-7, and 9-10. As the series slipped into the seventh game and Americans reveled in the intrigue of their famous Fall Classic, the Cardinals were conscious of the old adage, "Revenge is a dish best served cold," as they faced their rival A's, a superb team which had beaten them six times in the previous year to become the first team in baseball history to win the World Series twice back-to-back. Was the revenge sweet? The Cardinals returned to the World Series three years later and the A's, well . . . they did not return to the World Series for 41 years. (Charles S. Borjes, photographer.)

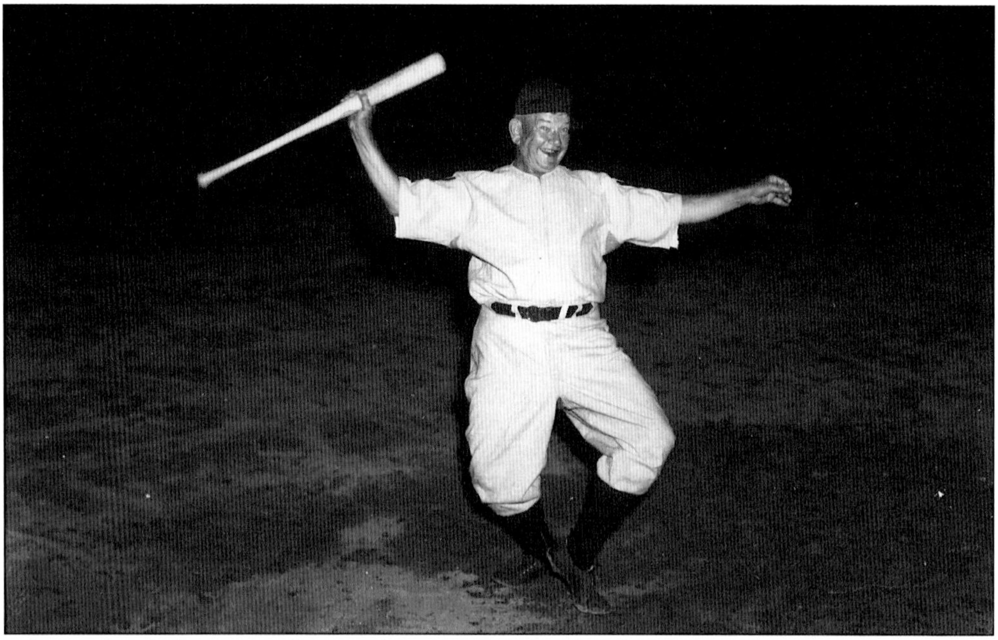

What's a baseball game without a clown? Nick Altrock, a baseball clown, entertained crowds at Norfolk's Bain Field for many years, and stories passed down over the years indicate he was a crowd favorite. Charles S. Borjes captured Altrock in one of his lighter moments during a game in 1933.

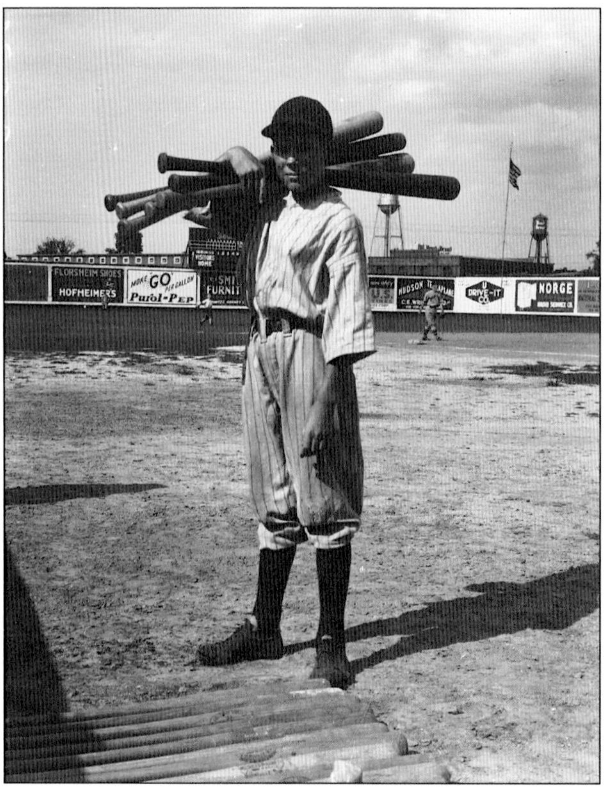

Batboy Junior Ewell, pictured on August 9, 1934, worked for the Norfolk Tars during the baseball season. (Charles S. Borjes, photographer.)

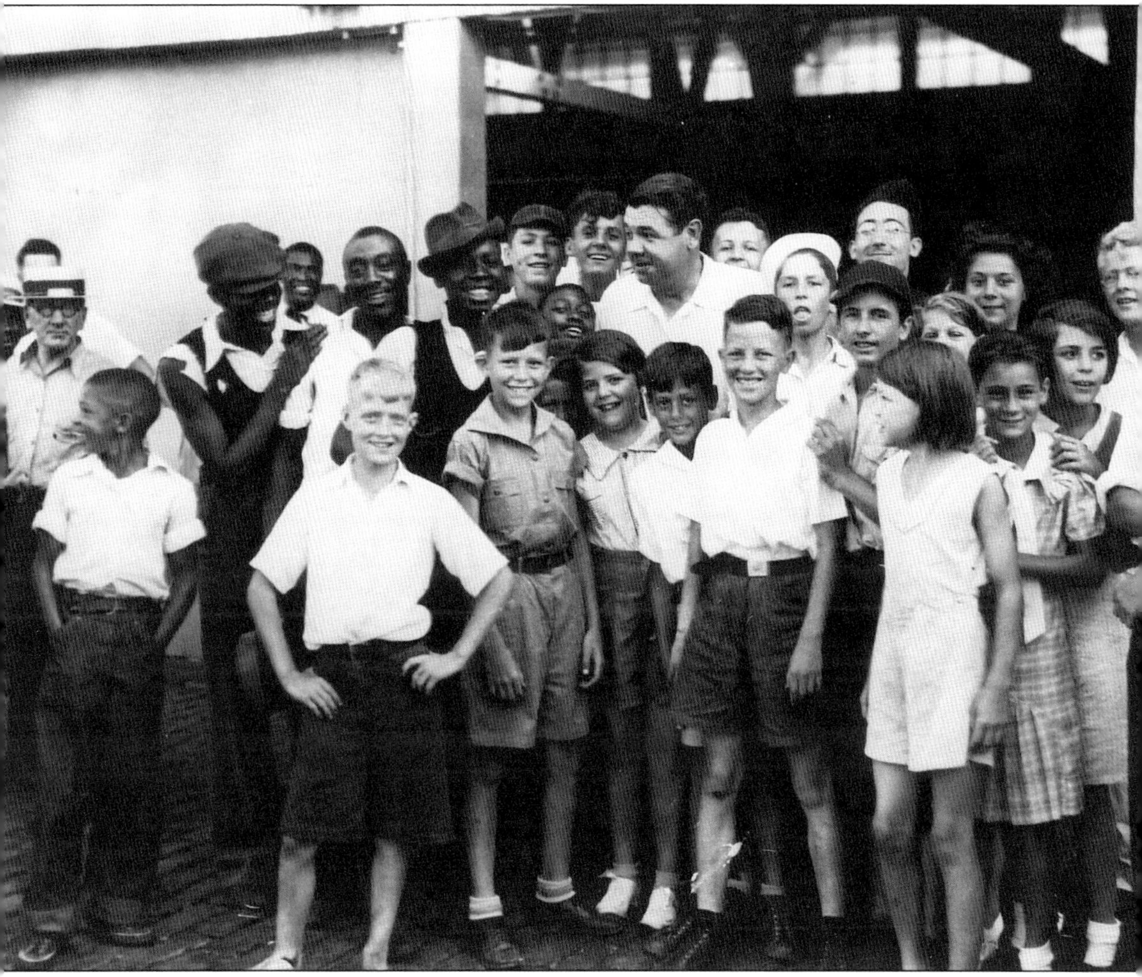

The great "Sultan of Swat" visited Norfolk in the summer of 1934. Babe Ruth delighted children at the Washington Boat Docks, located at the foot of Colley Avenue and Front Street. Identifiable children are J.C. Larkin (white shirt with hands on his hips in left foreground), H.D. Vollmer Jr. and Clara J. Vollmer (just behind Larkin), David Costas (standing directly next to Babe), and Woodie Kite (wearing the sailor's hat to the right of Ruth). Babe Ruth played for the New York Yankees from 1920 to 1934. This picture is both a priceless piece of the Babe's greatest years in baseball, demonstrating his popularity with his fans, and his swan song with Yankees management. At his zenith, Babe Ruth was baseball's best performer, and in his later years, its best ambassador. (H.D. Vollmer, photographer.)

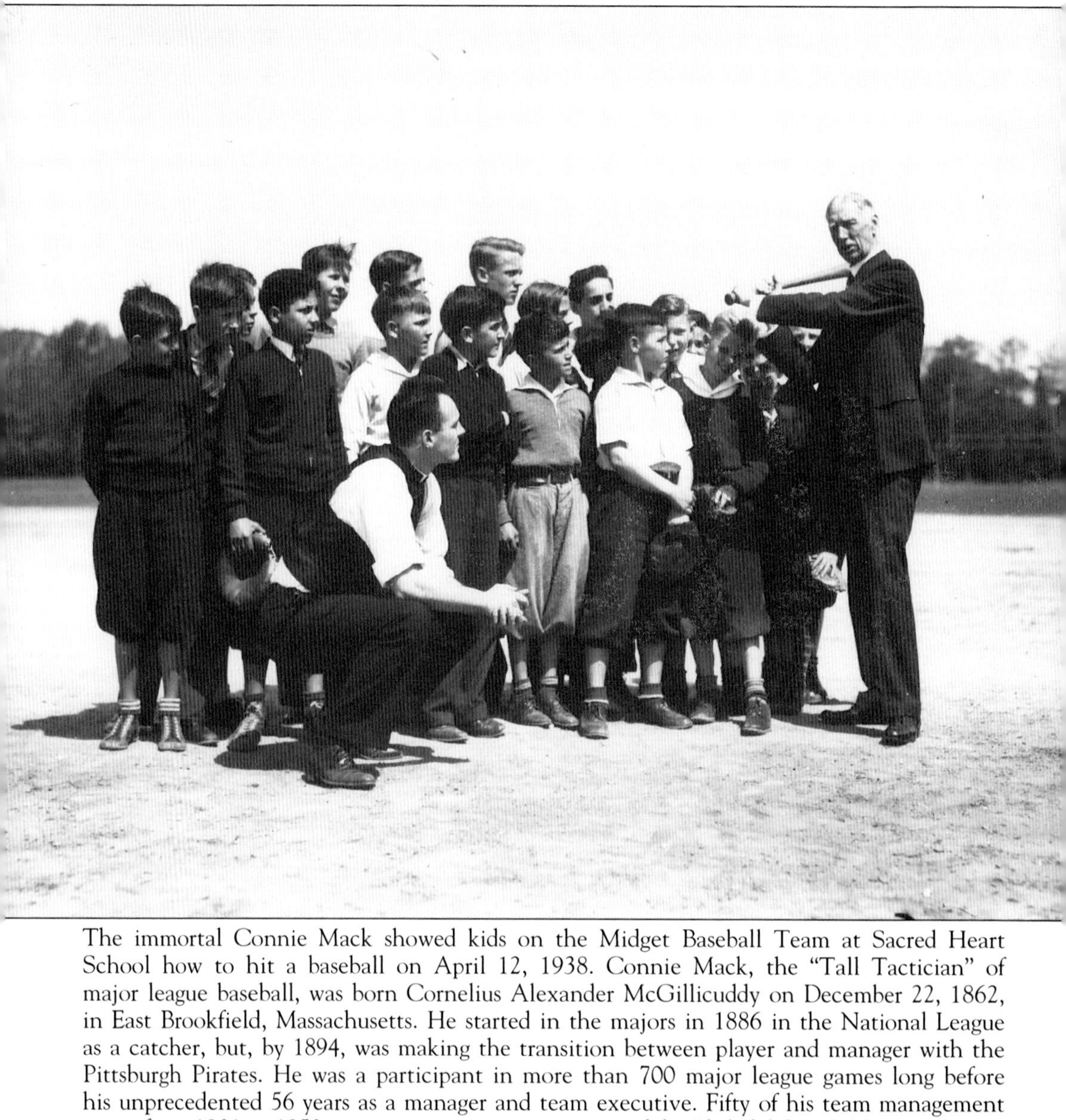

The immortal Connie Mack showed kids on the Midget Baseball Team at Sacred Heart School how to hit a baseball on April 12, 1938. Connie Mack, the "Tall Tactician" of major league baseball, was born Cornelius Alexander McGillicuddy on December 22, 1862, in East Brookfield, Massachusetts. He started in the majors in 1886 in the National League as a catcher, but, by 1894, was making the transition between player and manager with the Pittsburgh Pirates. He was a participant in more than 700 major league games long before his unprecedented 56 years as a manager and team executive. Fifty of his team management years, from 1901 to 1950, were spent as owner-manager of the Philadelphia Athletics. The A's won nine American League championships and five World Series under Mack's leadership. This legend of baseball, who purportedly shortened his name to Mack so it would fit on the scoreboard, was elected to the National Baseball Hall of Fame in 1937. The business suit Mack is wearing in this photograph was indicative of his dress for every game as manager of the A's. Fans identified him by it, respectfully referring to him as "Mr. Mack." He retired after the 1950 season at the age of 88, and died on February 8, 1956. Perhaps his bust in the Hall of Fame says it best of all as the self-proclaimed "Mr. Baseball" will live on forever in the memory of all the children he influenced in the game and the enduring class with which he carried himself. (H.D. Vollmer, photographer.)

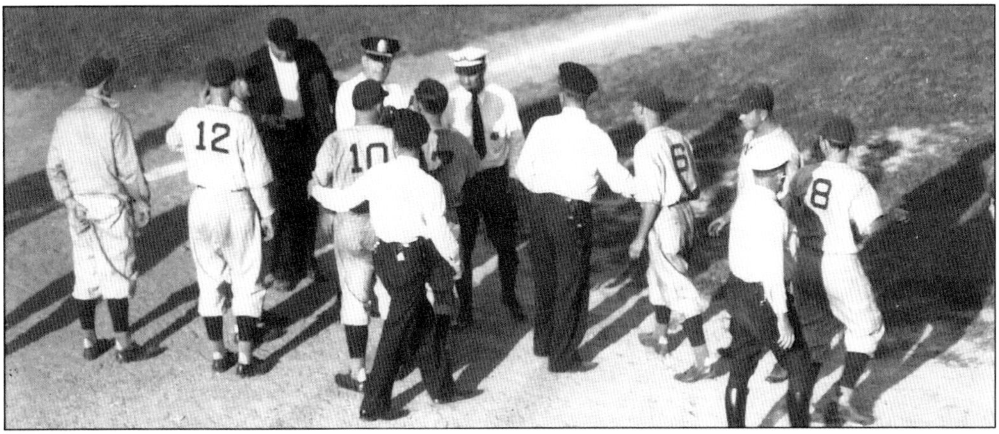

Norfolk police were called in to protect an umpire after Portsmouth players attacked him for a bad call in a game against the Norfolk Tars held at Bain Field on September 14, 1937. Fights were not unusual. One of the most well-remembered fights occurred in 1916 in the fourth inning of a game in Norfolk. Count Manuel Cueto, a Portsmouth centerfielder, tried to flog the umpire with a baseball bat. After getting in a couple of vicious blows, Cueto, a Cuban player who would later become famous playing for the Cincinnati Reds, was escorted from the field by Norfolk policemen. Cueto was fortunate he left the field in one piece. "Lynch the dirty roughneck!" was the pervasive sentiment of onlookers, and the last words anyone heard resonating from the stands as he departed the park. (H.D. Vollmer, photographer.)

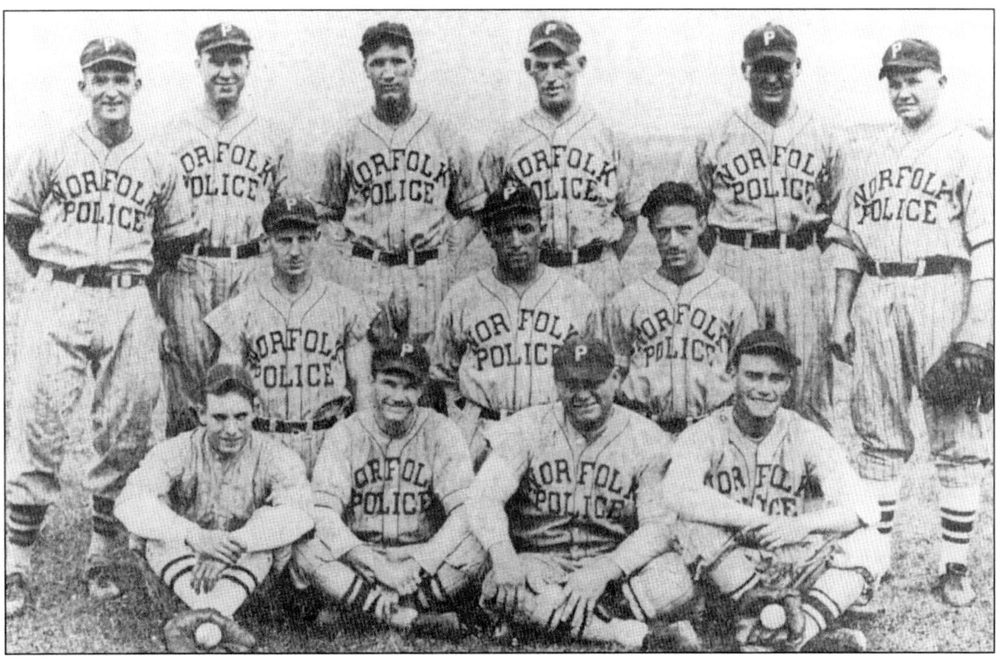

The Norfolk Police Baseball Team, pictured as they appeared in the *Ledger-Dispatch* newspaper on July 29, 1938, were among the better amateur teams to play in the city. The players were, from left to right, as follows: (front row) Harold Predmore, Tommy Nee, Mullett Saunders, and LeRoy Perry; (center row) Al Zeher, Ham Callahan, and Pinkie Fisher; (back row) Red Keller, Doug Berry, Bubber Staylor, Pinkie Lindsay, Jimmy Mayo, and team manager Mason Holland. (Photographer unknown.)

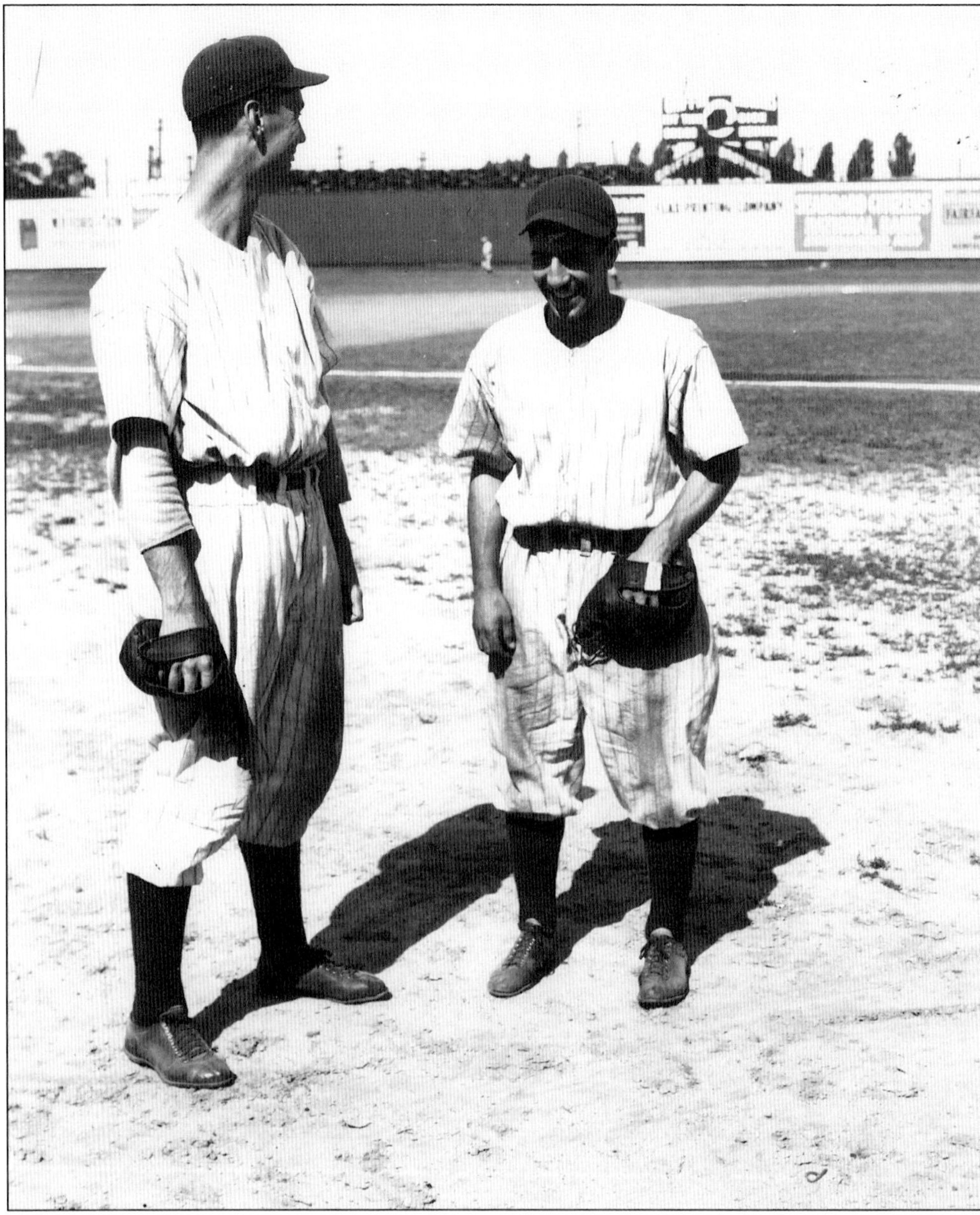

"The long and the short of the Tars," Jack Graham, 6 feet, 2 inches, and Phil "Scooter" Rizzuto, 5 feet, 6 inches, poked fun at one another at Bain Field on June 13, 1938. Jack Graham, born John Bernard Graham, on December 24, 1916, in Minneapolis, Minnesota, played in the minors until his major league debut with the Brooklyn Dodgers (National League) on April 16, 1946. Graham was traded the same year to the New York Giants, and, in 1949, to the St. Louis Browns, his first stint in the American League. Rizzuto, an excellent-fielding shortstop, was named Minor League Player of the Year while playing for Kansas City two years after this picture was taken, and he went on to play for the New York Yankees from 1941 to 1942, and again, from 1946 to 1956. During WW II, Rizzuto and his Brooklyn Dodgers' rival, Pee Wee Reese, joined the U.S. Navy and played for the same team, the Naval Air Station Norfolk Fliers. (Charles S. Borjes, photographer.)

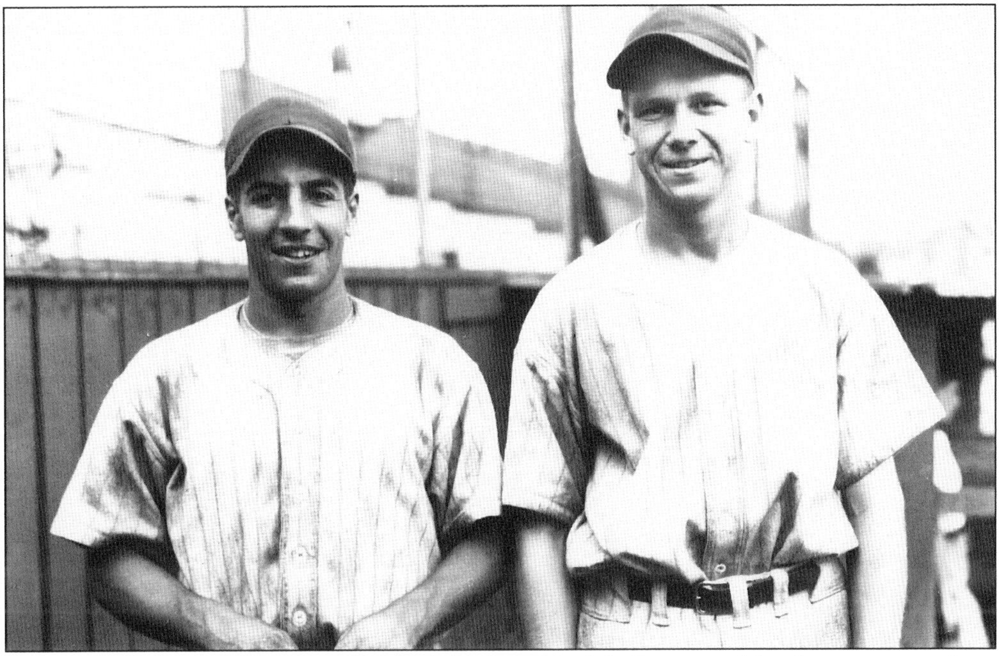

Phil Rizzuto (left) and Gerry Priddy (right) of the Norfolk Tars posed for this picture on June 27, 1938. Priddy turned the ripe old age of 18 while playing for the championship Tars in 1938, one of the best teams the Tars ever fielded. He batted .323, hit 9 home runs, and had 73 RBIs. Overall, Priddy had great hands and a fantastic throwing arm. Priddy, like his teammate, Rizzuto, would later play for the New York Yankees in the 1942 World Series against the St. Louis Cardinals. The Yankees lost the series four games to one. Priddy switched off playing first and third bases for the Yankees, while Rizzuto played shortstop. Priddy and Rizzuto played 11 and 12 years, respectively, in the majors after leaving Norfolk. (Charles S. Borjes, photographer.)

Bud Metheny, the former Old Dominion University coach, was showing off his Norfolk Tars uniform, August 1, 1938. Metheny came to the Tars out of the College of William & Mary. He played 89 games with the Tars in 1938, batting .338 and hitting 21 home runs. Metheny did not finish the season with the team because the New York Yankees moved him up to the majors that year. He went on to become a major league star. (Charles S. Borjes, photographer.)

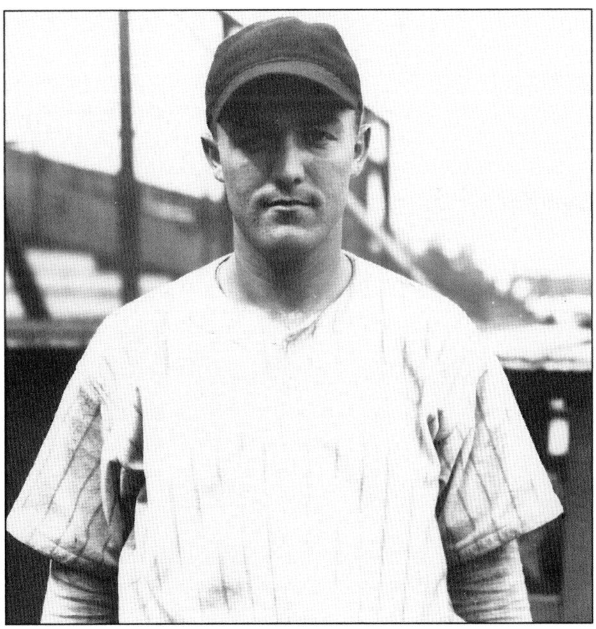

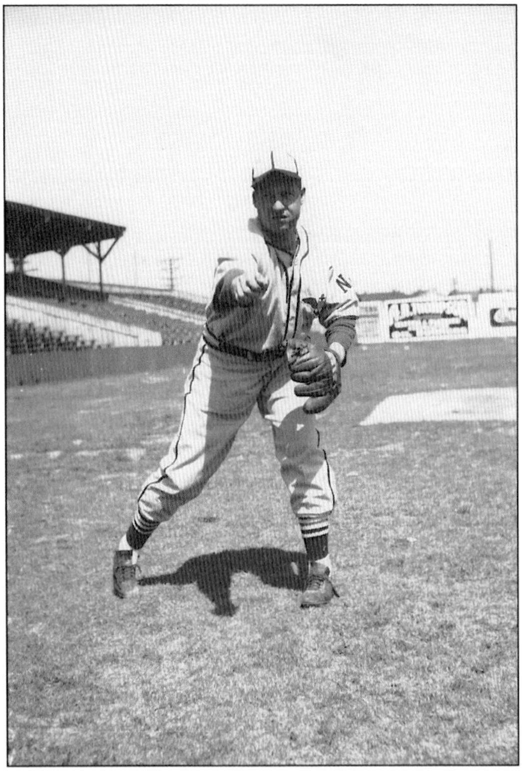

Naval Air Station Norfolk Fliers pitcher Hugh Casey (1913-1951), a pitcher for the Brooklyn Dodgers before the war, was a world-class catch for his Navy team. He had pitched for the Dodgers in the 1941 World Series against the New York Yankees, and, though his team lost the Fall Classic, it was not due to Casey's rapid-fire pitches over the plate. Casey's pitching was pure perfection most of the time. He was a tough competitor, but a heavy drinker who savored his talent and his victories in a bottle of booze. This would explain why Casey became fast friends with author Ernest Hemingway. During the Dodgers' spring training in Cuba, Casey frequented Hemingway's house. It was on one of those visits that Casey and Hemingway elected to don boxing gloves and, totally drunk, knocked one another senseless. Sadly, Hugh Casey took his own life in 1951, distraught over the break up of his marriage. The picture shown here was taken on April 13, 1943. (Charles S. Borjes, photographer.)

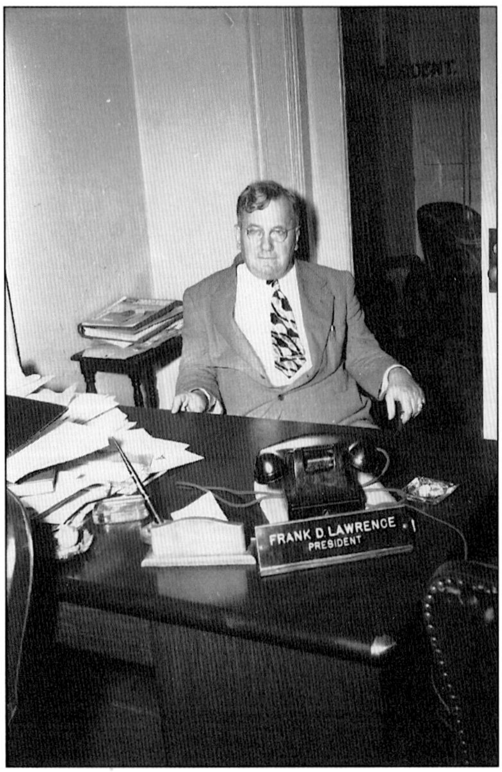

Frank D. Lawrence, dubbed the "Stormy Petrel of the Minors," was a banker better known as the owner of the Portsmouth Merrimacs, a minor league baseball club in the Piedmont League. Lawrence spent nearly 50 years in the business of managing his Portsmouth clubs, but in 1943, this contentious icon of Virginia baseball garnered national attention when the prestigious baseball publication, the *Sporting News*, named him Minor League Executive of the Year after the Merrimacs took the Piedmont League pennant. This was Portsmouth's first championship since 1927. Lawrence is shown here in his office on June 12, 1947. As major league management began to withdraw its investment in the Piedmont League, Lawrence fought them until the day the league eventually folded on July 14, 1955. His pugnacious personality made him come by the adjective "stormy petrel," a rather old-fashioned term indicative of an omen of something troublesome on the horizon. (Charles S. Borjes, photographer.)

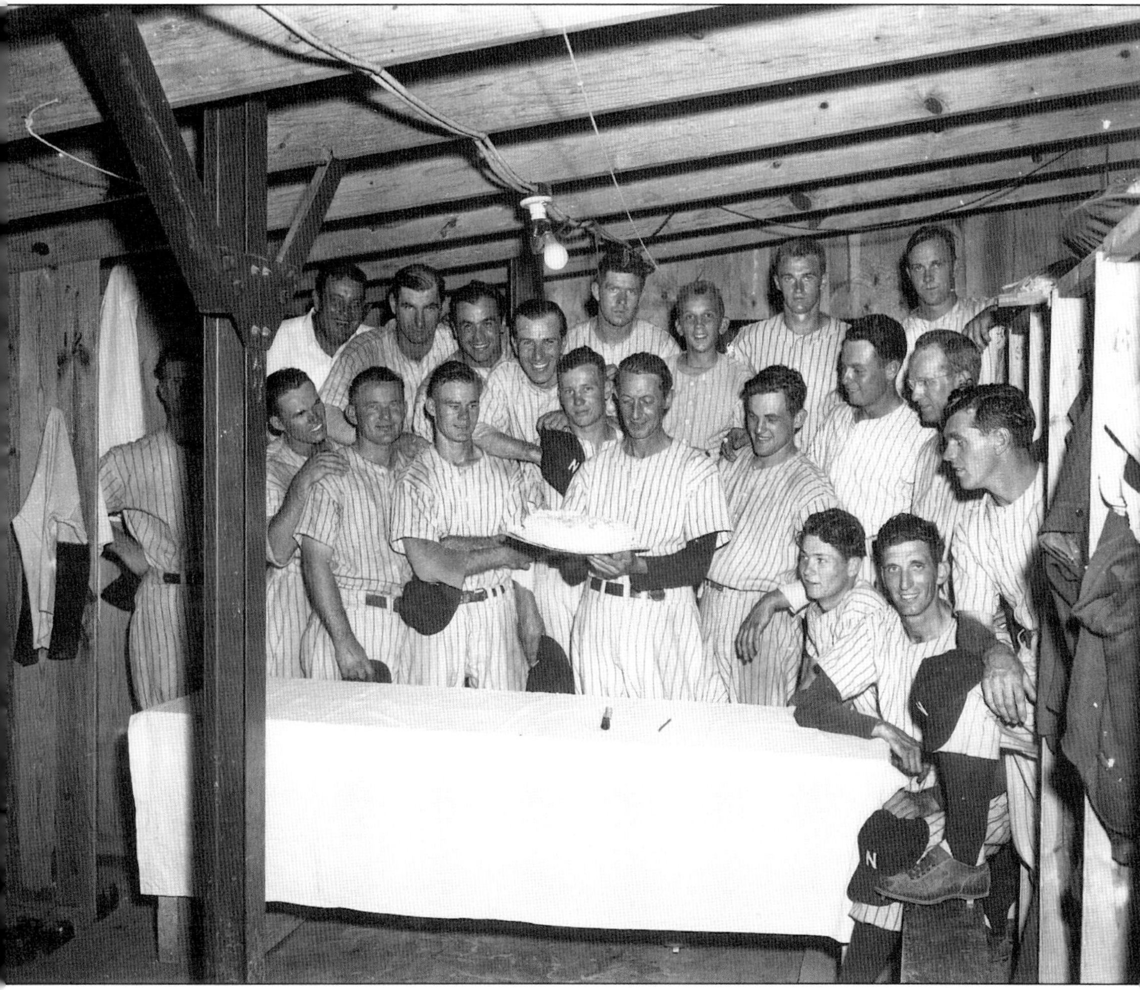

Manager Garland Braxton (center, holding the cake) was photographed with his Norfolk Tars team on June 10, 1944. The Norfolk Tars represented a colorful chapter in the area's baseball history. Begun in 1896 as Norfolk's entry in the Virginia League, the Tars continued to play on and off in the league until 1916, with one complete departure to the short-lived Atlantic League between 1898 and 1900. The Tars returned to the Virginia League after WW I, but the league folded in 1928, leaving Norfolk without a minor league ball club. Then, in 1930, a group of citizens started the Eastern League, a good-natured effort to revive the sport that died less than two years later. By 1934, Jacob Ruppert, owner of the New York Yankees, resurrected the Tars and entered them in the Piedmont League. The team experienced great success from that time on, bringing to Norfolk some of baseball's greatest talent. Garland Braxton played ten years in the majors as a pitcher before being sent to Norfolk to manage the Tars. At the age of 43 in 1943, he was still playing the game with even greater precision and style than in his earlier days. Garland Braxton's Tars won the Piedmont League pennant in 1945. (Charles S. Borjes, photographer.)

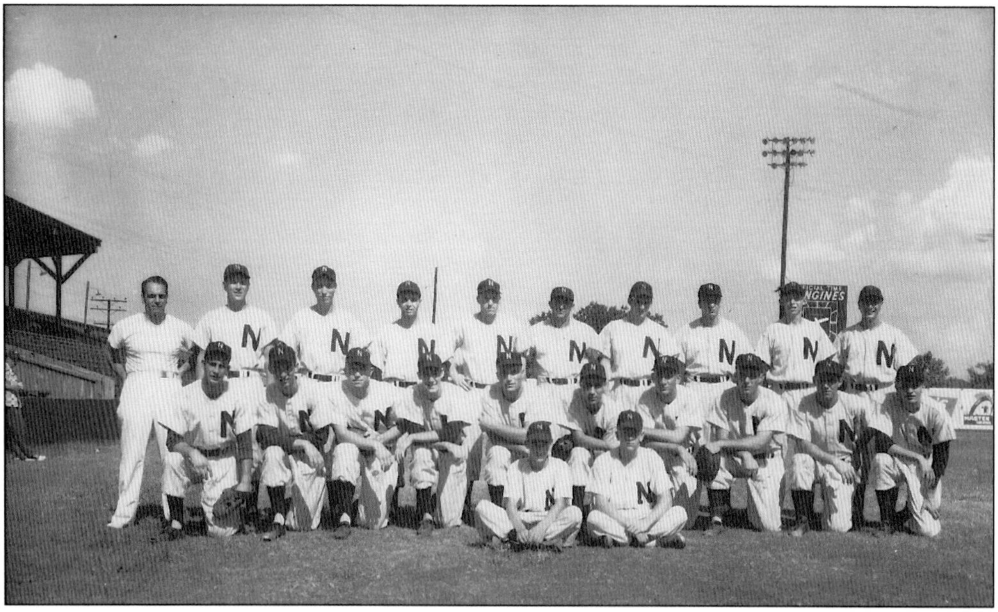

The Norfolk Tars are seen here September 3, 1950. Of all the greats to play with the Norfolk Tars prior to the team becoming a New York Yankees farm club, the name which should be remembered is that of Christy Mathewson, one of the greatest pitchers in baseball history. Mathewson was a phenomenon in Norfolk in 1900, compiling a 21-2 record. Sold to the New York Giants not long after, Mathewson garnered national acclaim by pitching three shutouts in the 1905 World Series. Mathewson, with 373 wins to his credit, was one of the first five players to be inducted into the Baseball Hall of Fame in 1936, along with Walter Johnson, Ty Cobb, Babe Ruth, and Honus Wagner. (Jim Mays, photographer.)

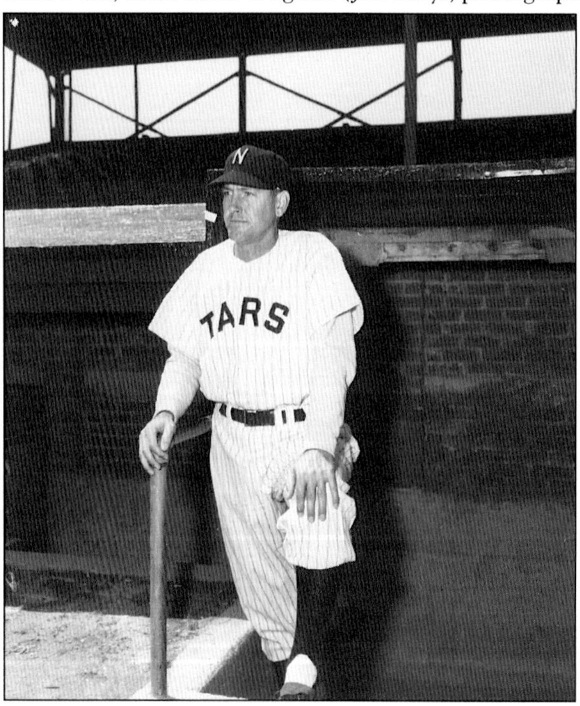

Mayo Smith, manager of the Norfolk Tars, was photographed on April 18, 1951, by Charles S. Borjes. Smith was the only manager of the Tars to have won back-to-back pennants in 1951 and 1952. He eventually earned his way from the minors to the major league management, coaching the Detroit Tigers to a World Series championship in 1968.

Six

To the Mountains and Sea

"The spring has departed, the Summer has come,
And autumn ere long its appearance will make:
So now's a good time to say good-bye to home,
And a trip to the White Sulphur take.

Chorus:
Then heigh-ho! to the Springs let us go,
To drink of the water and flirt with the girls:
To merrily prance as cotillions we dance,
Or gyrate in gay waltzing whirls.

'Tis said sulphur water for some things is good,
And girls, too, are good for a good many things;
While a waltz or cotillion, 'tis well understood,
Much comfort to many folks brings."

—From *The White Sulphur Springs*, August 1897
John Thomas Watson, American poet (1822–1905)

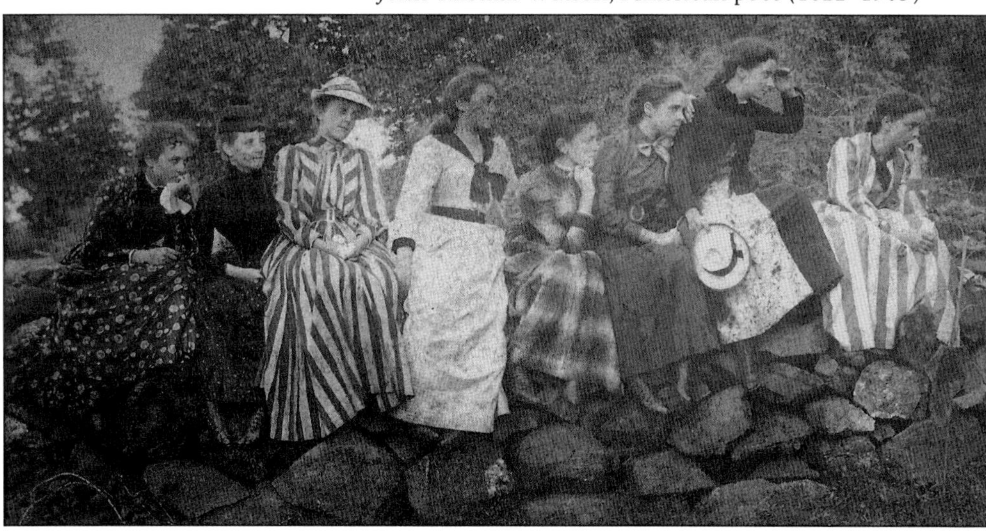

Looking for high adventure, the "gang" posed for this picture atop a stone wall at Monterey Springs in August of 1888. From left to right, they are as follows: Nina Tomlin, Mrs. George McIntosh, Bessie and Patty Taylor, Nina Whitehead, Elizabeth Taylor, Sally Walke, and Bland Taylor.

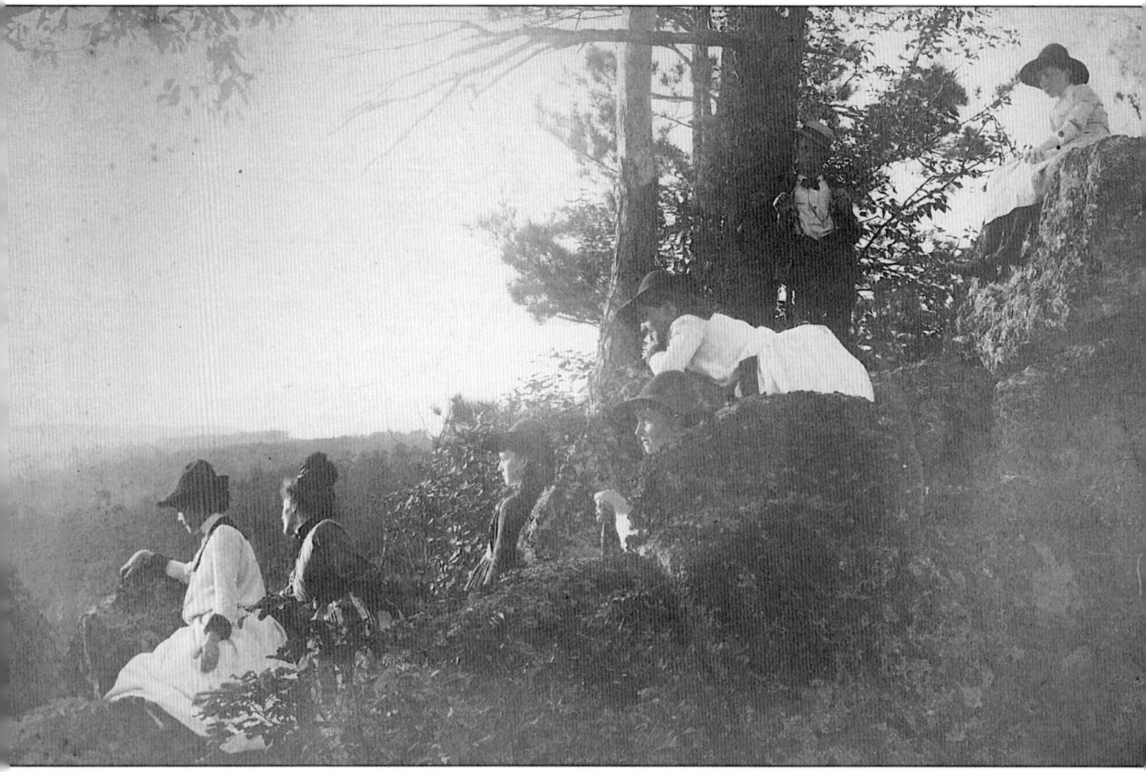

Members of the Taylor and Walke families spent the late afternoon of July 1, 1888, gazing at the Blue Ridge and a beautiful sunset from Echo Peak, Pennsylvania. The Walke family had ties to the Blue Ridge dating back to the 18th century. Captain Anthony Walke was chosen by the governor of the Virginia colony, Alexander Spotswood, to explore the reaches of the mountains in the western part of the commonwealth. Spotswood had become governor in 1710 and remained so until 1722. His tenure as governor was devoted to westward settlement and securing Native American trade from the French. Walke and a gentleman named Colonel Edward Moseley (who had married the widow of Bartholomew Taylor of the Eastern Shore) were part of Spotswood's 1716 expedition of 63 men. Eight days after the expedition departed Germanna, they reached the highest point of the Blue Ridge at Swift Run Gap. From this vantage point they looked down into the beautiful Shenandoah Valley, and, from there, they gazed upon the Massanutten, the Native American name given to one of the mountains. Far to the west, the men of Spotswood's group saw the Allegheny Mountains. Walke would return to Princess Anne County with fond tales of his adventure with Governor Spotswood, as well as an abiding love of the mountains he explored on his journey. To commemorate the expedition, Governor Spotswood gave each of the members of his party a golden horseshoe encrusted with jewels which bore the Latin motto, *Sic juvat transcendere montes*, meaning "How delightful it is to cross the mountains." To date, only one of the horseshoes was ever seen in the 20th century, and that one was exhibited in the New World building at the Jamestown Exposition in 1907.

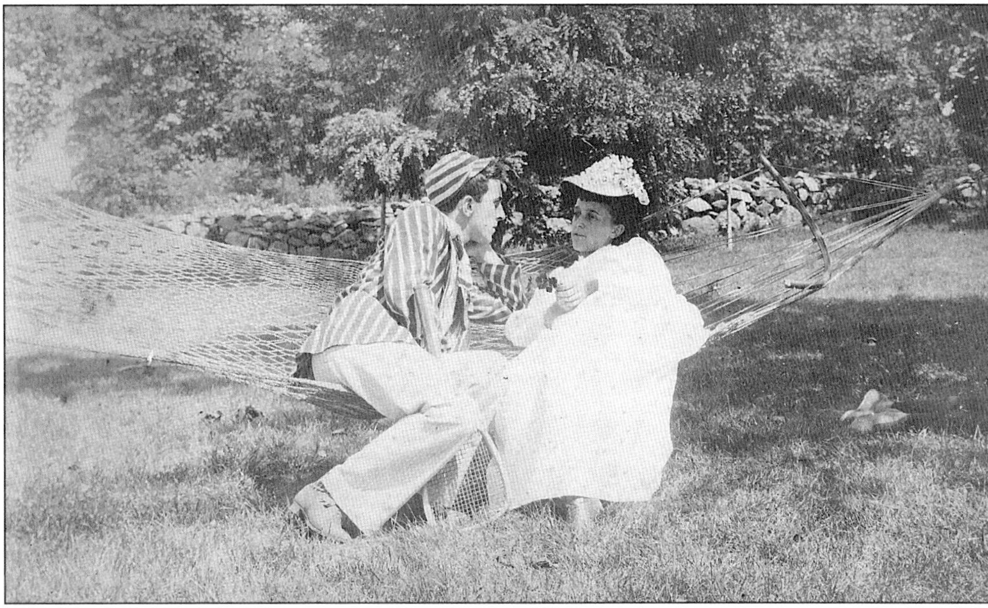

Dr. Robert Tunstall "Bob" Taylor and Bessie Taylor (late Mrs. William B. Baldwin) posed in a hammock at the Blue Ridge Summit in August 1888. Bessie Taylor was a mere 21 years of age when this picture was taken on the summit. She died in Norfolk on November 21, 1948, at the age of 81.

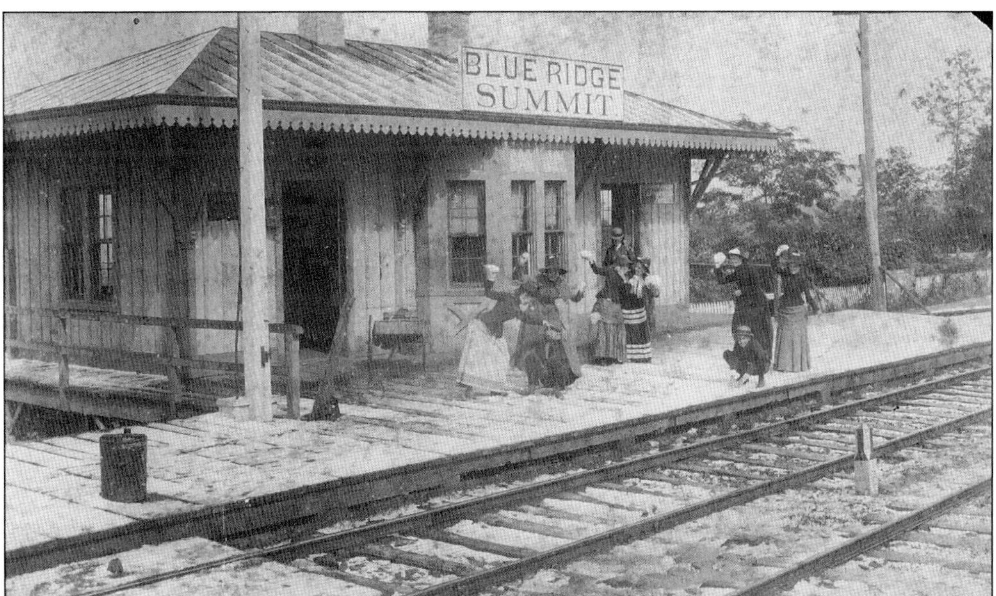

The train station at the Blue Ridge Summit was photographed by an unknown photographer on September 29, 1888, while Taylor family members mugged for the camera.

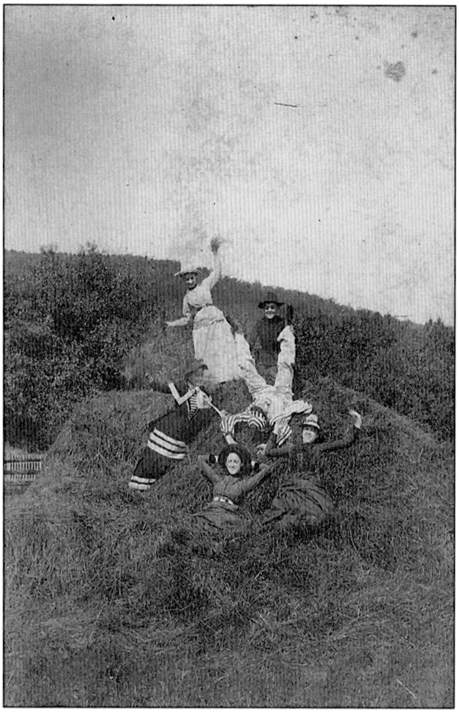

Bob Taylor was tossed headfirst into a hay pile by Bland Taylor, Sally Walke, Bessie Taylor, and Nina Whitehead at the Monterey Springs property, August 1888.

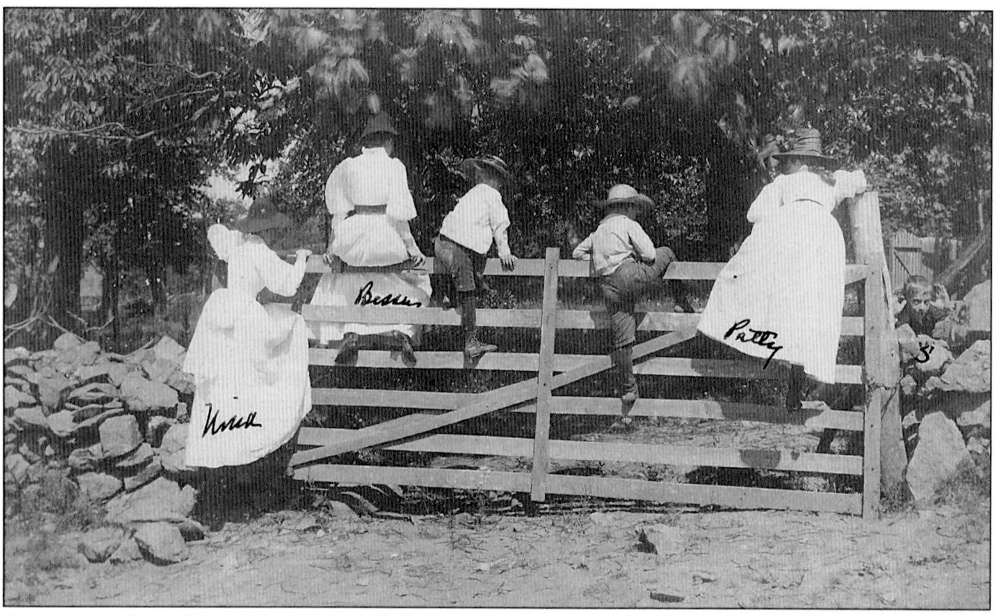

Going over the split rail fence, from left to right, Nina Tomlin, Bessie Taylor, two unidentified little boys, Patty Taylor, and, to the far right, poking fun at the photographer, "S" (Sinclair Taylor) decided to play a game of hide-and-seek. The picture was taken in August 1888 at the Blue Ridge Summit.

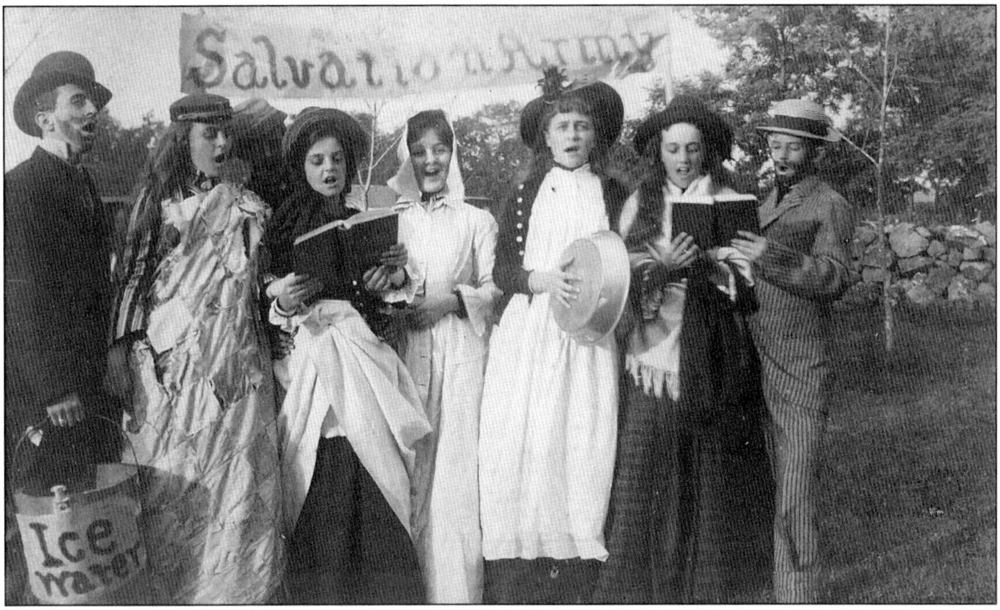

Spoofing the Salvation Army during their stay at the Blue Ridge Summit in August 1888, the young people of the Taylor and Walke families, from left to right, are as follows: Robert Tunstall "Bob" Taylor, Patty, Dick, and Bland Taylor, Ethel Neely, Nina Tomlin, and Bessie and Lee Taylor. "Dick" is Richard Cornelius Taylor, born in 1874 and died on July 21, 1936, at the age of 62. Ethel Neely never married. She passed away in Norfolk at the age of 72 on January 12, 1943.

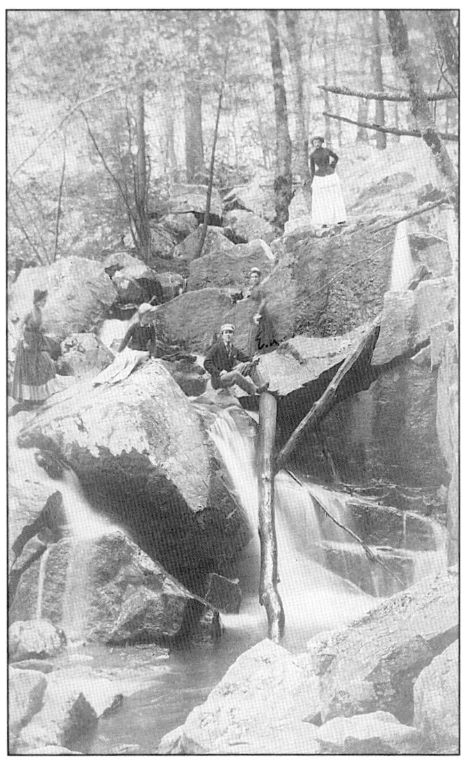

The Cascades were part of the Taylor and Walke families' trek to the Blue Ridge Summit for summer vacation. This picture, taken in August of 1888, is indicative of the rocky terrain the young people of these two prominent Norfolk families so enjoyed climbing as part of their holiday to the mountains.

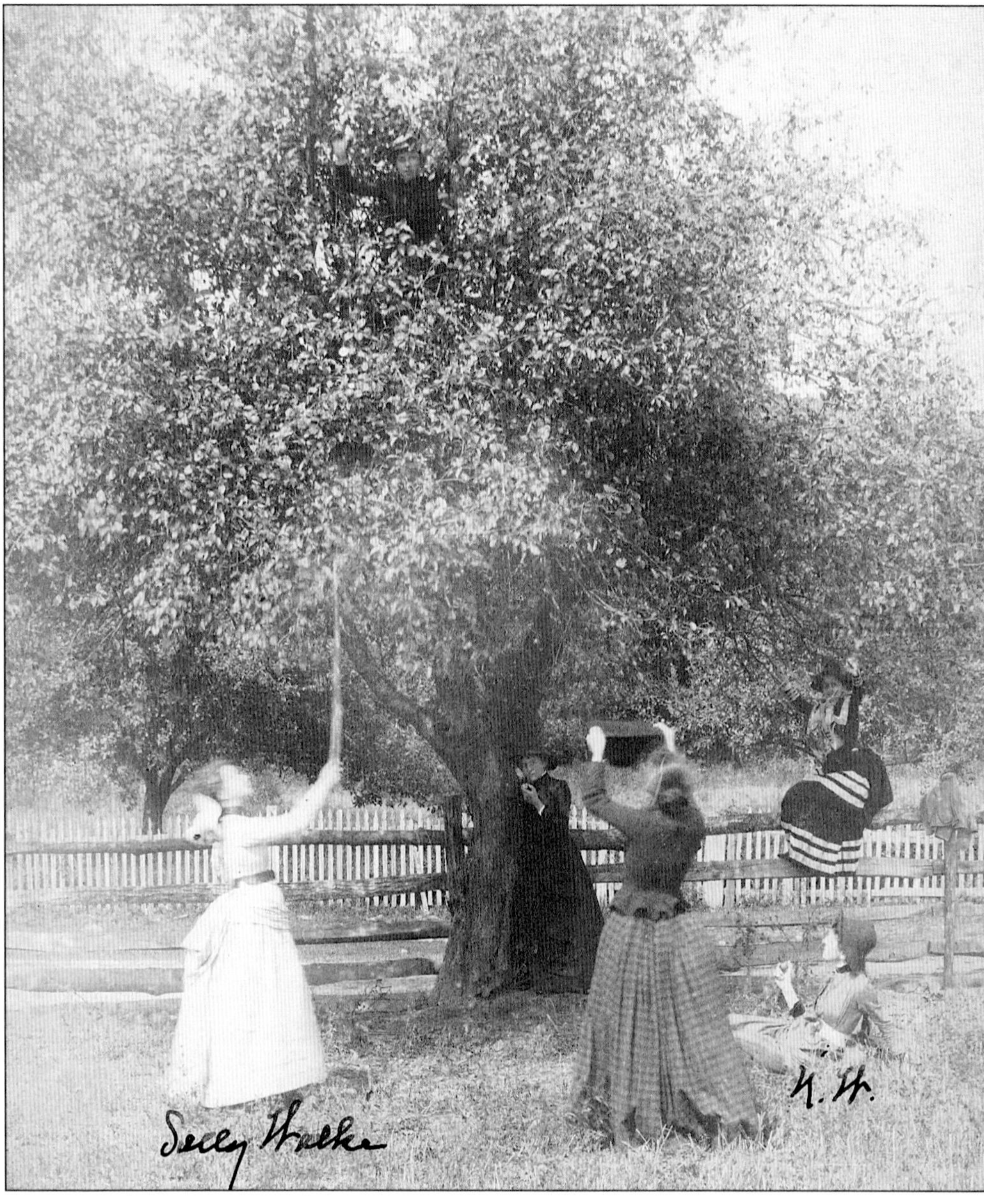

Picking apples was a team effort on the Taylors and Walkes's trip to Monterey Springs on the Blue Ridge Summit during September of 1888. One person dutifully climbed the tree while Sally Walke beat the lower branches to jar loose apples for a friend to catch in her hat. Nina Whitehead (right, sitting in the tall grass) decided she had had enough picking apples and that eating one was more to her liking. When John Thomas Watson composed his poem *Know Ye the Land Where the Peach Tree and Apple* . . . in 1842, he must have had this scene in mind down to the smell of the apples and the buzz of the bees. He penned the following: "Know ye the land of the oak and the pine / Where the flowers yearly blossom and yearly decline? / Where the light wings of Zephyr, oppress'd with the scent / Of distilleries, invade every house, field and tent? / Where the apple and peach are the fairest of fruit? / Where the voice of the guinea-fowl never is mute? / Where the tints of the earth and the hues of the sky / I color though varied, in beauty ne'er vie."

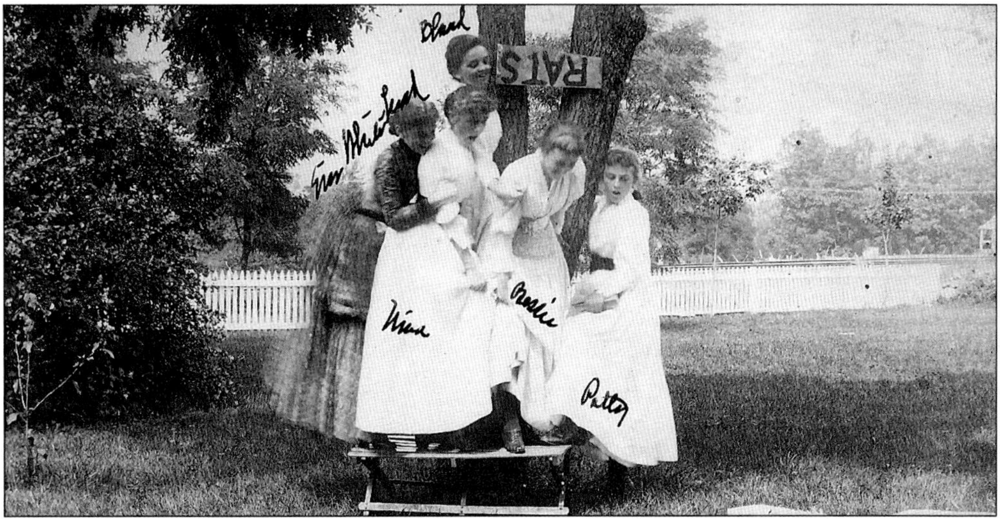

"Oh, what happened to Ethel?!?" exclaimed the giggling group of her friends who, in Ethel's absence, laid one of her dresses on the ground and pretended she had just disappeared! The skit was obviously for fun. From left to right, the girls are as follows: Elizabeth Whitehead, Nina Tomlin, Bland Taylor, Bessie Taylor, and Patty Taylor, August 1888, at Monterey Springs. The springs of western Virginia were believed to be good for one's health as well as spirit. By 1859, travel to Virginia's springs had grown rapidly as vacationers sought the curative and comforting powers they believed to be found in the waters. At the time the pictures shown here were taken, families not only visited, but owned properties near the springs.

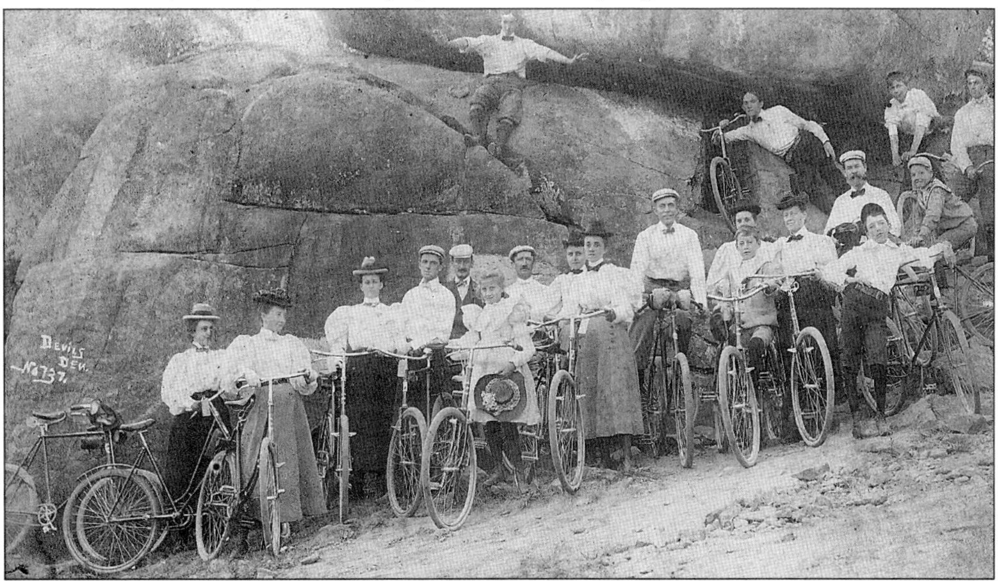

Devil's Den at Gettysburg, Pennsylvania, was the scene of this bicycle outing, which included members of Norfolk's Taylor family in 1889. This area of rocks, formed during the Ice Age, became famous for its position at the base of Little Round Top during the bloody engagement of Union and Confederate forces at the Battle of Gettysburg in 1863. First contact was made at Devil's Den on July 2 in which the Confederates, despite resistance from Union troops, quickly overtook this advantageous position. Confederate sharpshooters picked off Union soldiers on Little Round Top from these haunted rocks. (J.I. Mumper, photographer.)

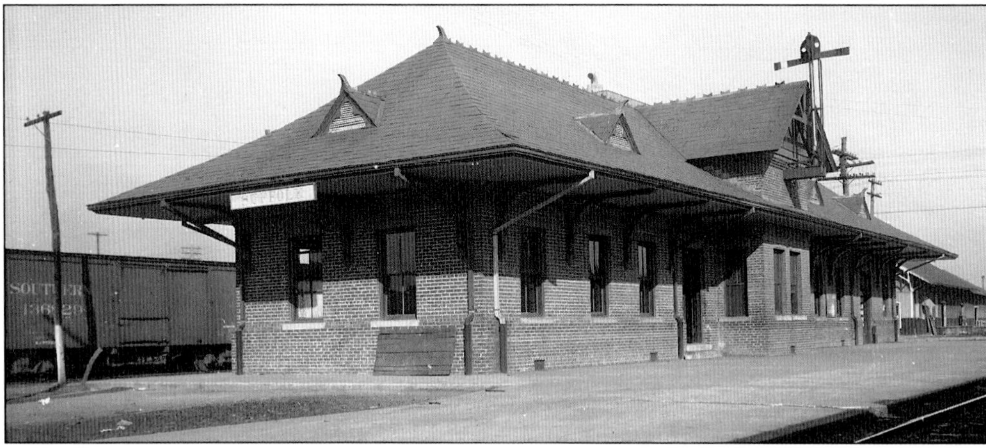

The famous lines from Henry David Thoreau's *Old Marlborough Road*, "When the spring stirs my blood, / With the instinct to travel," appropriately describe the exodus of families from the cities and counties on the southside who, like clockwork, left the trappings of their year-round homes to travel to destinations far and wide, such as the Blue Ridge and Allegheny Mountains or places closer to home such as Virginia Beach and Ocean View, or a bit farther away like Nags Head, North Carolina, for rest and recreation. In most cases, it was the women and children who remained on holiday through late-spring and summer, with husbands and fathers visiting in-between work and social obligations at home as time permitted. The old Suffolk train station, pictured here as it appeared in 1927, was the start of many such journeys to the mountains of Virginia. (Charles S. Borjes, photographer.)

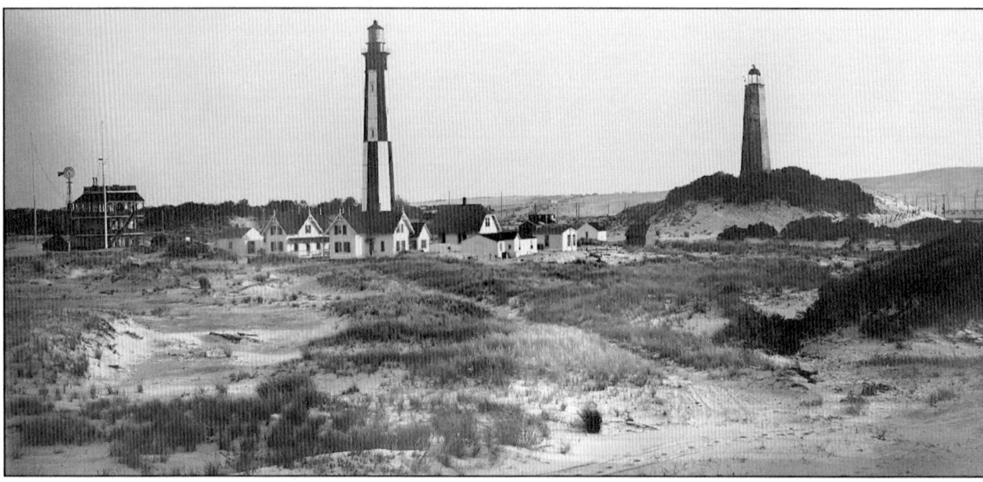

When the old Cape Henry lighthouse was built in 1791, the top of the dune where the octagonal tower stands was leveled some 75 feet from side to side. A bulwark 3 feet thick and 3 feet high—equivalent to the breastworks of a fort—and made of rough stone with foundations sunk below the surface was built around the edges. In the early days of the old lighthouse's existence, sand was almost always a problem. Benjamin Henry Latrobe (1764-1820), the most famous architect and engineer of his day, visited the lighthouse in 1798 and reported that the keeper's wooden, two-story house was overtopped by mounds of sand which, as Latrobe put it, "buried his kitchen to the eaves." This photograph depicts the new iron lighthouse, finished in 1881, on the left and the old lighthouse to the right. The three-story building to the far left of the new lighthouse is the old weather station. Harry C. Mann took this photograph about 1907. The residences of the keepers and weather station personnel dot the landscape around the lighthouses.

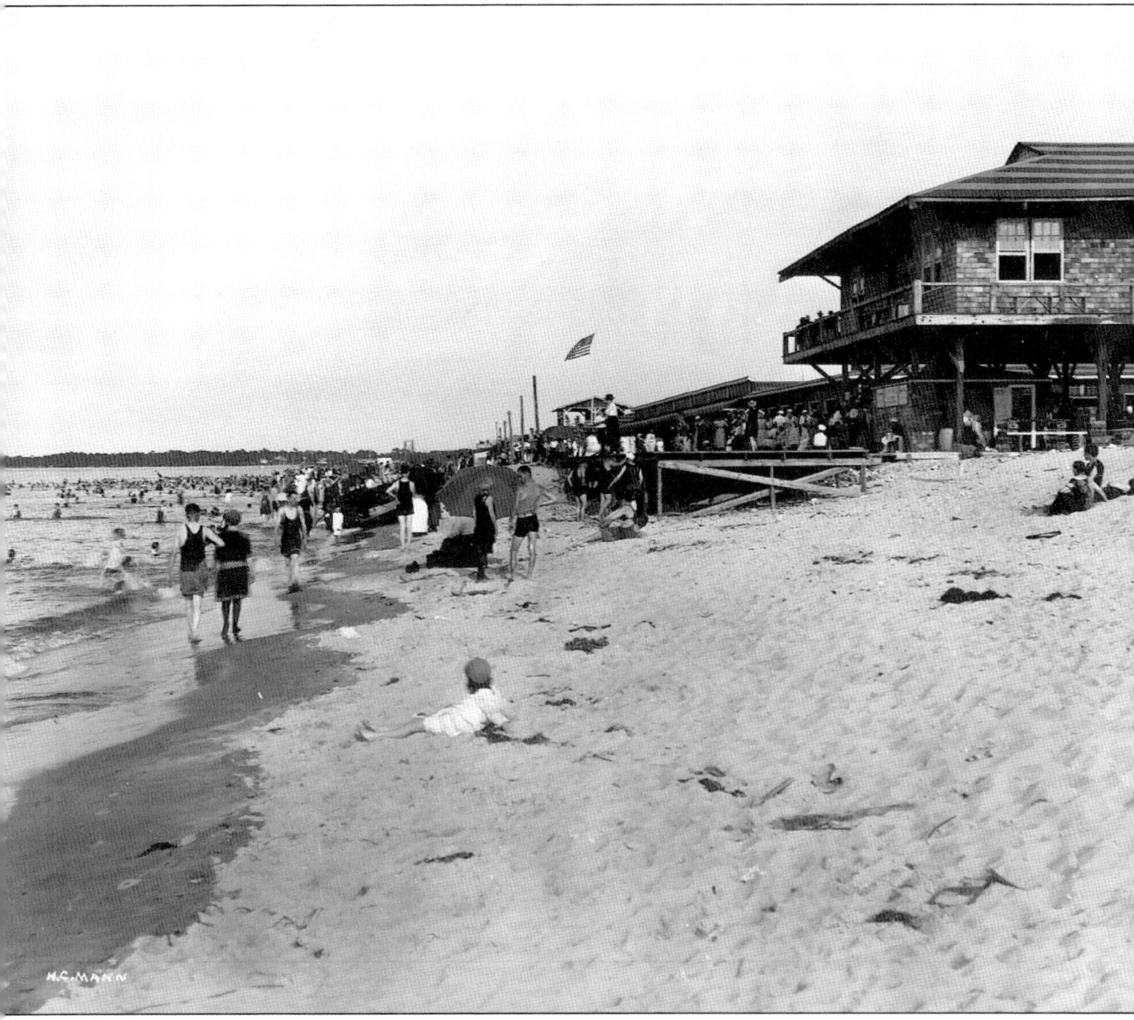

Ocean Park, located over the Lesner Bridge approximately where Duck-In Restaurant sits today, was photographed by Harry C. Mann in 1913, the year it opened its facilities to the public. The resort was nearly always crowded and remained a popular getaway for residents of southside cities and counties from 1913 into the early 1930s. The park was operated by the Ocean Park Corporation, headquartered in Norfolk, and owned by James W. Hough, a real estate developer who was also a principal in the firm of Bellamy & Hough, Inc., and Wayland W. Yoder. It is remarkable that Ocean Park was constructed near what had been a 17th-century fortification c. 1610. The fort was equal in age to what had been Forts Henry and Charles near Kecoughtan, and like the Kecoughtan sites, had been built on the site of a former Native American encampment, in this case, one belonging to the Chesapeake Indians. The location of their encampment and, later, the fortification, was between Ocean Park and Chesapeake Beach, roughly where Apasus is shown on John White's 1585 map of the area.

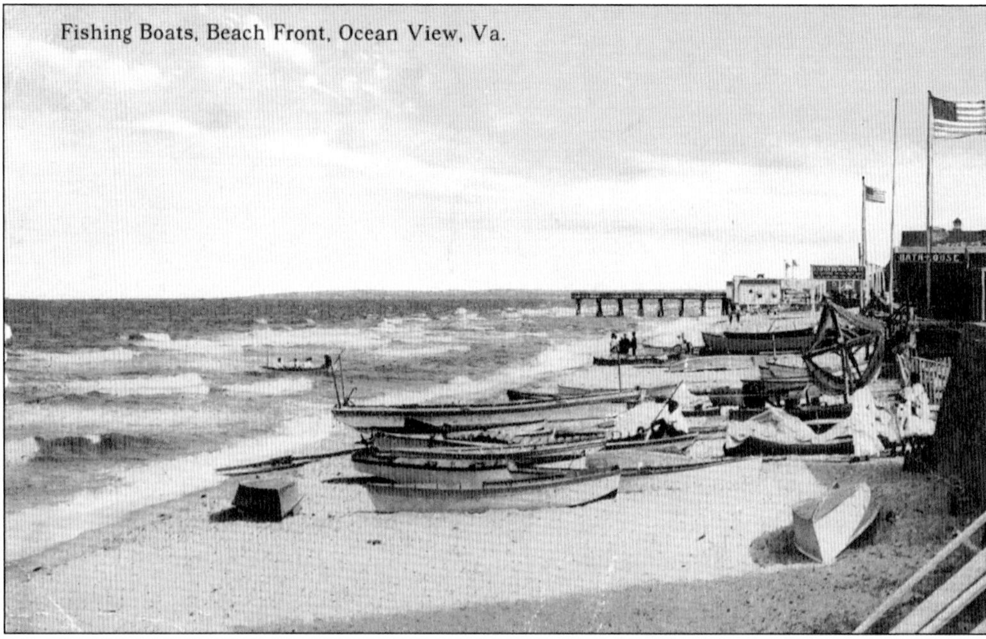

This penny postcard of fishing boats on the beach at Ocean View was postmarked September 2, 1912. Fishing at Ocean View was a fisherman's dream come true. The location of the boathouse was right off the old amusement park. Excursion boats took men, women, and children of all ages fishing for the famous Ocean View spot as well as croakers, flounder, and chub.

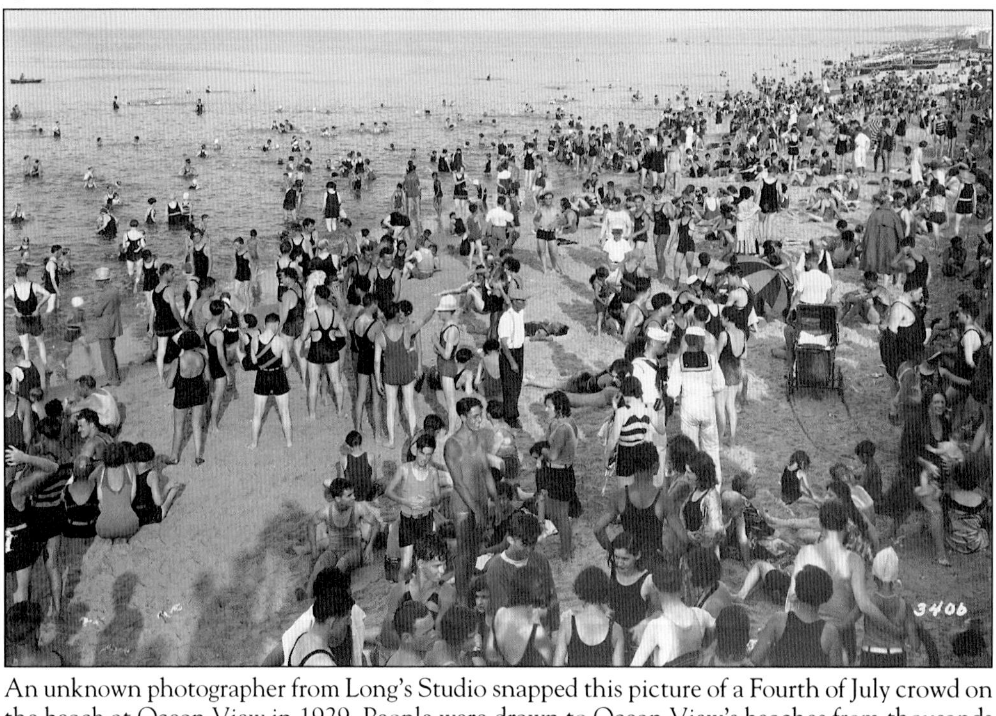

An unknown photographer from Long's Studio snapped this picture of a Fourth of July crowd on the beach at Ocean View in 1929. People were drawn to Ocean View's beaches from thousands of miles away—just for the opportunity to experience the thrill that comes with the splash of gentle waves on the Chesapeake Bay and a visit to Ocean View Amusement Park.

Seven

Toiling in the Sun

"The splendid raiment of the Spring peeps forth;
Her universal green, and the clear sky,
Delight still more and move the gazing eye.
Wide o'er the fields, in rising moisture strong,
Shoots up the simple flower, or creeps along
The mellow'd soil; imbibing fairer hues,
Or sweets from frequent showers and evening dews;
That summon from their sheds the slumb'ring plows,
While health impregnates every breeze that blows."

—From *The Farmer's Boy; A Rural Poem*, 1806
Robert Bloomfield, English poet (1766–1823)

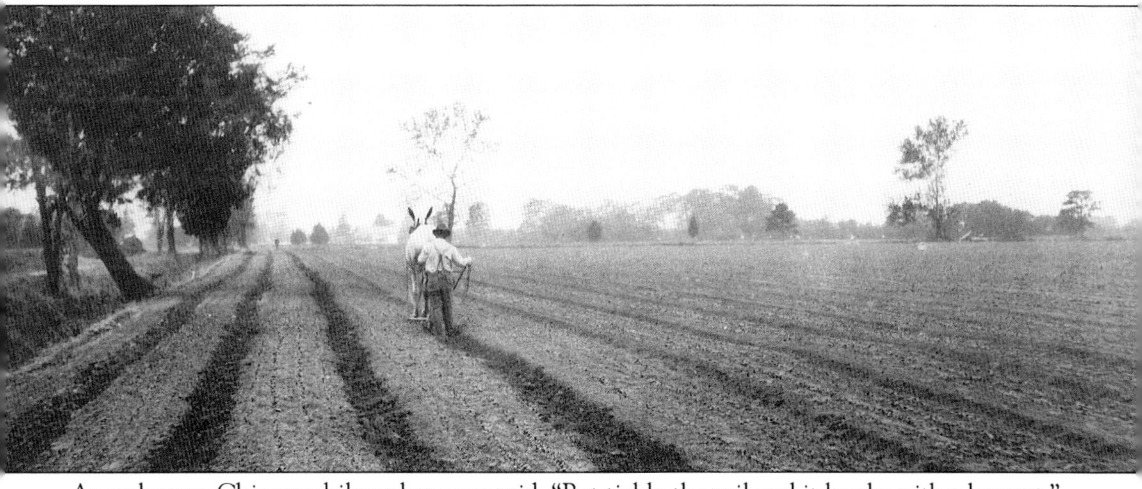

An unknown Chinese philosopher once said, "But tickle the soil and it laughs with a harvest." The farmer ploughing and cultivating this field with his mule in Lower Norfolk County (now Chesapeake) was but one of many such truck farmers whose farms supplied fresh produce to markets in Norfolk as well as areas of the country as far away as New York and New Jersey. The picture was taken about the turn of the century. (Photographer unknown.)

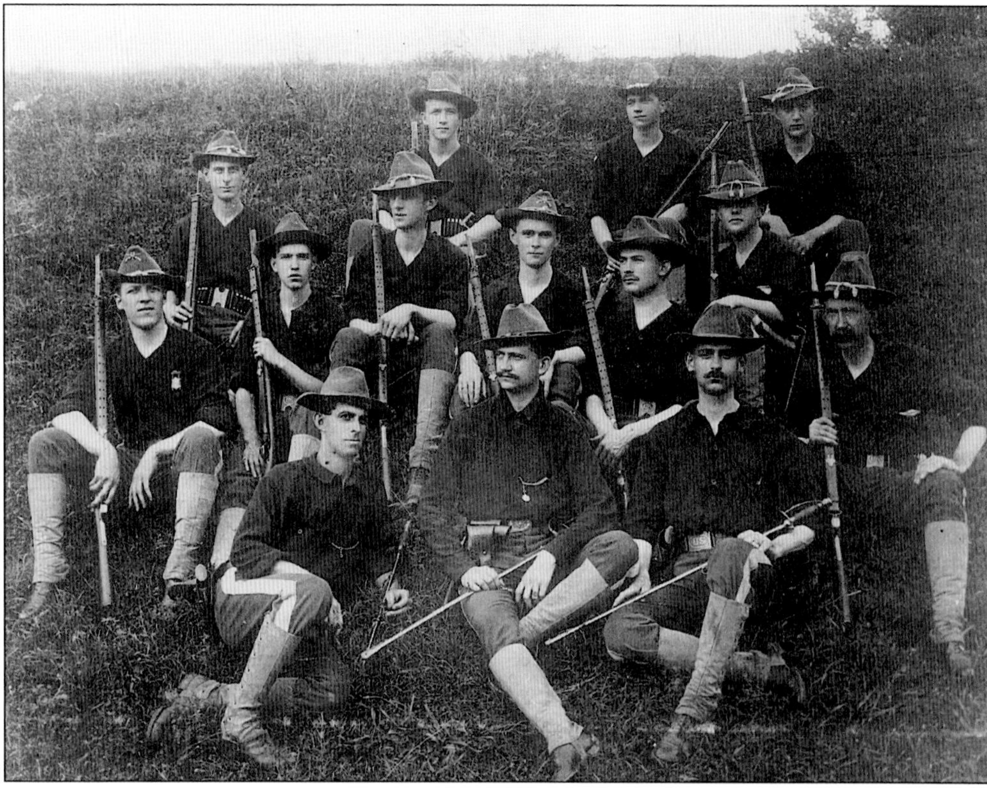

Members of the Lee Rifles, Norfolk Company A, 71st Regiment Infantry Virginia Volunteers were called to duty during the streetcar strike in Richmond, Virginia, during June and July of 1903. Captain Frederick L. Curdts (center row, fourth from the left) was in charge of the unit. Lieutenant John Creekmore (center row, far left) was second in command. (Photographer unknown.)

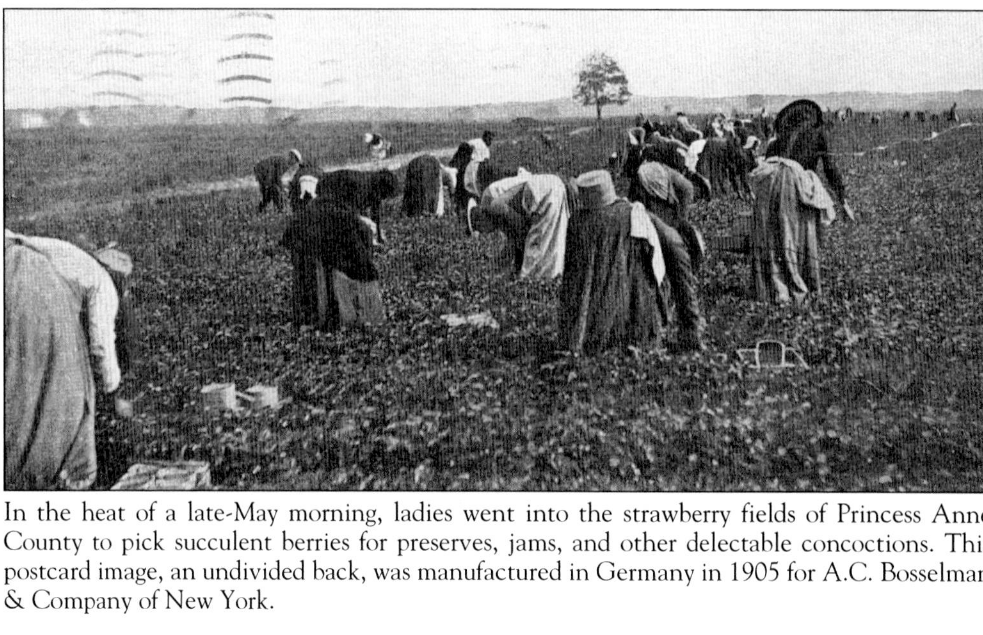

In the heat of a late-May morning, ladies went into the strawberry fields of Princess Anne County to pick succulent berries for preserves, jams, and other delectable concoctions. This postcard image, an undivided back, was manufactured in Germany in 1905 for A.C. Bosselman & Company of New York.

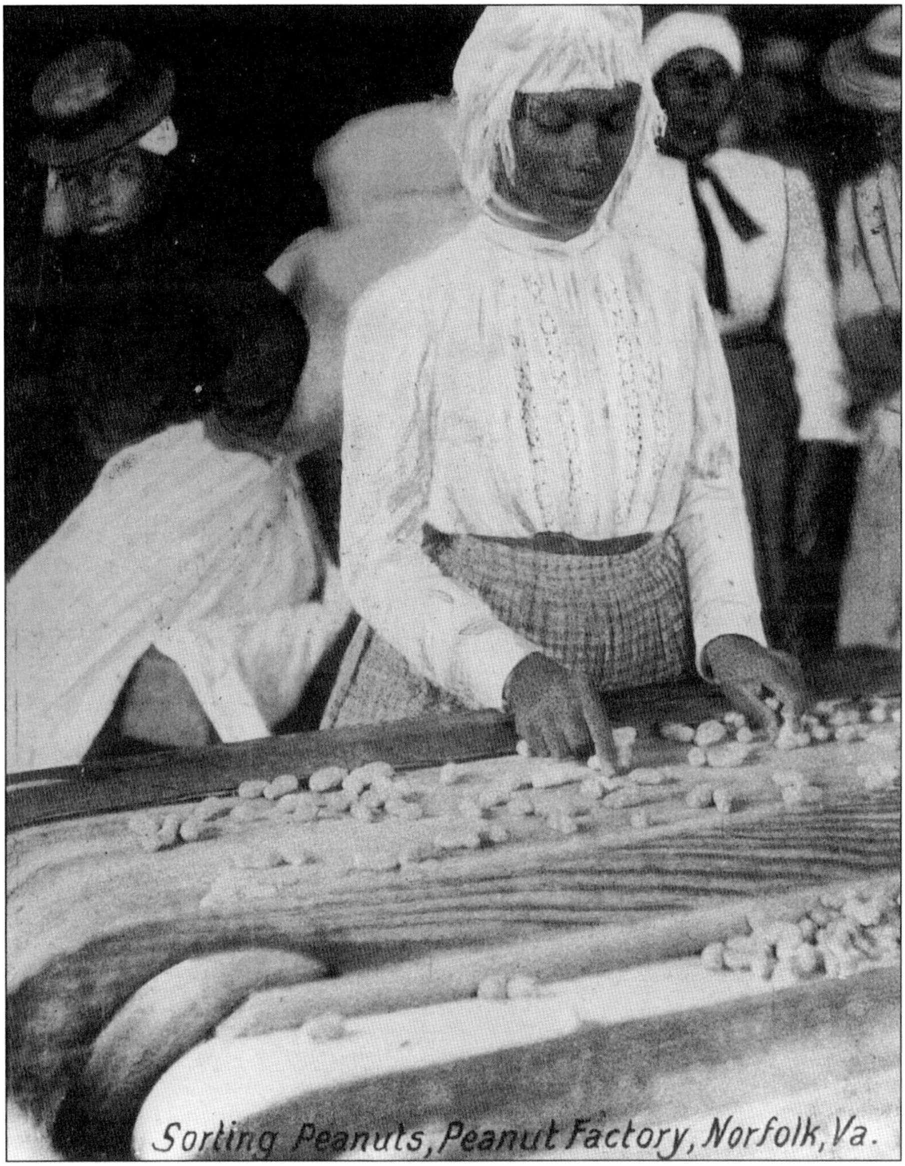

The job of sorting peanuts in a Norfolk factory belonging to the Columbian Peanut Company was tedious work for these women, *c.* 1910. The company had its beginnings in Norfolk in 1892 and was organized by John L. Roper and his partners. The company's first plant, in which this image was taken, occupied an entire block of Water Street in Norfolk, which at that time was the hub of the peanut-milling industry and the largest miller of raw peanuts in the United States. As production increased, peanuts began to be cultivated in North Carolina, and, by 1904, the center of the industry became centered around Suffolk. The company, which took its name from the fact that it was founded in the year of the Columbian Exposition, constructed a new plant in Suffolk—the heart of peanut-growing country—where it remained in operation until the plant was sold to John King Peanut Company in 1913. The Columbian Peanut Company subsequently built another plant in Suffolk.

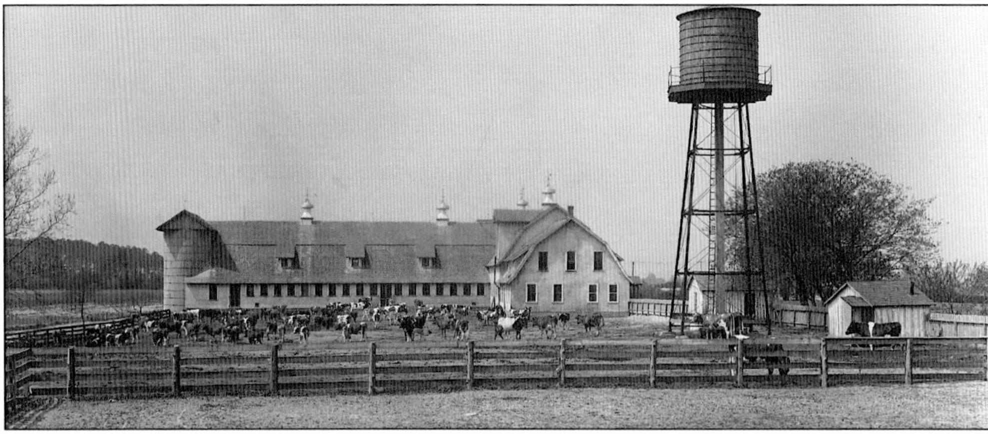

Foxhall Farm Dairy, built along the old Princess Anne Turnpike, was one of Harry C. Mann's favorite subjects to photograph. Morris S. Secord was superintendent of the farm. Taken about 1914, this image projects the bucolic life on a dairy farm which, in those days, was an important supplier of dairy products to people living in and around downtown Norfolk. The Fox Hall section of Norfolk bears the name of the farm which was tucked between the southern end of Sewell's Point Road where it once enjoined the eastern end of Princess Anne Road near the head of Broad Creek. Princess Anne Road ran into the county also bearing the name Princess Anne. Princess Anne County was formed in 1691 with the division of Lower Norfolk County into Norfolk and Princess Anne Counties. The farm was on the north side of old Princess Anne Road.

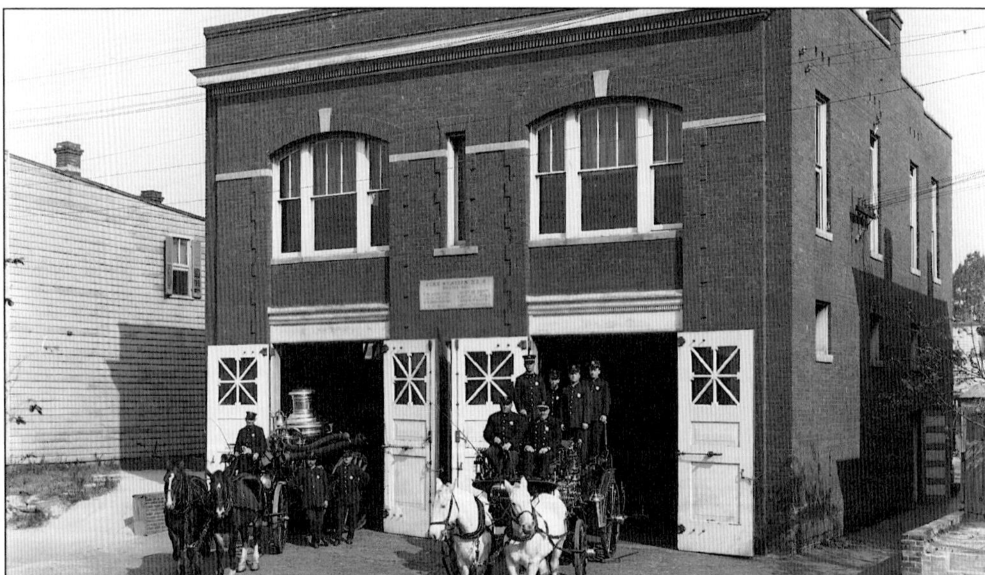

The Norfolk Fire Department's Fire Station No. 4 was located on East Olney Road. Harry C. Mann took this photograph c. 1908. The early fire engines were horse-drawn water-pumping machines manned by black men until about 1849, when whites began taking over positions on the engines. The very first fire company in Norfolk was established in 1797 by Robert Archer and was called the Union Fire Company of Fire Company No. 1. The firemen were completely volunteer before the City incorporated the fire department in 1871. Only the fire wardens were paid prior to incorporation.

Chemical Company No. 10 of the Norfolk Fire Department was still using horse power when this picture was taken outside the station, located at Thirty-eighth Street near Bowden's Ferry Road, about 1912. This print was made from the original glass plate, which had broken into two pieces. (Harry C. Mann, photographer.)

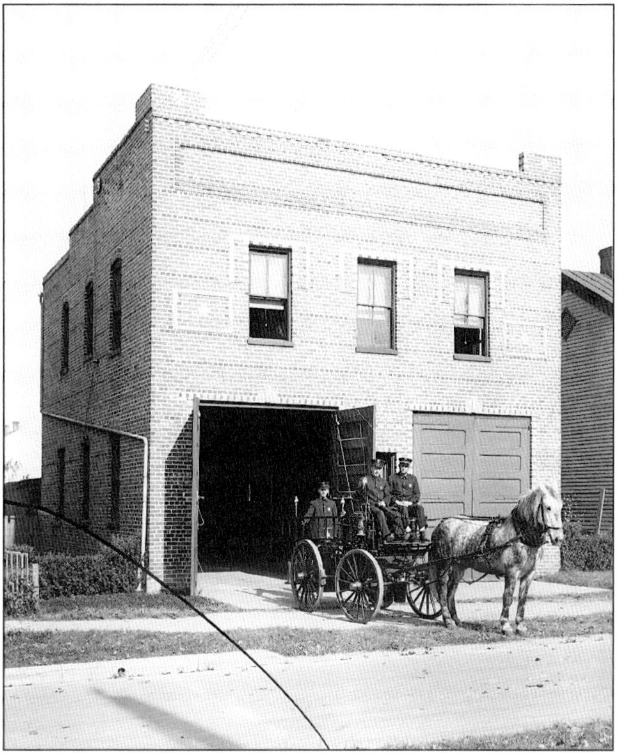

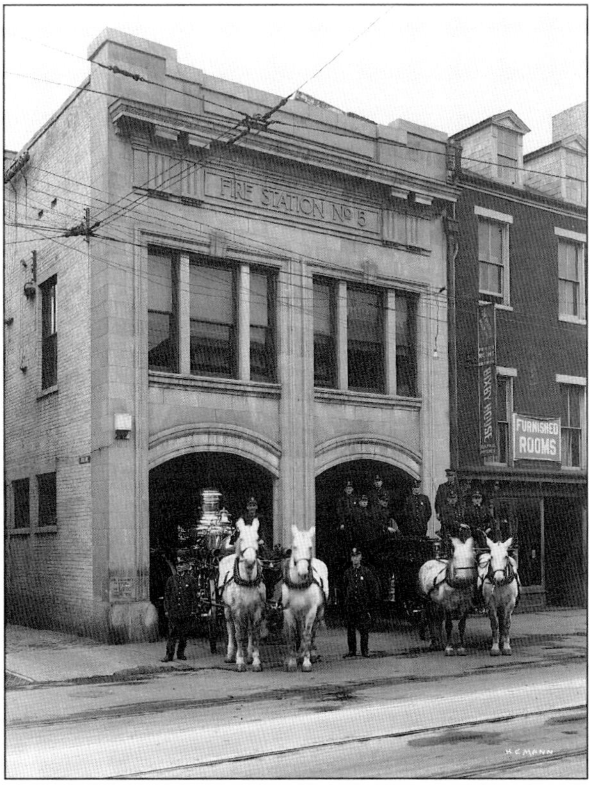

The horses would not be still for Harry C. Mann to take this picture, c. 1910, of the Norfolk Fire Department's Fire Station No. 5, situated at 733 East Main Street. George W. Stone Jr., a former assistant fire chief, once recalled that two fire horses, Clydesdales named Thunder and Lightning, had had long careers pulling steam engines to fires for the Norfolk Fire Department. With the advent of motorized firetrucks, Thunder and Lightning's services were no longer needed, so they were sold to a Norfolk dairy in 1923, only a few months after the city finally phased out horse-drawn engines. Every time the horses heard the fire bells wail, they would run off after the fire wagon, spilling milk down the streets of Norfolk. The dairy promptly returned the horses to the city, where they were assigned to walk ahead of the men who cleaned the streets.

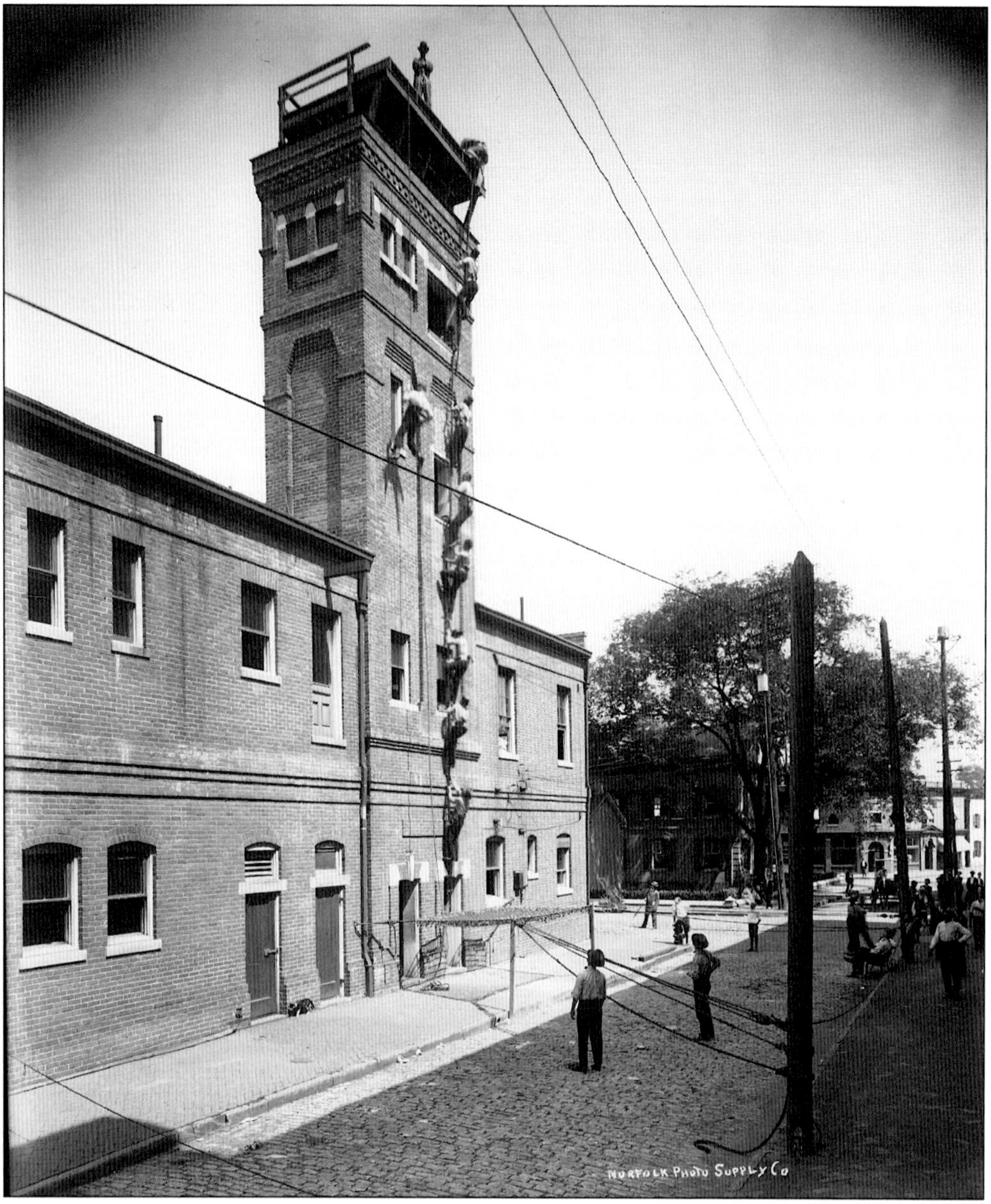

Firemen practiced on the tower of Norfolk's Fire Station No. 1, located on Plume Street at the corner of Talbot Street, July 1910. (Harry C. Mann, photographer.)

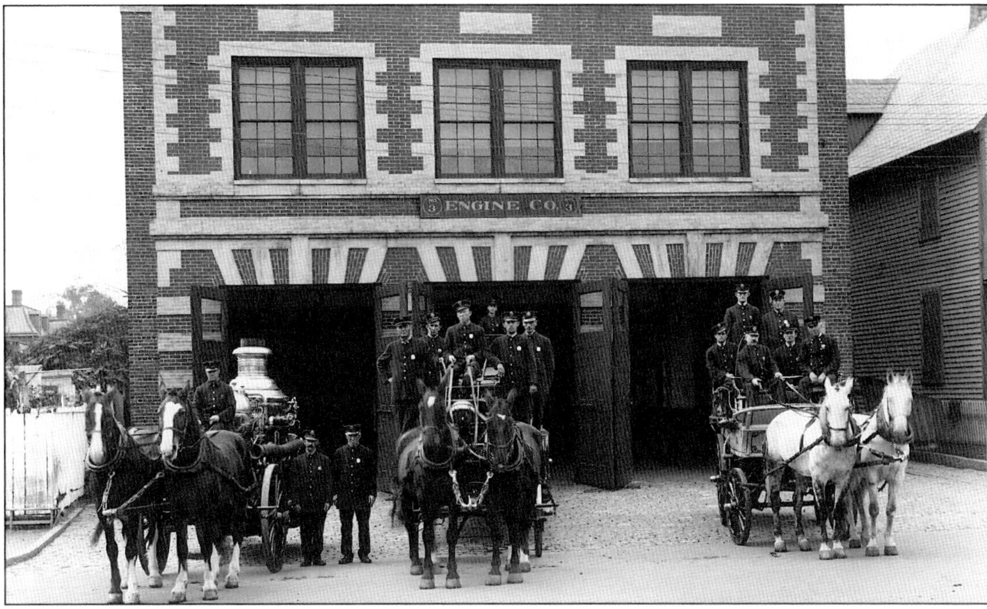

Firemen of Fire Station No. 3, situated in Norfolk's Atlantic City section on West Fairfax Avenue near Colley Avenue, show off their equipment to photographer Harry C. Mann, *c.* 1912. The steam engine to the far left is engraved with Thomas Kevill's name. The fire department was incorporated as part of city government in 1871, and its firemen compensated by the city for their services. The department's first fire chief after incorporation was Thomas Kevill, a personage already famous in Norfolk and vicinity as a volunteer gunner aboard the Confederate ironclad CSS *Virginia* when she engaged the Union fleet in Hampton Roads on March 8-9, 1862, and specifically, the USS *Monitor* on the second day of the battle. Kevill, a member of the United Fire Company at the start of the Civil War, was joined by several firemen from his unit, each of whom served alongside him manning the guns of the *Virginia*.

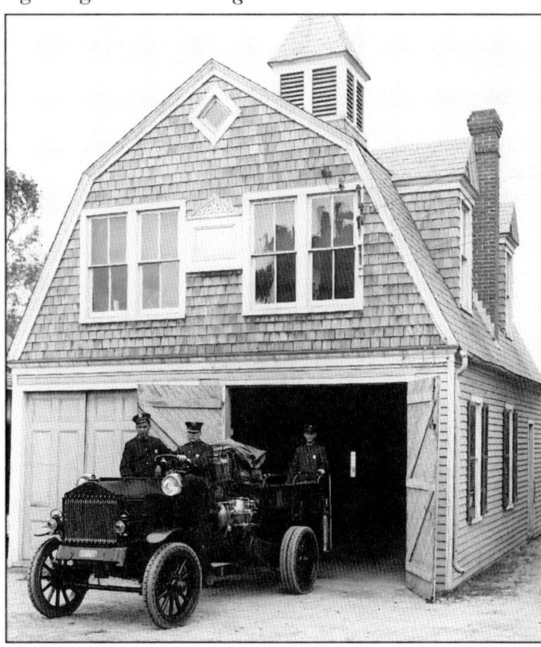

Members of the Norfolk Fire Department, Chemical Company No. 7, located on Old Ocean View Road, show off their REO firetruck in front of the station house, *c.* 1913. The truck was manufactured by REO Motor Car Company, founded by Ransom Eli Olds in 1904. About 1912, Olds's automobiles and trucks were using acetylene headlights and kerosene lamps as sidelights or, as is evident in this picture, as lights mounted on either side of the radiator grill. The steering wheel of this firetruck is wooden. Olds, an inventor, machinist, and manufacturer, founded the Oldsmobile Company in 1897, a progeny he would leave seven years later to start his new motor car company. (Harry C. Mann, photographer.)

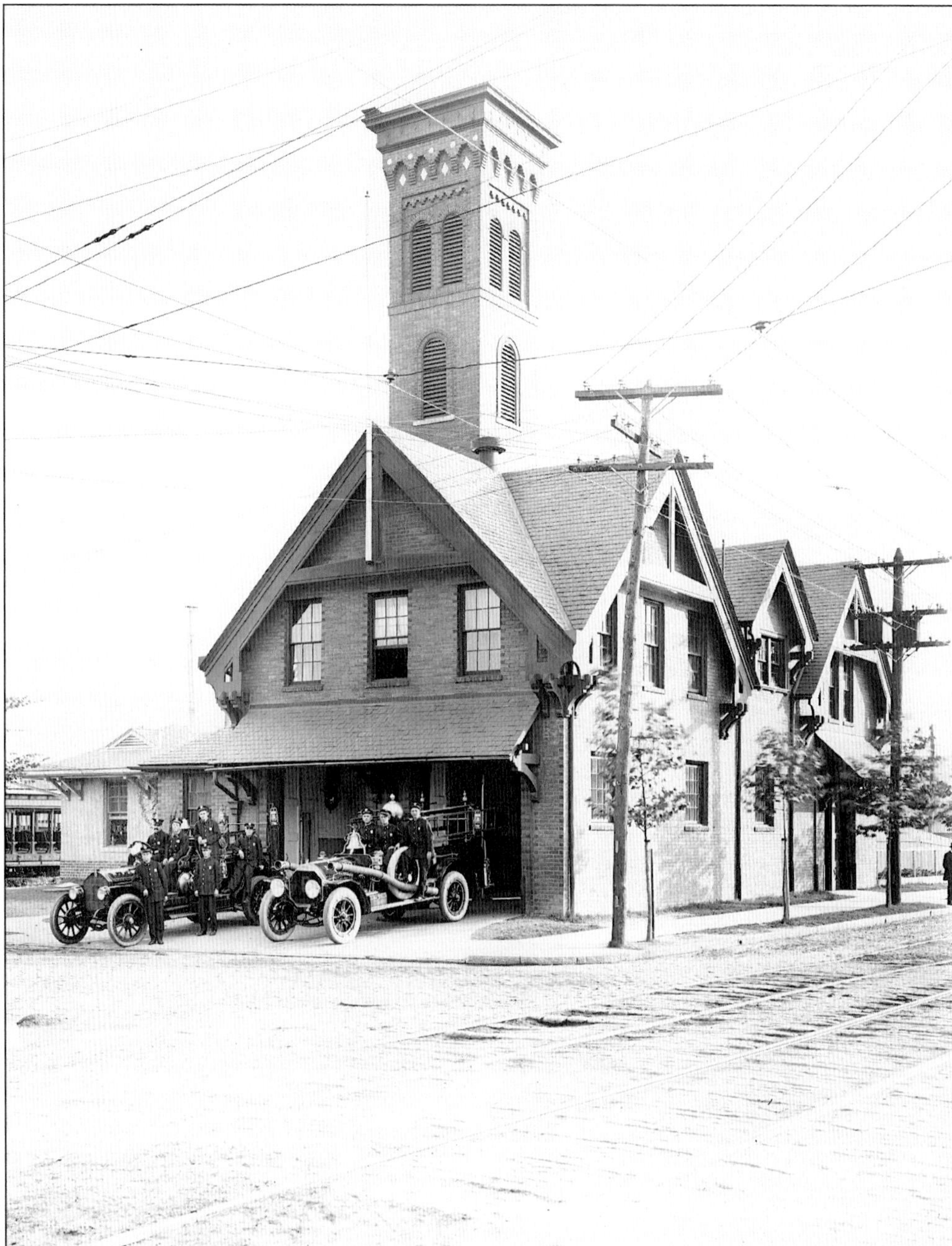

The first motorized vehicle purchased by the Norfolk Fire Department was a car for the fire chief in 1911. By 1912, the chief's car was joined by a motor tractor, the first firefighting equipment not drawn by horses. Two more motorized engines were added in 1913. Each year or so more motorized equipment was bought by the fire department until horse-drawn engines disappeared for good in 1923. Fire Station No. 6, located on the corner of Twelfth Street and Monticello Avenue, was built in 1911. The 70-foot tower was designed for drying hoses and conducting fire drills. The picture was taken about 1915. (Harry C. Mann, photographer.)

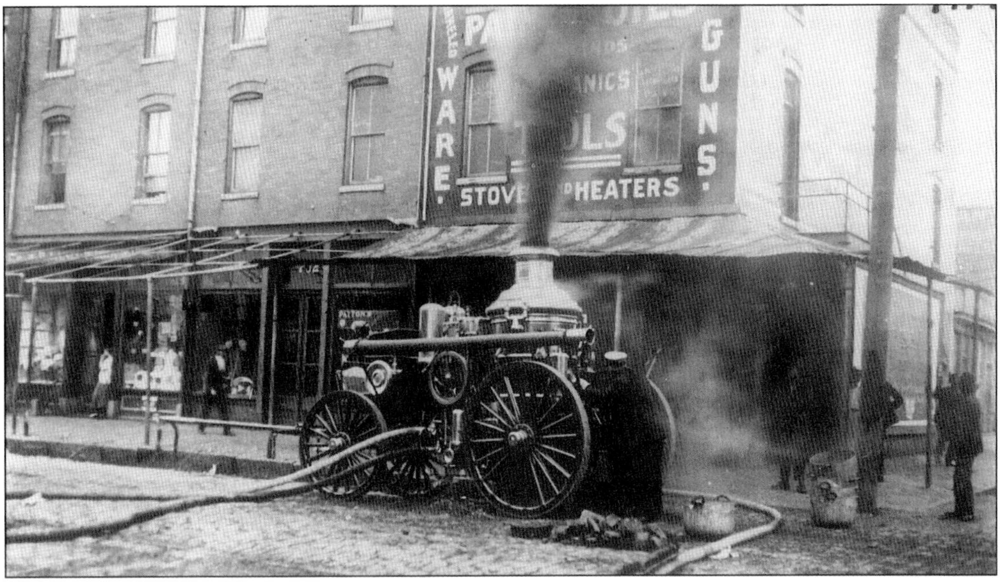

When fire erupted at the corner of Crawford and County Streets in Portsmouth on June 14, 1917, firemen manning the firetruck seen here, Chambers Fire Engine Company No. 2 from Fireman's Hall at 501 Court Street, responded.

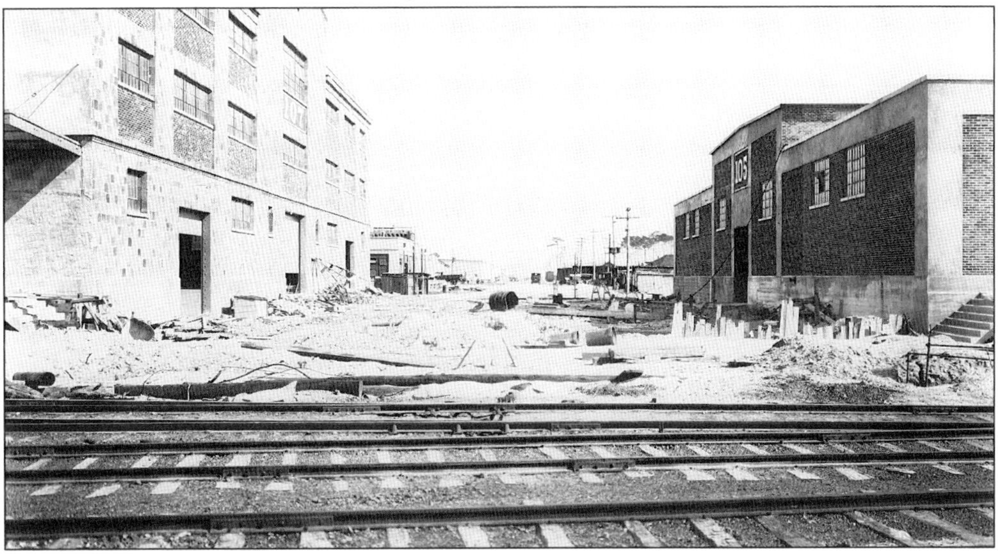

Construction of storehouses on the Naval Operating Base Norfolk was at its peak when an unknown photographer took this picture looking north between Buildings 107 and 105 on April 24, 1920. Both of the buildings in this photograph became part of the Naval Supply Station, commissioned into service on March 1, 1919, with Commander E.H. Van Patten of the supply corps as the command's first officer-in-charge. This command eventually became known as today's Naval Supply Center, also called "The Biggest Store in the World." Though the command was not inaugurated until 1919, its first building, Building 100, was begun on October 11, 1917, on land occupied by the Pine Beach Hotel and the Piney Beach Amusement Park, one of the southside's finest resorts prior to the sale of its land to the United States Navy to construct the naval base. The tall pines which once stood thick along the shore of Pine Beach are visible in the background.

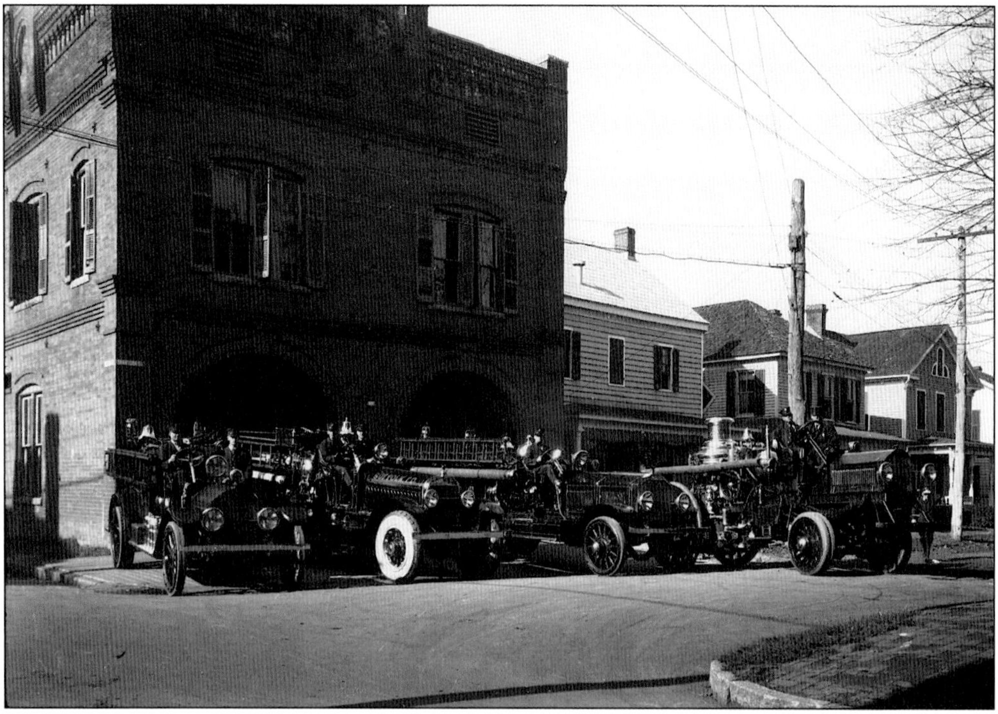

The Suffolk Fire Department was enlarged and improved in the early years of the 20th century. The station on Saratoga Street was photographed in 1927 by Charles S. Borjes. This fire station was a reflection of the progress that had been made since the city of Suffolk was established on October 1, 1910.

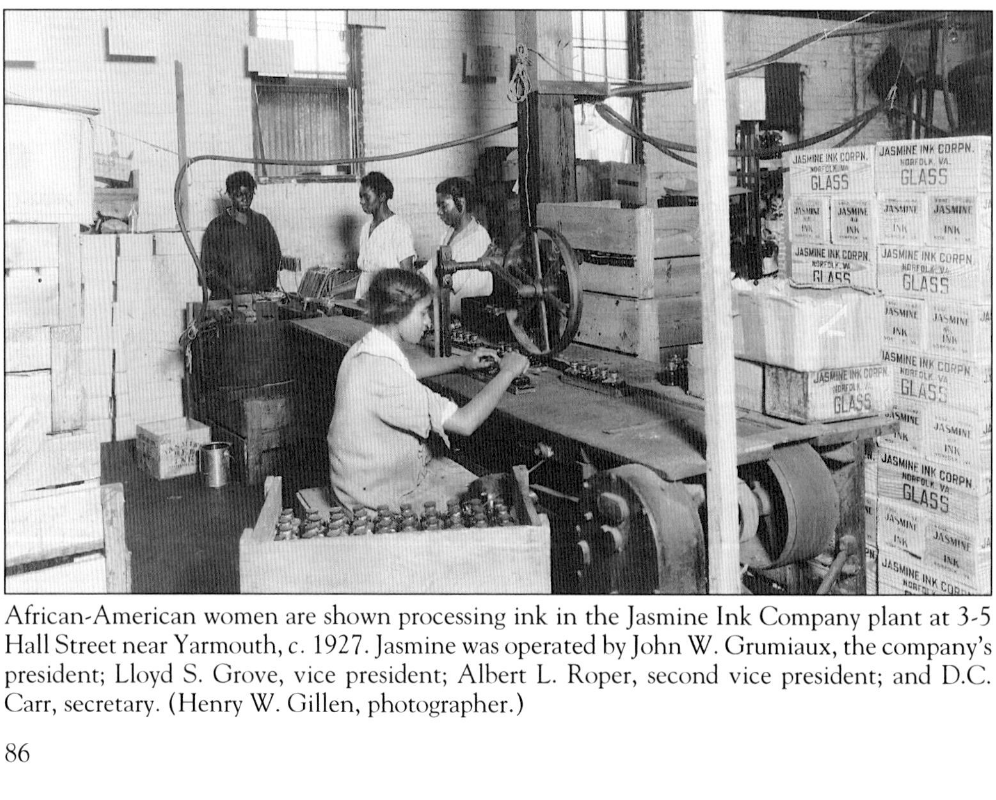

African-American women are shown processing ink in the Jasmine Ink Company plant at 3-5 Hall Street near Yarmouth, *c.* 1927. Jasmine was operated by John W. Grumiaux, the company's president; Lloyd S. Grove, vice president; Albert L. Roper, second vice president; and D.C. Carr, secretary. (Henry W. Gillen, photographer.)

Eight

ON THE WATER

"Leafy-with-love banks and the green waters of the canal
Pouring redemption for me, that I do
The will of God, wallow in the habitual, the banal,
Grow with nature again as before I grew."

—From *Canal Bank Walk*, 1960
Patrick Kavanaugh, Irish poet (1904–1967)

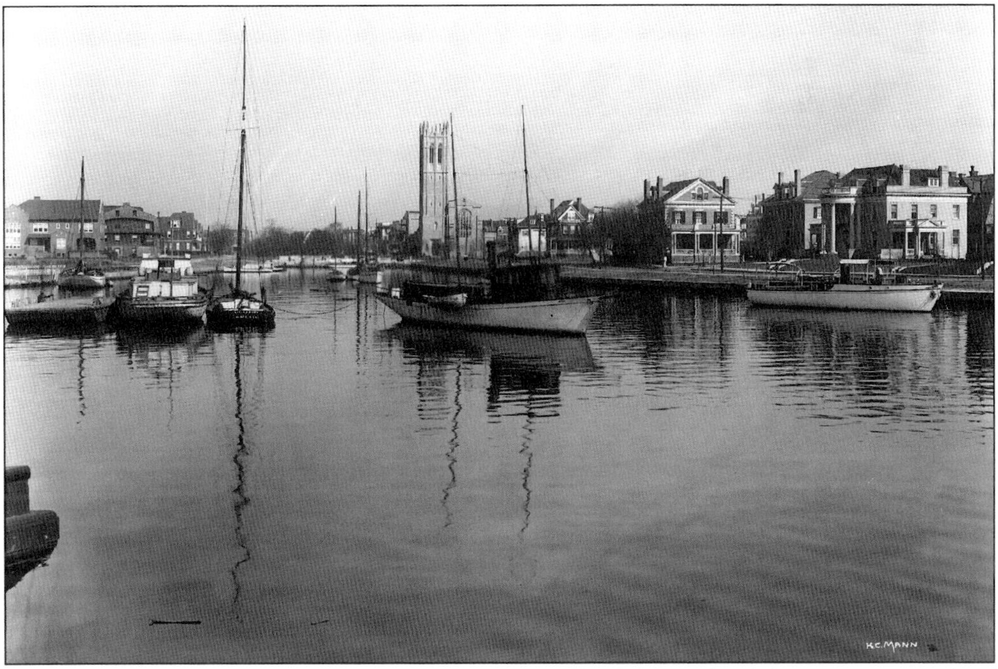

The Hague, also once called Smith's Creek, is a small tidal branch of the Eastern Branch of the Elizabeth River. Its shorter end skirts the old Stone Park near the Chrysler Museum of Art while the other end, shown here *c.* 1910, comes up to Olney Road facing Stockley Gardens. The large houses on the right abutted Mowbray Arch. The Hague was a popular anchorage for working watermen and pleasure boaters. In its heyday, there was always an abundance of sail and power yachts, oyster boats, fishing trawlers, knockabouts of just about every kind, tugs, and barge hulks. It is almost impossible today to envision the Hague full of boats such as the ones in the photograph or Atlantic City bustling with activity on the shoreline across the waterway from Mowbray Arch, but the Atlantic City Bridge used to have a draw to admit waterborne traffic, and Norfolk's "Yacht Haven" was full. Famous yachts from up and down the East Coast frequented the Hague, which contributed to Norfolk being called the "Venice of the New World" in bygone days.

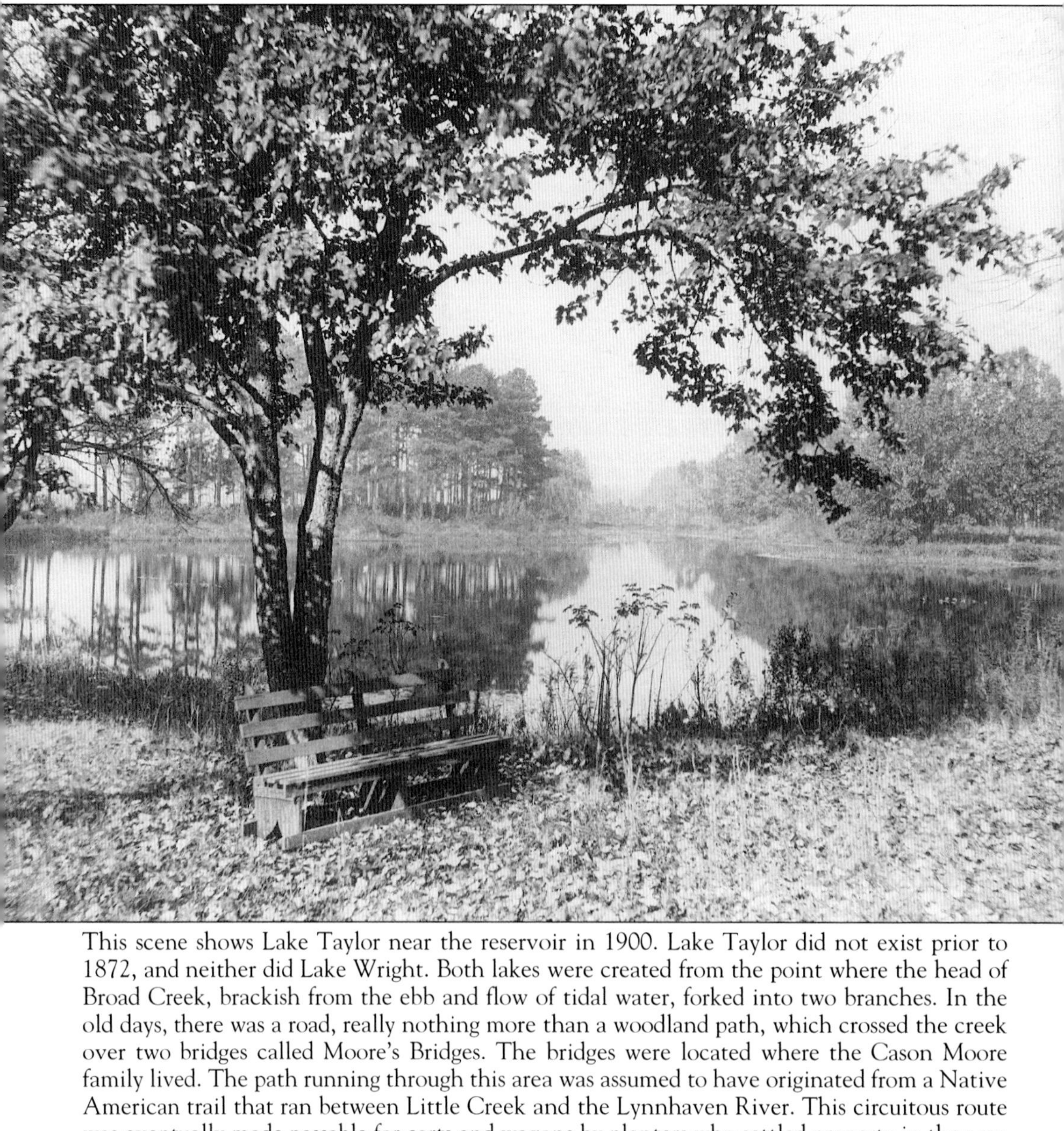

This scene shows Lake Taylor near the reservoir in 1900. Lake Taylor did not exist prior to 1872, and neither did Lake Wright. Both lakes were created from the point where the head of Broad Creek, brackish from the ebb and flow of tidal water, forked into two branches. In the old days, there was a road, really nothing more than a woodland path, which crossed the creek over two bridges called Moore's Bridges. The bridges were located where the Cason Moore family lived. The path running through this area was assumed to have originated from a Native American trail that ran between Little Creek and the Lynnhaven River. This circuitous route was eventually made passable for carts and wagons by planters who settled property in the area around Moore's Bridges, by then incorporated as part of Princess Anne County. The branches were dammed to provide the city with a supply of pure water, and, subsequently, increased in size. The lakes were created as a result. The Moore's Bridges Pumping Station, an essential part of the city's early waterworks system and still its headquarters, was established in 1872. (Photographer unknown.).

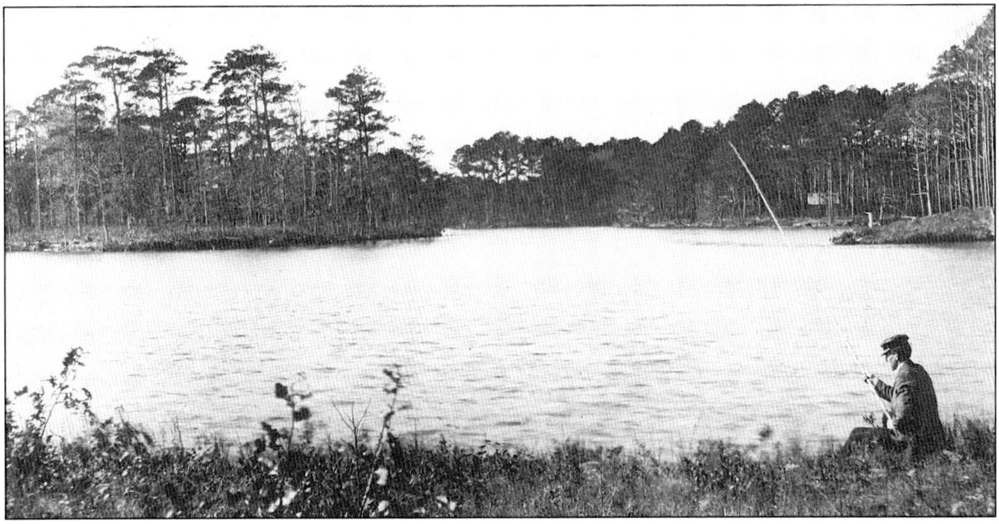

Fishing on Lake Holly, located about two blocks inland from the Virginia Beach shoreline, was a pleasant excursion in 1900. This fisherman brings to mind these lines from a John Thomas Watson poem, *Fishing Tommy*, composed in 1897: "He ought not to wonder that fishes should, under / Such circumstances, conclude not to bite. / They had no inducement. With them to refuse meant / That they were too wise or had no appetite." (Photographer unknown.)

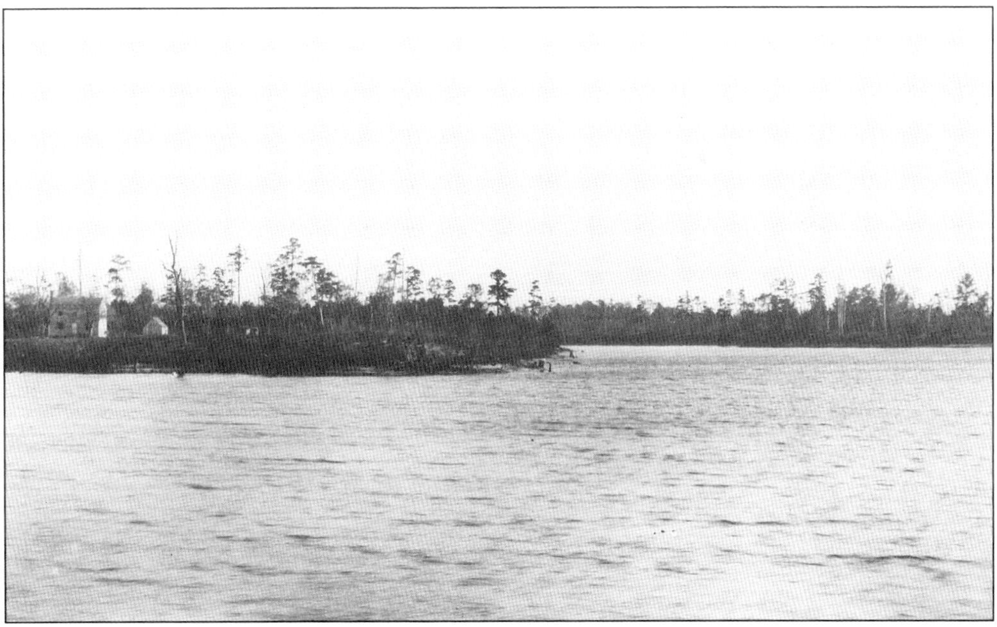

Lake Joyce, shown here as it appeared in 1900, was at one time part of the continuous waterway system extending from Little Creek to Lynnhaven. Chesapeake Indians forged woodland paths along its edges as they moved in and out of their village of Apasus. Amateur archaeologist Floyd Painter found evidence of the Chesapeakes' habitation around the lake during his excavations of the area in 1955 and 1956. The city of Norfolk purchased Lake Joyce by 1899, at which time it was incorporated in the waterworks system. (Photographer unknown.)

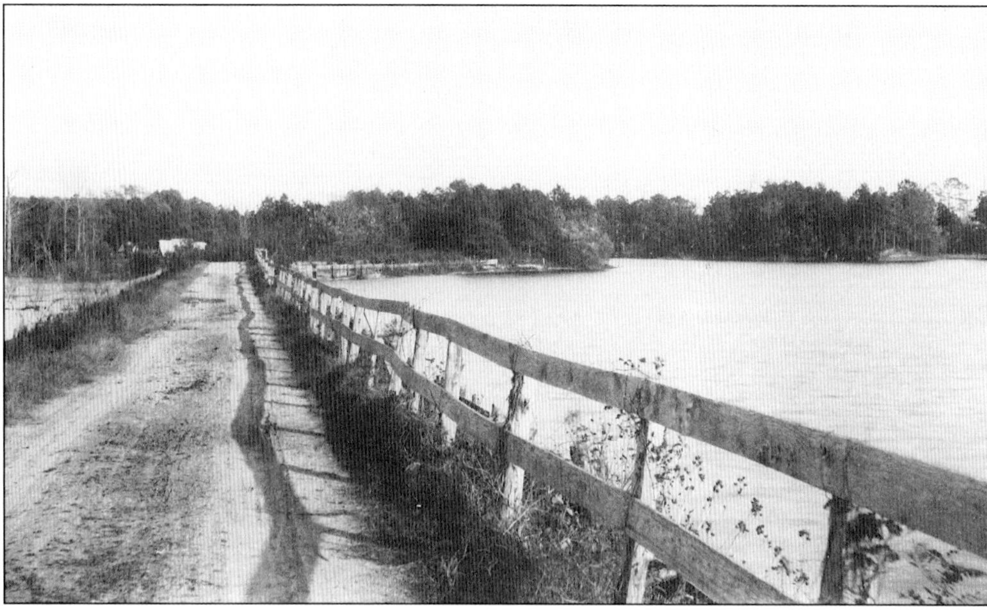

Lake Smith, rural and untouched when this photograph was taken in 1902, is owned by the city of Norfolk, but located in the city of Virginia Beach. The photographer of this picture was standing on top of the low-level dam used to secure the natural water stream that created the lake about 1890. The dam is located where present-day Northampton Boulevard crosses between the lake and reservoir. The picture was also taken just after the of Norfolk built the Little Creek Reservoir on the north side of the dam between 1900 and 1901. The city purchased Lake Smith in 1901 for incorporation into the waterworks system. (Photographer unknown.)

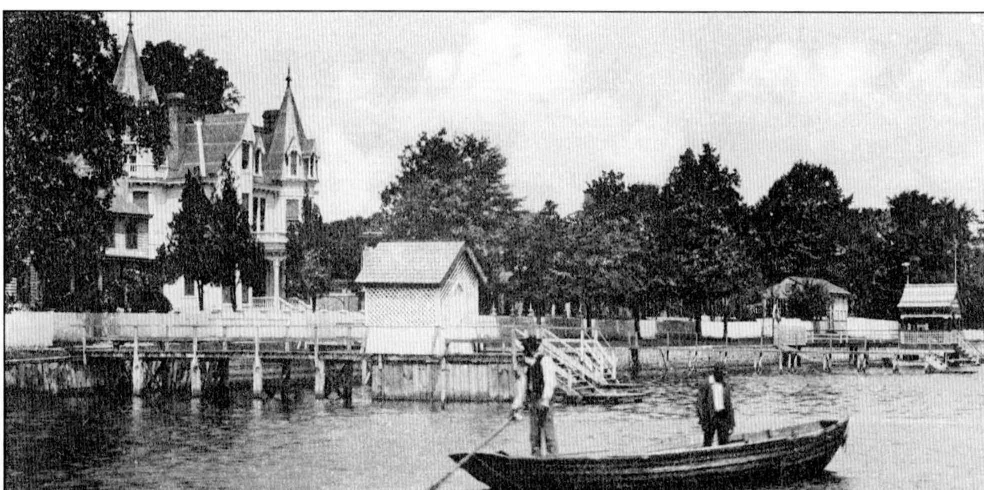

Two fishermen worked their boat along the shore of Portsmouth near the city's Olde Towne section. The picture was taken in 1902 by an unknown photographer.

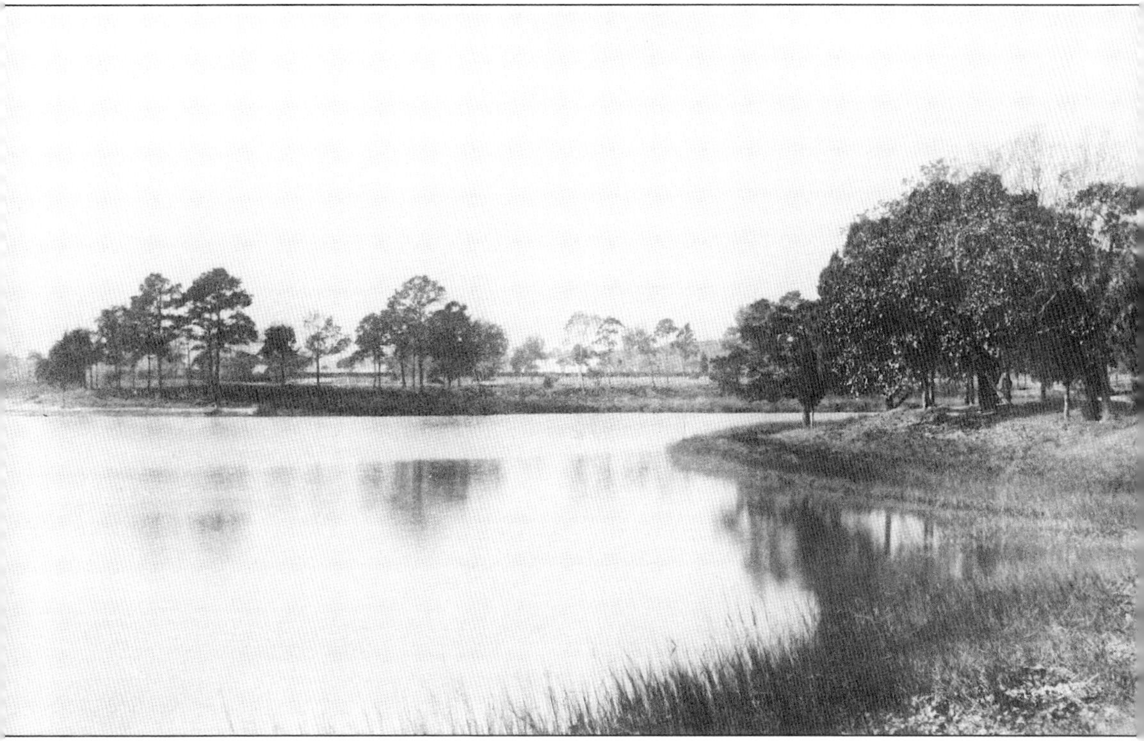

Lafayette Park, abutting Tanner's Creek (now called the Lafayette River), was a tranquil scene in this 1901 photograph by an unknown cameraman. The park rolled gracefully to the water's edge. The creek was named for Daniel Tanner, and, though there are no surviving copies of early grants to him, a description of a grant issued to William Croutch by him on November 21, 1637, described Tanner's association to the river in this manner: "In the great creek on the lefthand going into the mouth of the Elizabeth River about two miles on the north side from Daniel Tanner," lies the land of the aforesaid Croutch. A grant issued two years later mentioned land adjoining Daniel Tanner. What became of Daniel Tanner? A British document issued by William Stanley, mayor of the city of Canterbury, on August 10, 1654, and entered into the records of Lower Norfolk County court on January 1, 1654-55, documents the marriage of Daniel and Charity Tanner on November 26, 1614, as well as the birth of their son John, on October 14, 1627. Daniel died in December of 1653, leaving no heirs to his property. The document was likely filed as part of the process to dispose of his land and personal effects. Daniel Tanner's creek was renamed the Lafayette River in the 19th century.

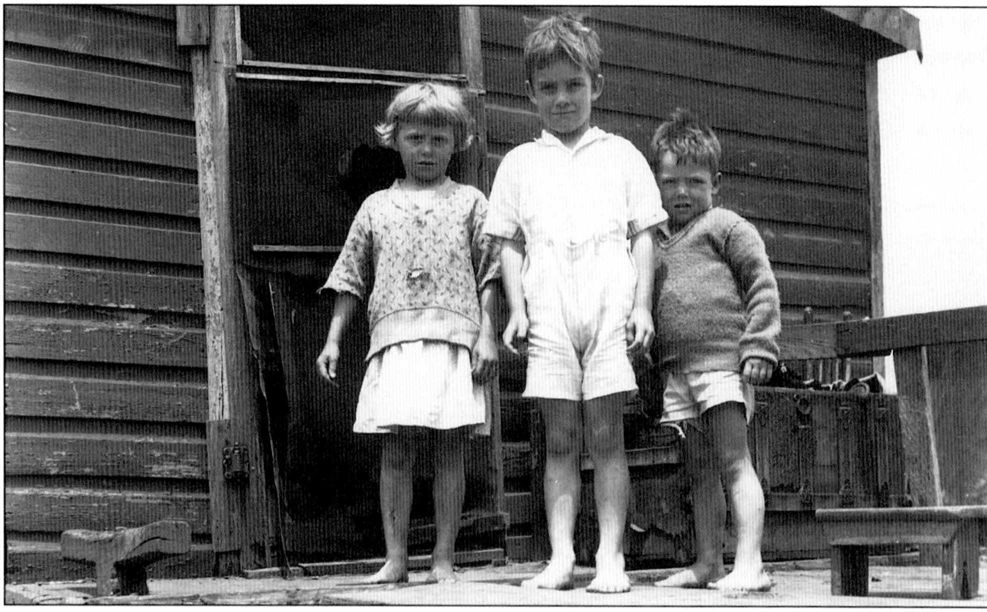

The children in this photograph, taken May 23, 1934, lived on a houseboat in Berkley's Pescara Creek. Pescara Creek is located in the Berkley section of Norfolk, and it was in this waterway that a houseboat "city" arose in the early decades of the century. The living conditions for relatively low-income families aboard the houseboats was poor. (Charles S. Borjes, photographer.)

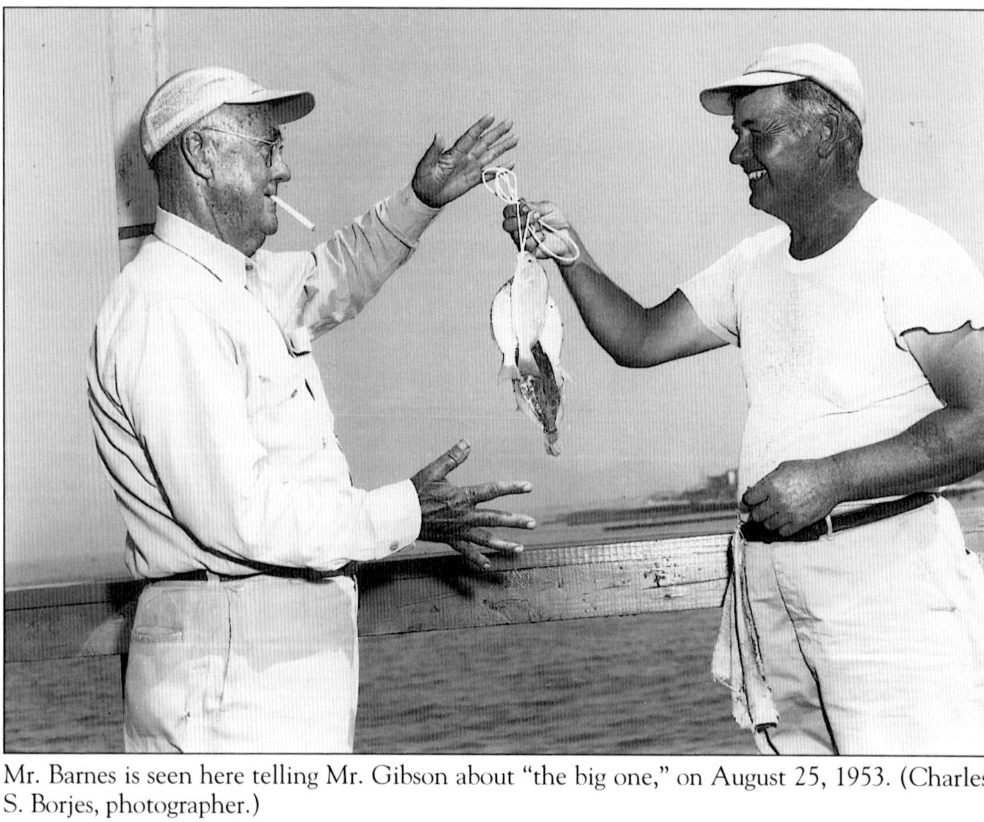

Mr. Barnes is seen here telling Mr. Gibson about "the big one," on August 25, 1953. (Charles S. Borjes, photographer.)

Nine

All the Fun We Had

"Scarce in the shade, nor in the scorching day,
Stretch'd on the turf he lies, a peopled bed,
Where swarming insects creep around his head.
The small dust-colour'd beetle climbs with pain
O'er the smooth plantain-leaf, a spacious plain!
Thence higher still, by countless steps convey'd,
He gains the summit of a shiv'ring blade,
And flirts his filmy wings, and looks around,
Exulting in his distance from the ground.
The tender speckled moth here dancing seen,
The vaulting grasshopper of glossy green,
And all prolific Summer's sporting train,
Their little lives by various pow'rs sustain."

—From *The Farmer's Boy; A Rural Poem*, 1806
Robert Bloomfield, English poet (1766-1823)

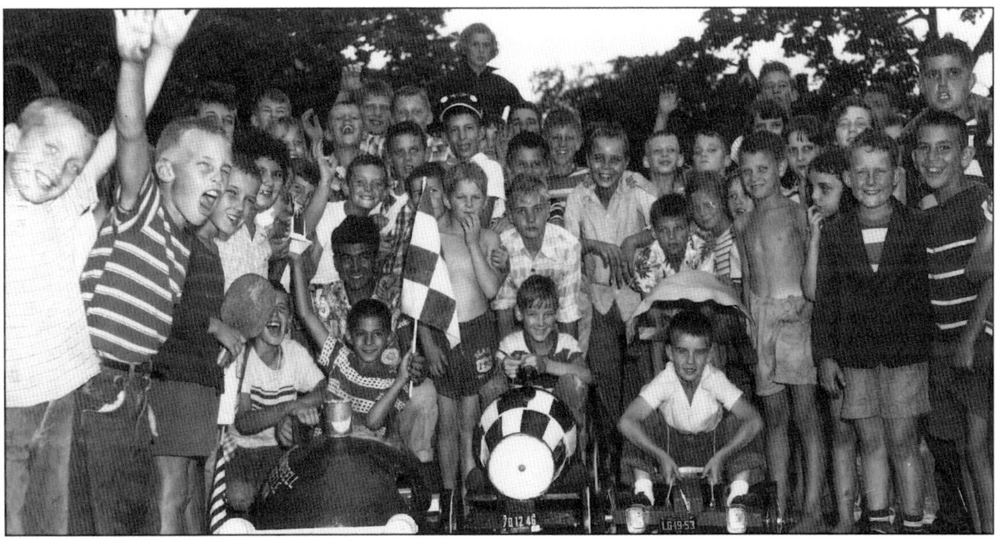

Charles S. Borjes captured the drama of the finish line at this soap box derby race held at Robert E. Lee School on August 13, 1953. Coincidentally, soap box derbies originated with a newspaper photographer named Myron Scott, who was covering a race, just as Borjes did in Norfolk, of boy-built cars in Dayton, Ohio. Scott was so taken with the event that he acquired a copyright for the idea and began developing a similar program at the national level. Soap box derbies have been run nationally since 1934, with the exception of the WW II years. World championship finals are still held each August at Derby Downs in Akron, Ohio. Derby Downs was built as a permanent track site for the youth racing classic under the auspices of the Works Progress Administration (WPA) in 1936.

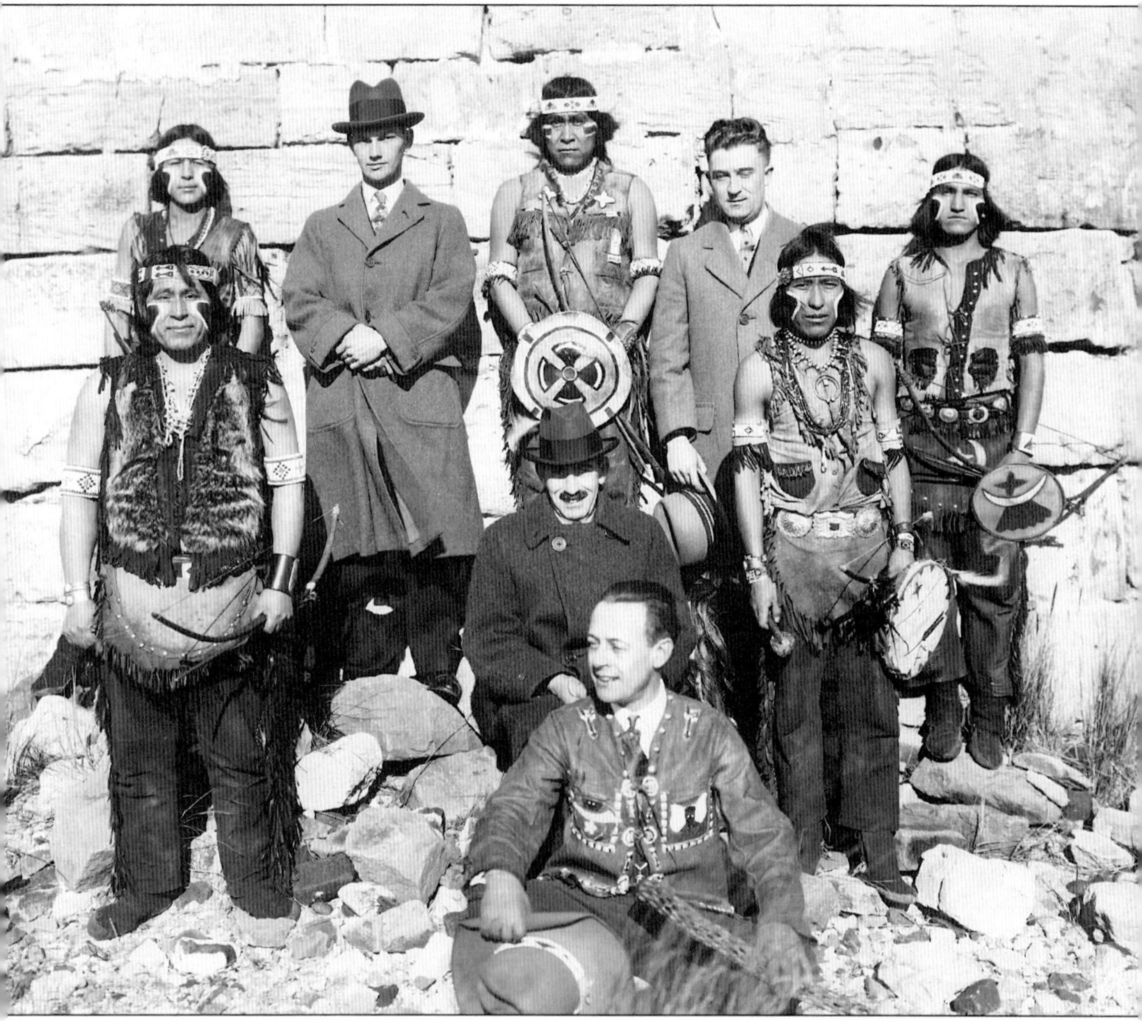

The Wild West Show came through Norfolk and the Virginia Beach resort in the fall of 1927. The show's promoters and performers staged promotional photographs at the base of the old Cape Henry lighthouse. These large outdoor arena extravaganzas were modeled after Buffalo Bill's Wild West Show, which, under various names, he ran from 1883 to 1913. After breaking up his own show, William F. "Buffalo Bill" Cody (1845-1917) joined the Sells Floto Circus for the 1914 and 1915 seasons. Though Buffalo Bill subsequently traveled with the Miller Bros. 101 Ranch Shows in 1916, the year before his death, he was tiring of travel and physically exhausted after performances. He died on January 30, 1917. The performers in this photograph are believed to have originated with the Miller Bros. 101 Ranch Shows, which was known to frequent the area in the 1920s. By the 1930s, most of the large outdoor wild west shows, such as the Miller Bros. 101 Ranch Shows and the short-lived Colonel Tim McCoy's Wild West Show, had ended due to poor financial management. (Henry W. Gillen, photographer.)

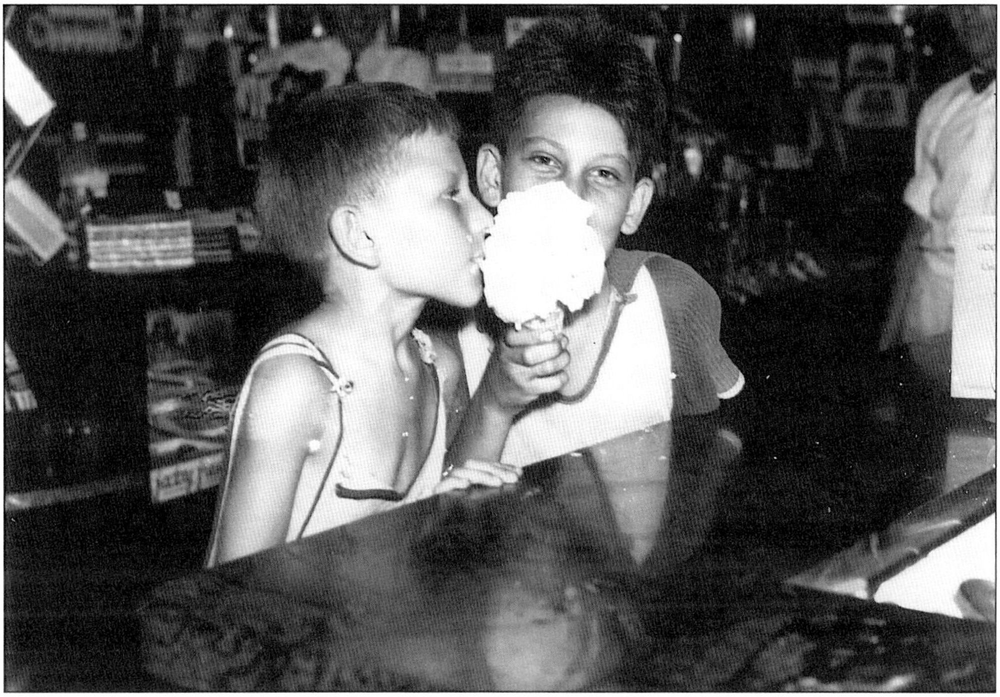

Wilbur and Douglas Bowden dove into a drugstore for ice cream during one of Norfolk's worst summer heat waves. The picture was taken by Charles S. Borjes on July 10, 1937.

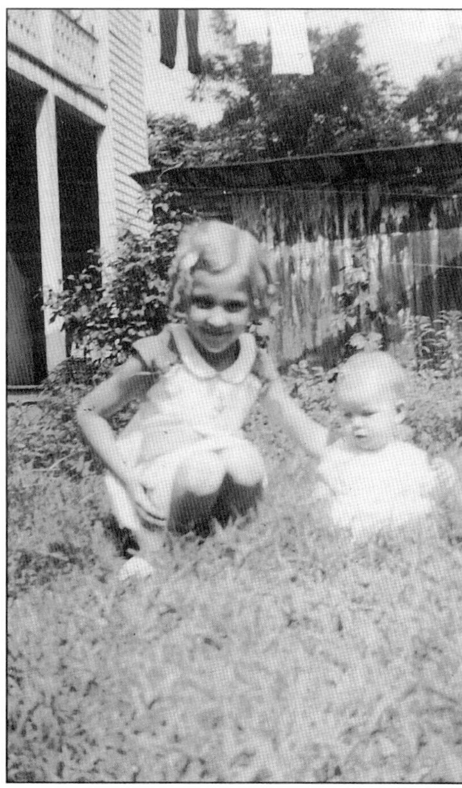

An unidentified child (left) played with Elizabeth Fentress (baby sitting in the grass) during the summer of 1938. The house in the background was located on Park Avenue in the Brambleton section of Norfolk and belonged to Elizabeth's grandparents, John Thomas and Mary Beulah O'Reilly. "The tall trees stood in the sunlight / As still as still could be, / But the deep grass sighed and rustled / And bowed and beckoned me." [From *Summer Sun Shone Round Me*, 1885; Robert Louis Stevenson, Scottish poet (1850-1894).]

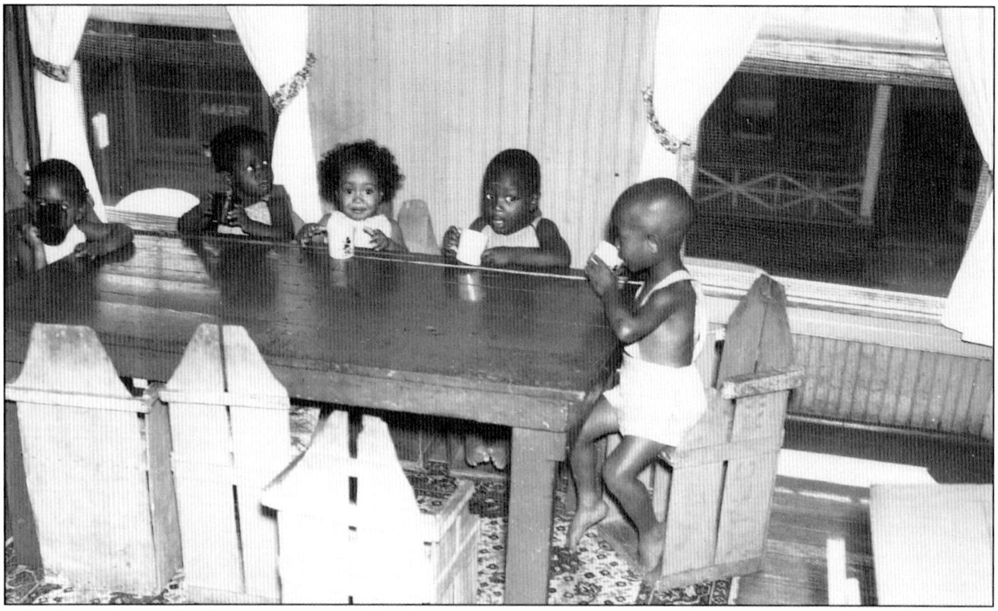

Children in a black nursery school on Chapel Street played happily as Charles S. Borjes photographed them on July 7, 1939. Borjes took many photographs he knew would never run in the newspapers, but he continued to take them to record important moments—and glimpses—into the life of people on the southside, particularly those out of the mainstream. Some of Borjes's best and most compelling photographs were taken of African Americans, and it is because of his belief that history belonged to everyone in the diverse communities of the region that he diligently continued to take pictures of people and events who were never featured as front-page news—or who were deemed unsuitable to cover because of their race or religious preference.

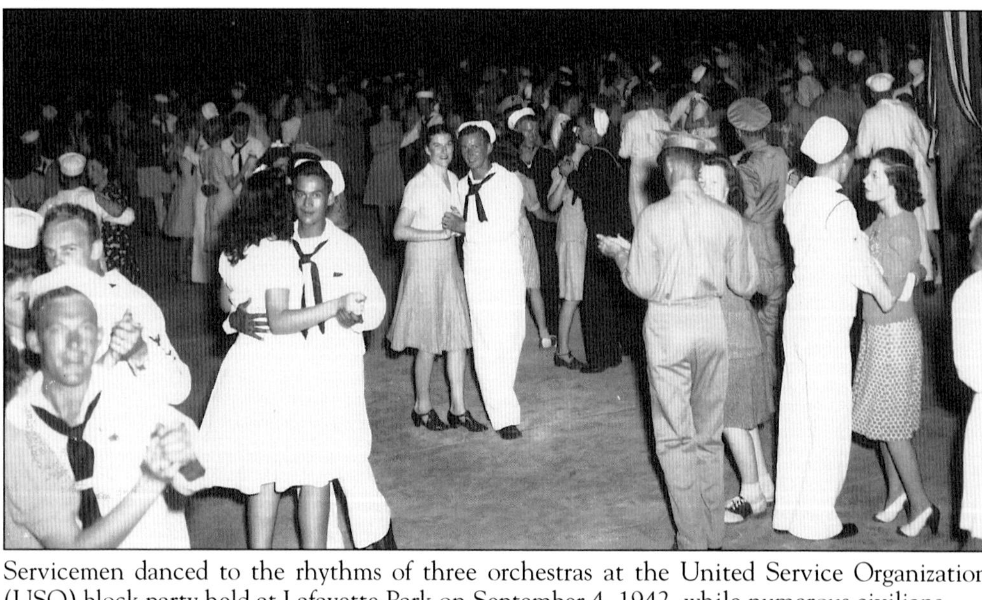

Servicemen danced to the rhythms of three orchestras at the United Service Organization (USO) block party held at Lafayette Park on September 4, 1942, while numerous civilians looked on. The dance, billed as the largest ever given at the park, was staged by all the USO clubs in and around Norfolk. (Charles S. Borjes, photographer.)

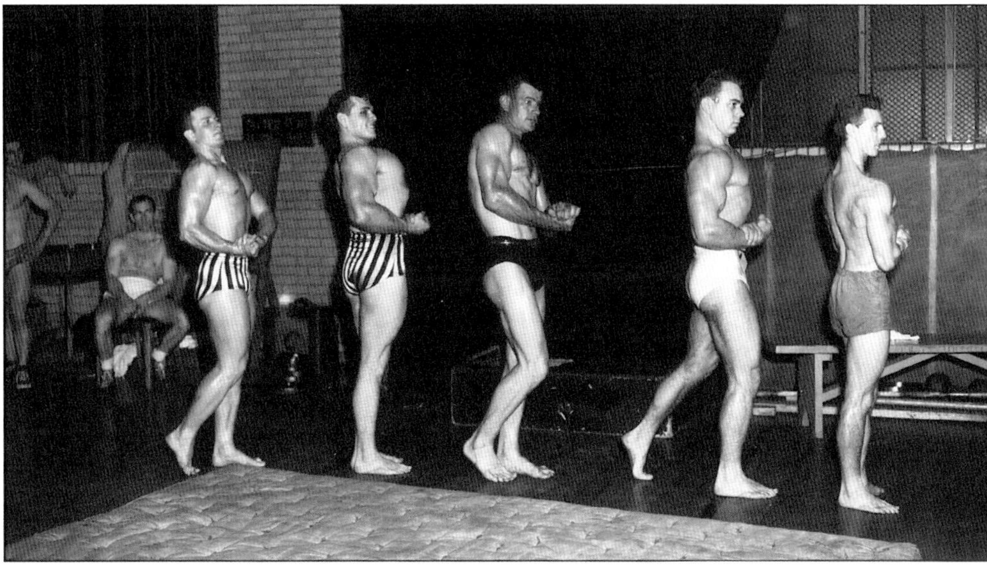

Contestants in the Mr. Virginia contest sported their muscular physiques before a good-sized crowd at the Navy YMCA, located on Brooke Avenue in downtown Norfolk, the evening of March 26, 1949. Willard Logwood, of Lynchburg, won the title of Mr. Virginia. Wilkes Robinson, a resident of Charlottesville, was second, and Willford B. Houghton, of Newport News, was third in the tournament to decide the most perfectly built man in the Commonwealth of Virginia. This competition was the climax of the state Amateur Athletic Union (AAU) weightlifting contest, also being held at the Navy "Y." Norfolk's own Edward Edney placed fourth in the competition. (Charles S. Borjes, photographer.)

The lovely Miss Virginia and former Miss Norfolk, Shirley Bryant, posed for this photograph just prior to her departure for the 1952 Miss America pageant in Atlantic City, New Jersey. The date was September 3, 1951, five days before the new Miss America was to be crowned. Shirley Bryant did not place in the national competition. Twenty-five-year-old Miss Utah, Colleen Kay Hutchins, of Salt Lake City, won the 1952 Miss America title. Not only was Hutchins the oldest winner of the pageant at that time, but at 5 feet, 10 inches, she was the tallest Miss America winner since Bess Myerson, of New York, took the title in 1945. Hutchins was also the first blonde to win the competition since 1938, when Marilyn Meseke won the crown. (Charles S. Borjes, photographer.)

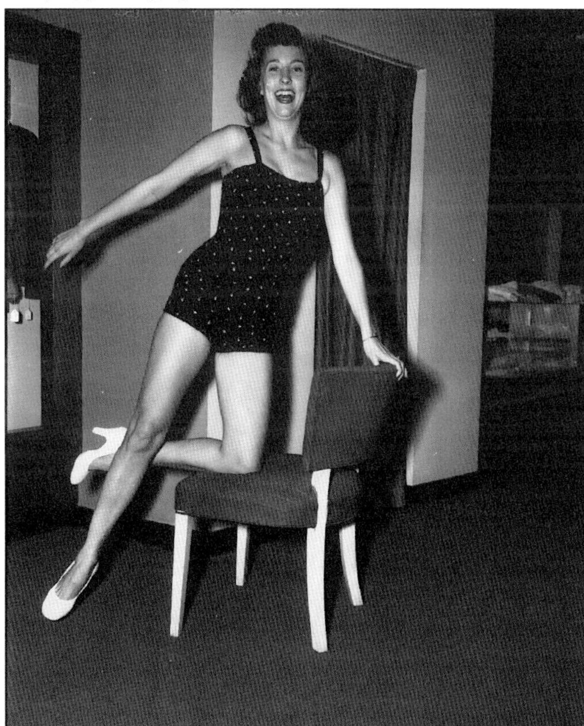

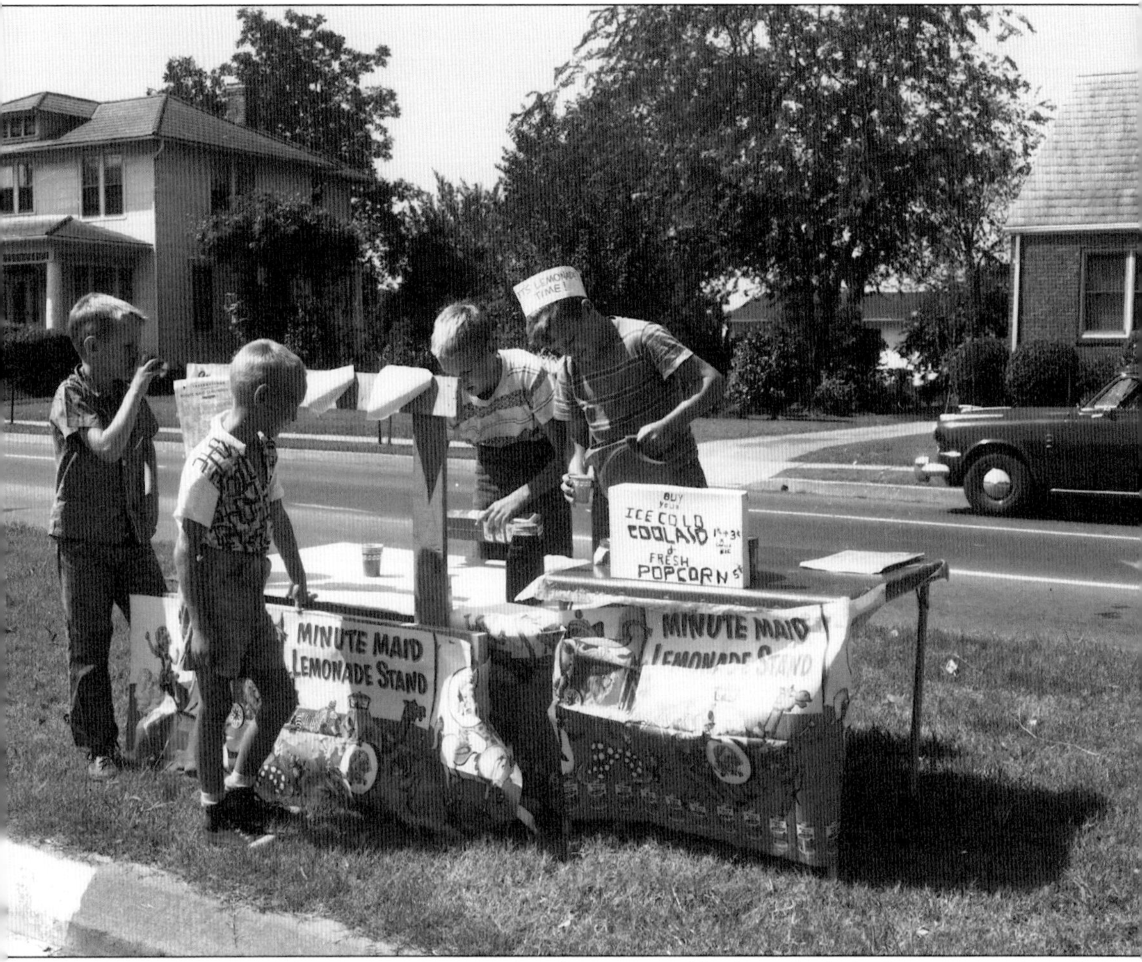

For lemonade stand partners Alex Ward and Tony Mecklenburg (right), the opening day of school was a business tragedy. Though they reported brisk sales from school-bound small fry on September 8, 1951, the day this picture was taken, their business would be closed the next morning because young Alex and Tony returned to school themselves that day. Billy Ward and Peter Mecklenburg (left) sampled the product on their brothers' last day in business. (Jim Mays, photographer.)

Ten

And Those Smiling Faces

"Happy hearts and happy faces,
Happy play in grassy places——
That was how in ancient ages,
Children grew to kings and sages."

—From *A Child's Garden of Verses*, 1885
Robert Louis Stevenson, Scottish poet (1850–1894)

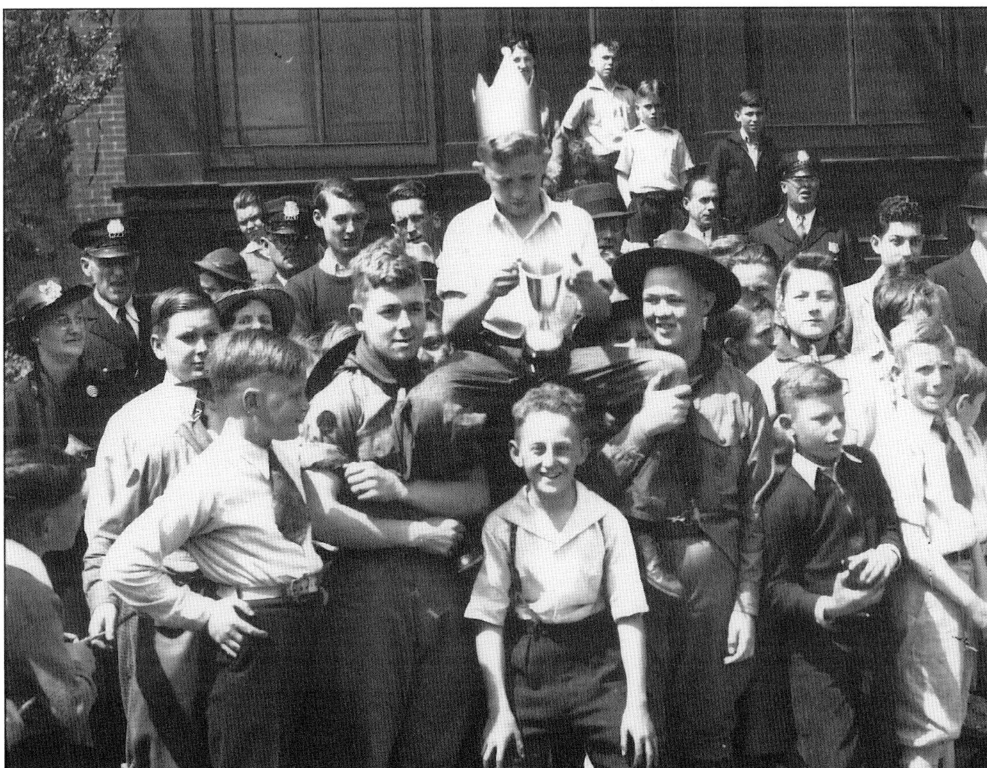

Sidney Tillim (wearing the crown), winner of the fifth annual *Ledger-Dispatch*-sponsored Tidewater Marble Tournament, was taken for a ride by fellow dinksters after winning the championship on April 16, 1938. Second place went to Meyer Pearlman (front, center), and third place, to Ernest Trueblood (front, left). Tillim represented the area in the finals of the national tournament at Wildwood, New Jersey, during the latter part of June. Young Sidney was a student at Ruffner Junior High School. (Charles S. Borjes, photographer.)

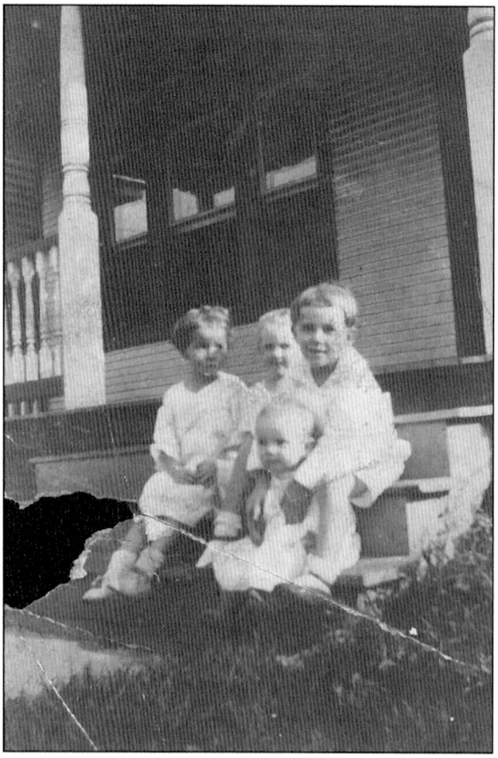

During the early summer of 1918, the first four children of Herbert Maitland and Edna Izora Bell Fentress posed on the steps of the family's house at 513 West Twenty-ninth Street in Norfolk's Park Place. The children sitting on the upper step are Mildred, Mabel Bell, and Walter Linwood. Herbert Maitland Jr., sitting on the lower step, is being held up by his brother Walter. Mabel Bell, precious child that she was, died on September 24, 1918, at the age of 3 years, 7 months, and 18 days. (Photographer unknown.)

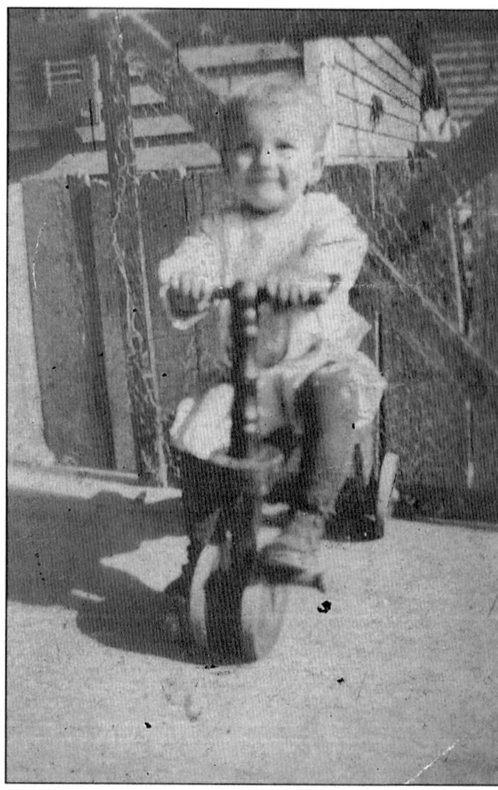

Herbert Maitland Fentress Jr. pedals on his tricycle, July 21, 1918, outside the family's house in Park Place. He was 22 months old when the picture was taken. Notice that the tricycle is made of wood. (Photographer unknown.)

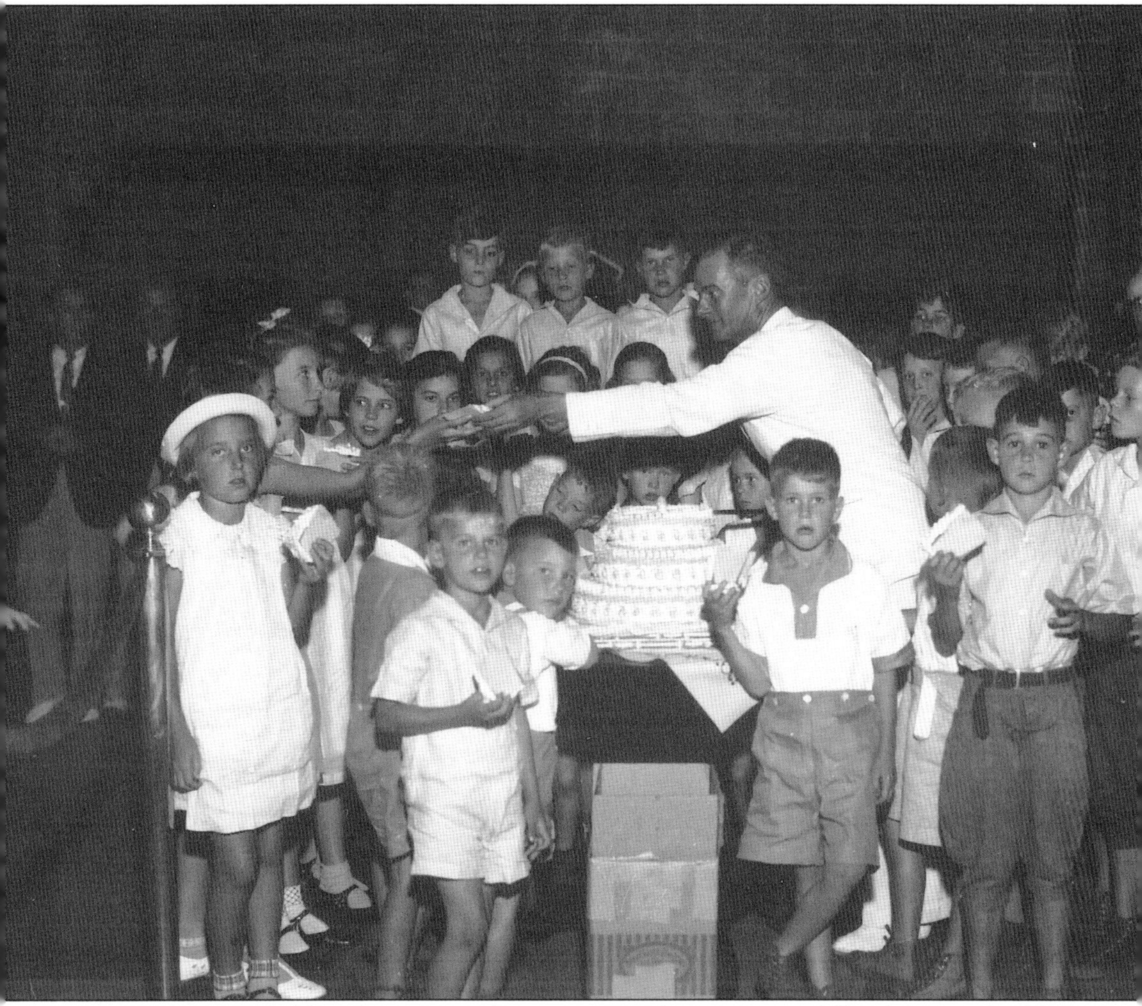

At a kiddie party held at the Loew's Theatre on Granby Street, Norfolk's director of public safety, Colonel Charles Barney Borland, passed out cake, August 21, 1934. Borland was born on January 8, 1886, to Thomas Riscius and Carrie Barney Borland. He attended Norfolk Academy, and, subsequently, the Horner Military School in Oxford, North Carolina. Though a businessman in his younger days, Borland had also joined the Virginia National Guard in 1908 and was on the rolls of the Fourth Virginia Infantry at the outbreak of WW I, where he held the rank of captain. By the end of the war, Borland was a major, and, with the reorganization of the 29th Division after the fighting had ended, he was ultimately promoted to colonel. By October of 1919, Borland was an inspector of police, and, in the fall of 1920, he received his first appointment as chief of police. In July of 1922, he was made director of public safety. He would serve again as chief of police before being appointed on September 16, 1938, as city manager, also serving as director of public safety, director of finance for the city, and chairman of port operations. He continued to oversee all these duties until his resignation on January 1, 1946. (Charles S. Borjes, photographer.)

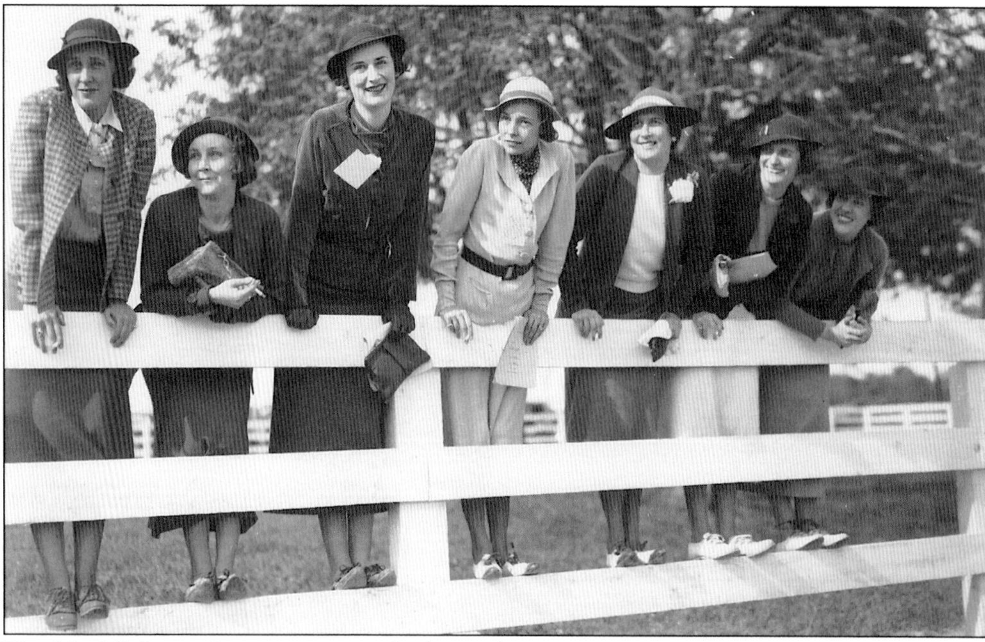

The Norfolk Junior League sponsored a horse show in Princess Anne County which attracted nearly a thousand people on May 11, 1935. The show was a great success. Norfolk society turned out for the event, going out to the show early in the morning, having lunch under the trees, and coming home after dark. From left to right are seven members of Norfolk's social set who spent that day watching the horses: Mary Dickson Cooke, Sarah Dryfoos Roper (Mrs. John L. Roper II), Mrs. Gordon Tyler, Mrs. Alfred Randolph, Mrs. Wilcox Ruffin, Mrs. Lenoir Chambers, and Edith Lewis. (Charles S. Borjes, photographer.)

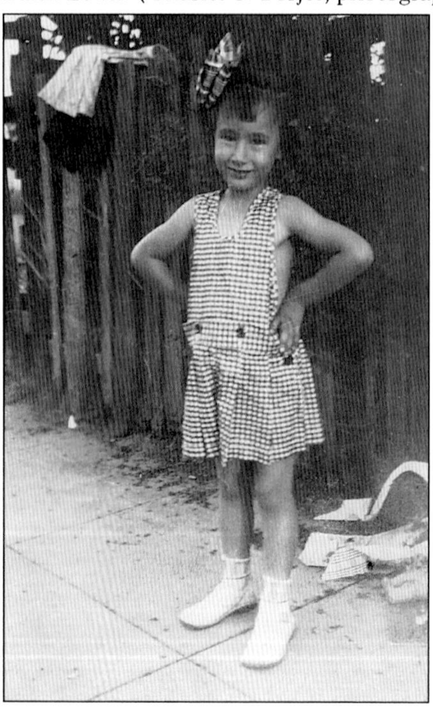

Marie Lanting lived next door to John T. and Mary Beulah O'Reilly's house on Park Avenue in Norfolk's Brambleton section at the time this picture was taken in August 1936. (Photographer unknown.)

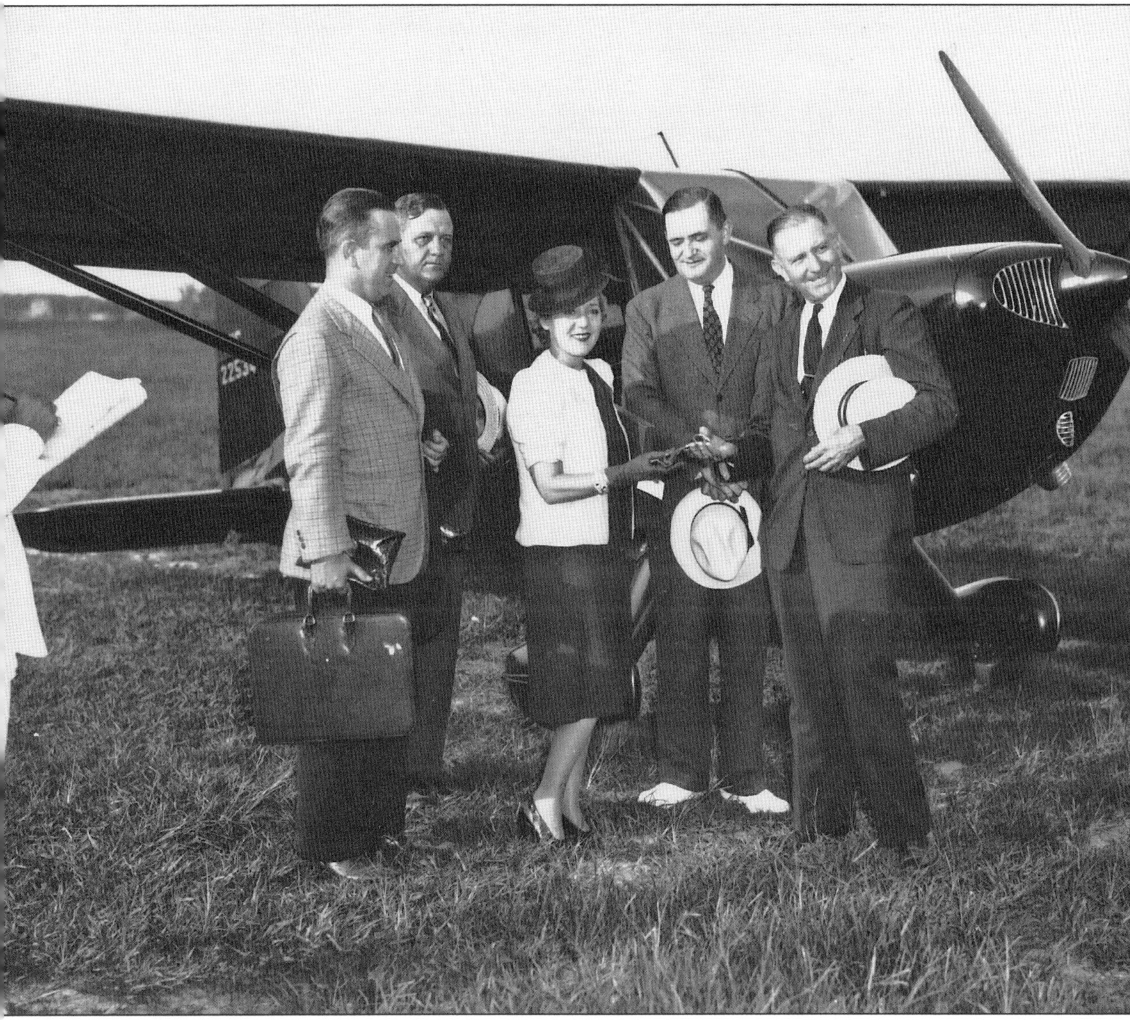

Norfolk Mayor John A. Gurkin presented Mary Pickford, "America's Sweetheart" in the days of silent movies, with the key to the city on September 6, 1939. Pickford had taken a cross-country flight from Hollywood, California, to Washington, D.C., then a car to Richmond. From Richmond, Pickford flew to Norfolk aboard her husband's Stinson airplane. Her reason for making the long trek was to be at the bedside of her husband, Charles "Buddy" Rogers, a film star and orchestra leader, who was recovering from a bout of pneumonia at the Cavalier Hotel at Virginia Beach. Rogers's orchestra was playing an engagement at the Cavalier Beach Club. Finding Buddy Rogers's condition had greatly improved, Pickford made arrangements to leave Glenrock Airport the next day and fly to South Boston, Virginia, where she was queen of the fifth annual National Tobacco Festival. The Rogers couple then met back at Glenrock on September 9, and departed for Newark, New Jersey. (Charles S. Borjes, photographer.)

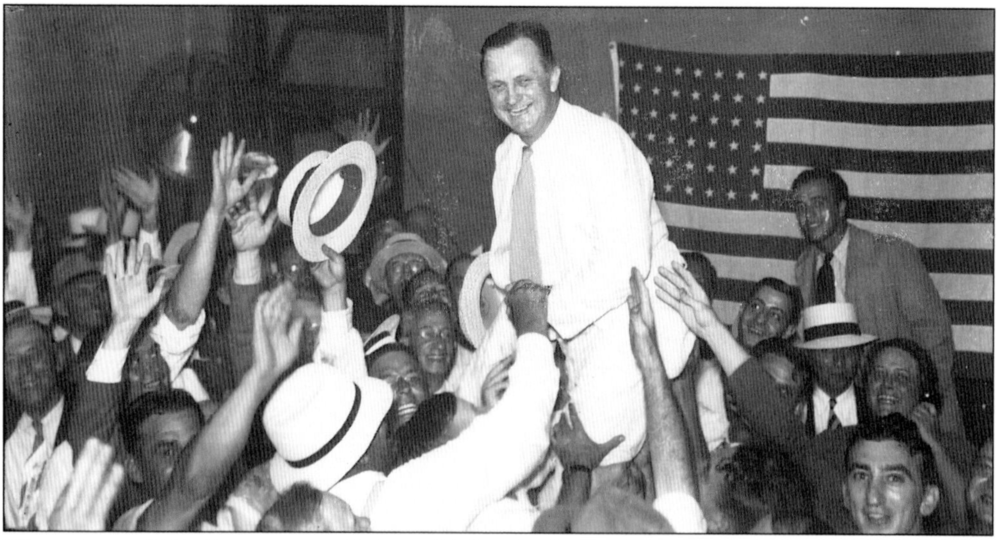

When former U.S. Congressman Colgate W. Darden Jr.'s nomination as the area's congressional candidate was made certain the evening of August 2, 1938, the throng that had stormed his headquarters on Plume Street raised him on their shoulders and paraded around the office as they shouted and sung hilariously. Darden had disavowed himself of any political affiliation in his campaign to win the nomination. He beat incumbent Representative Norman R. Hamilton for a chance at a congressional seat. (Charles S. Borjes, photographer.)

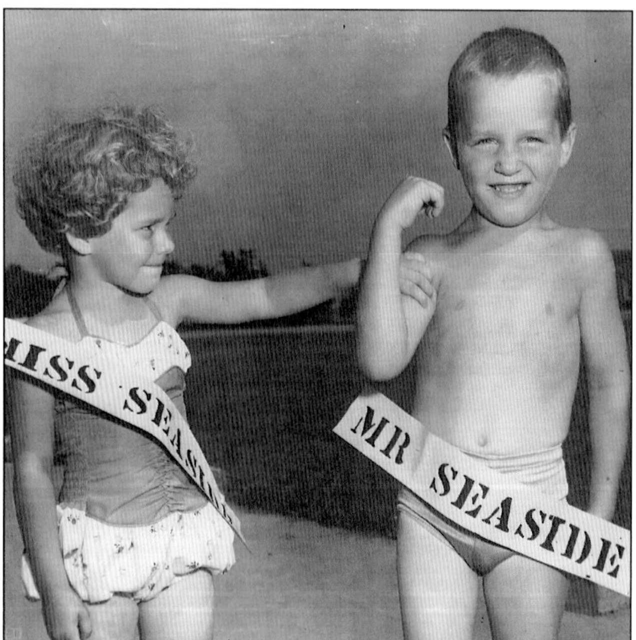

The Benmoreell Tiny Tots Bathing Contest of 1956 named two winners, Miss Seaside and Mr. Seaside. The contest was sponsored by the Norfolk Recreation Bureau for tenants of the Navy housing complex located off the east side of Hampton Boulevard near Naval Base Norfolk. Benmoreell was built in the early 1940s to alleviate the housing problem for enlisted Navy men and their families. It was named for Rear Admiral Ben Moreell, head of the Bureau of Yards and Docks, who successfully saw this test housing development come to fruition. (E.L. Trenchard, photographer.)

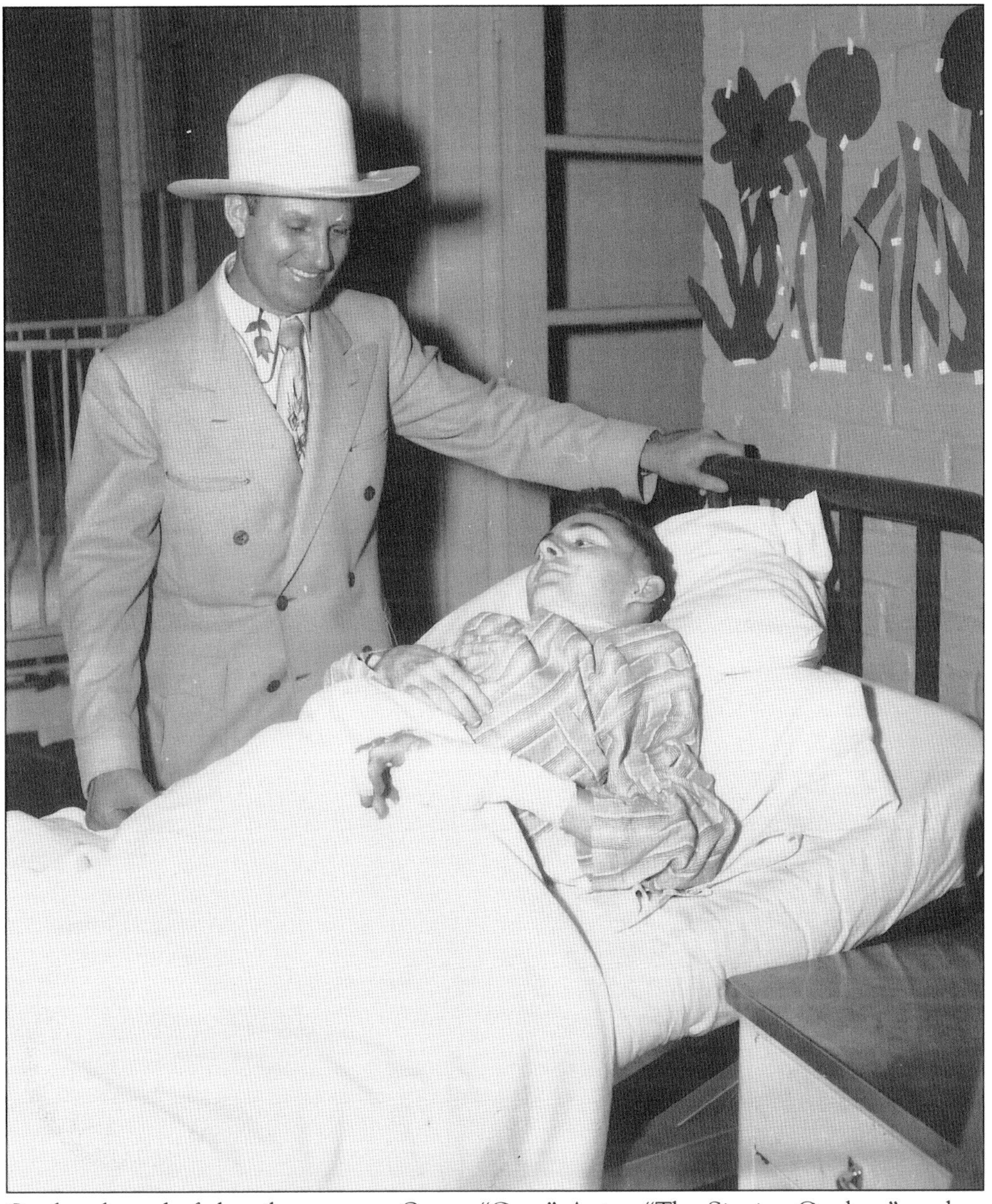

Cowboy legend of the silver screen, Orvon "Gene" Autry, "The Singing Cowboy," made a visit to Norfolk General Hospital on April 12, 1948. Autry was born on September 29, 1907, on a small farm in Tioga Springs, Texas. He appeared in over one hundred films and his horse, Champion, became a celebrity in his own right, carrying Autry through 93 movies and almost as many half-hour television adventures. Some of Autry's greatest single hits were "Mexicali Rose," "Tumbling Tumbleweeds," "Frosty the Snowman," "Here Comes Peter Cottontail," and his theme song, "Back in the Saddle Again." Autry, along with sidekicks Smiley Burnette and Pat Buttram, were popular with children around the world. Though he was a great vocalist, Autry also wrote nearly two hundred of the songs he would sing in his career, including "Tumbling Tumbleweeds," "Here Comes Peter Cottontail," and "Rudolph the Red-nosed Reindeer." He recorded over 625 songs. (Charles S. Borjes, photographer.)

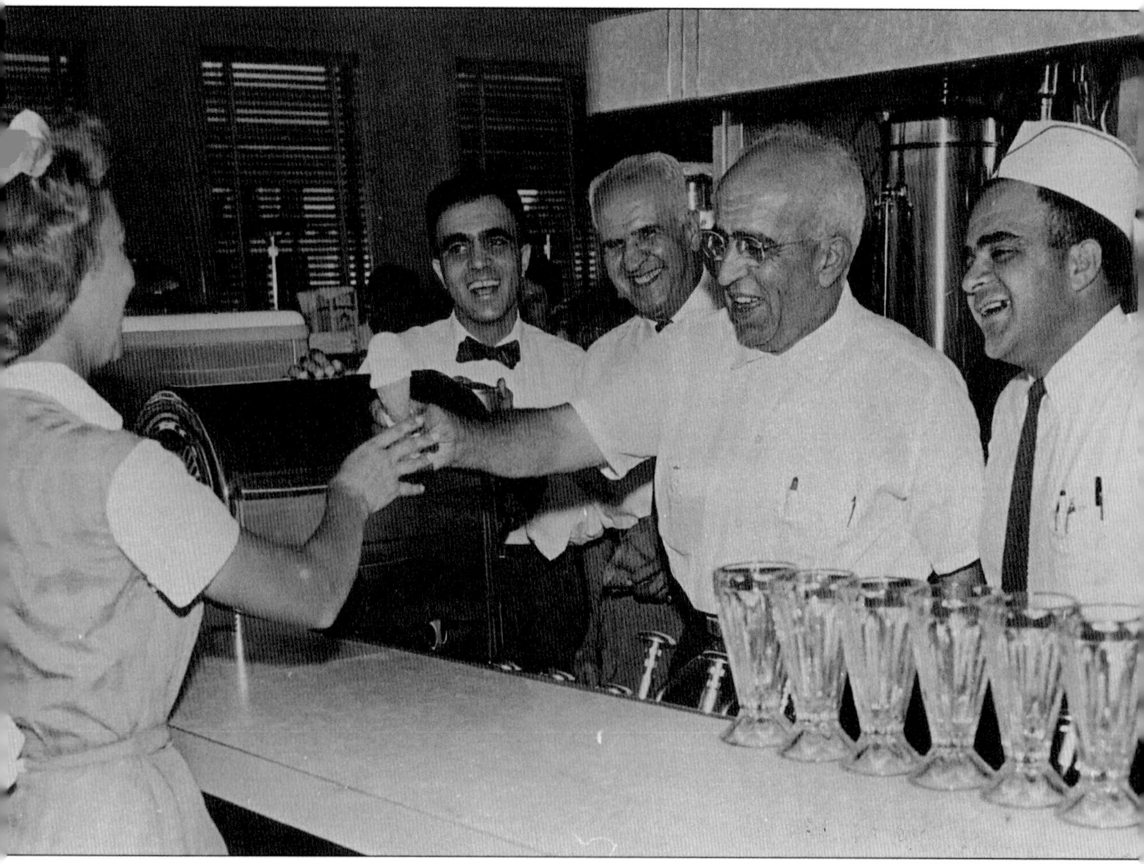

George Doumar serves an ice cream cone to waitress Inez Cuthrel as sons Al, John, and Victor look on. The picture was taken on a hot summer's day in 1957 at the Doumar's curb service restaurant on Monticello Avenue. George's brother Abe introduced the world to the ice cream cone at the St. Louis Exposition of 1904. Though the circumstances surrounding his invention of the ice cream cone have not always been clear, Abe Doumar is the cool confection's true creator. It was coincidence that Abe, himself a relatively new immigrant from Lebanon, met up with a Syrian vendor (who had only been in the country one year) at the exposition named Ernest Hamwi. Hamwi was selling Zalabia, a Persian wafer-thin waffle. Next to him was a vendor selling ice cream. The ice cream man ran out of bowls to serve his cold confection, so Abe suggested making a cone from the waffles and filling them with ice cream. He called it a "World's Fair Cornucopia" and sold it for 10¢. The ice cream cone was born. When the exposition was over, Abe returned to his home in New Jersey and, with the help of a nearby foundry, developed a four-iron baking machine to make the cones. By 1905, he was selling cones at New York's famous Coney Island. George Doumar and two other brothers arrived from Lebanon and were put to work at stands in other locations. Abe was initially drawn to Norfolk by the Jamestown Exposition of 1907, but could not secure a vending location on the exposition grounds. He found the perfect spot, however, at Ocean View Amusement Park, and, because he liked the area so much, moved his family from New Jersey to Norfolk. In 1913, he opened a second location on Virginia Beach's boardwalk. Since 1934, the only Doumar's location has been on Monticello Avenue at Twentieth Street. The restaurant building currently on the site was constructed in 1949. Abe Doumar's original cone-making machine is still used to make handmade cones at Doumar's.

Eleven

The Way We Were

"Oh, dear old yesterday! What store
Of joys for men you hold!
I'm sure there is no day that's more
Remembered or extolled."

—From *Yesterday*, unknown
Edgar Albert Guest, American journalist (1881–1959)

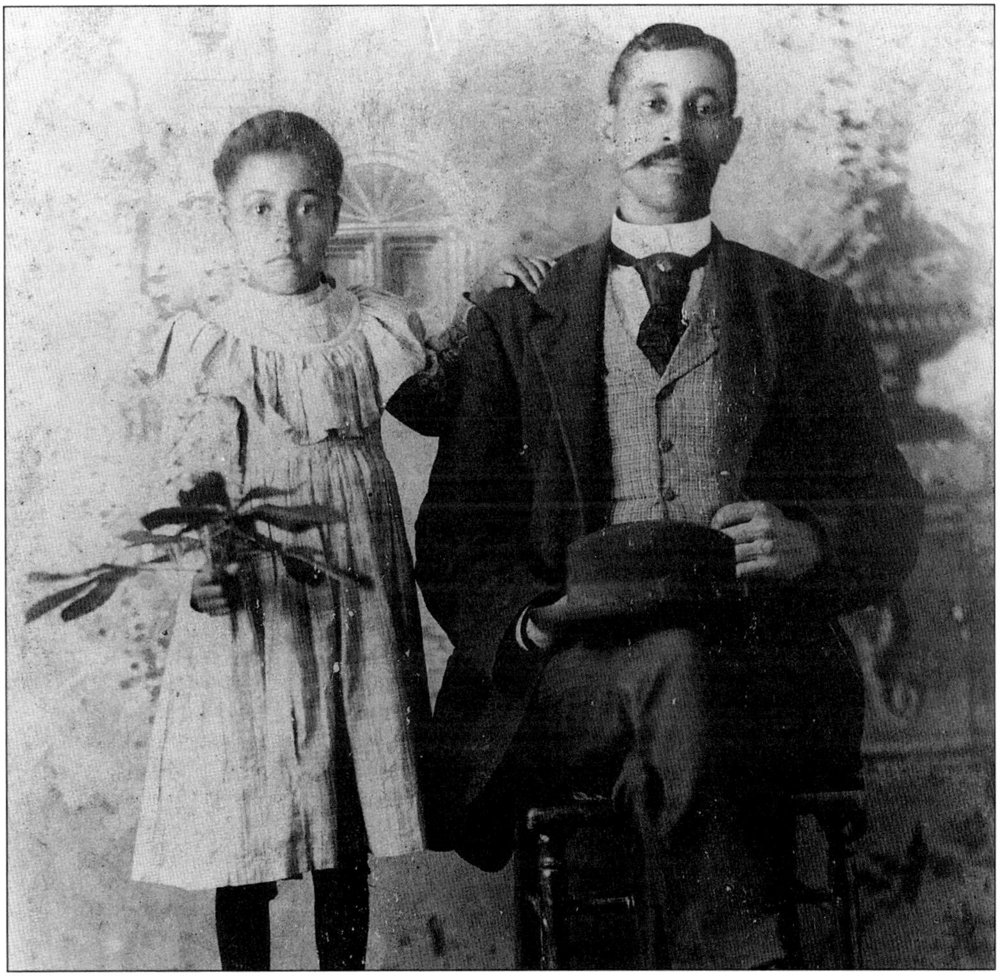

This photograph was taken about 1900 by J.H. Daniels, a photographer located at 488 Church Street. Little is known about the finely dressed gentlemen and his daughter.

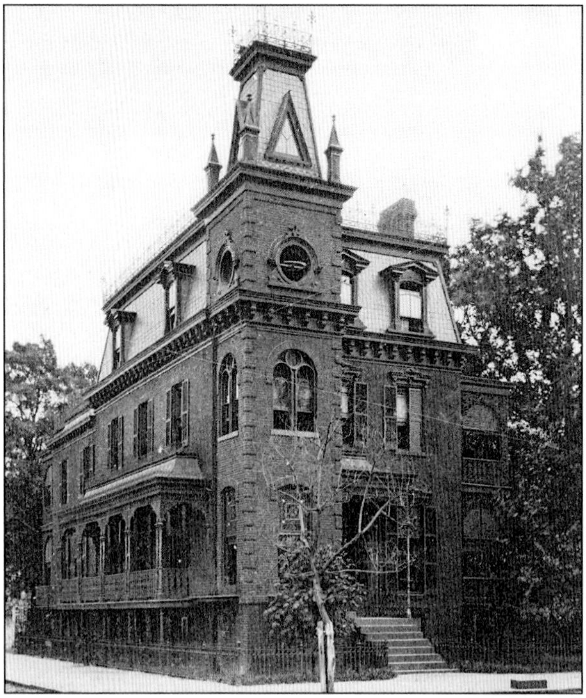

The Merrimack Club, pictured as it appeared in 1895, once stood at the corner of Freemason and Granby Streets. The club was erected in 1892 to immortalize the famous battle between the CSS *Virginia* and USS *Monitor* at Hampton Roads on March 9, 1862. One of the most interesting items once in the possession of the club's members was a gavel made from a piece of wood off the *Virginia*. The wood had been beautifully turned and mounted in silver. On one side it read *Virginia*, and on the other, *Merrimack*, the U.S. Navy's name for the ship prior to its conversion to a Confederate ironclad. The club was razed to make way for Norfolk's new Young Men's Christian Association (YMCA), which constructed a new building on the site in 1912.

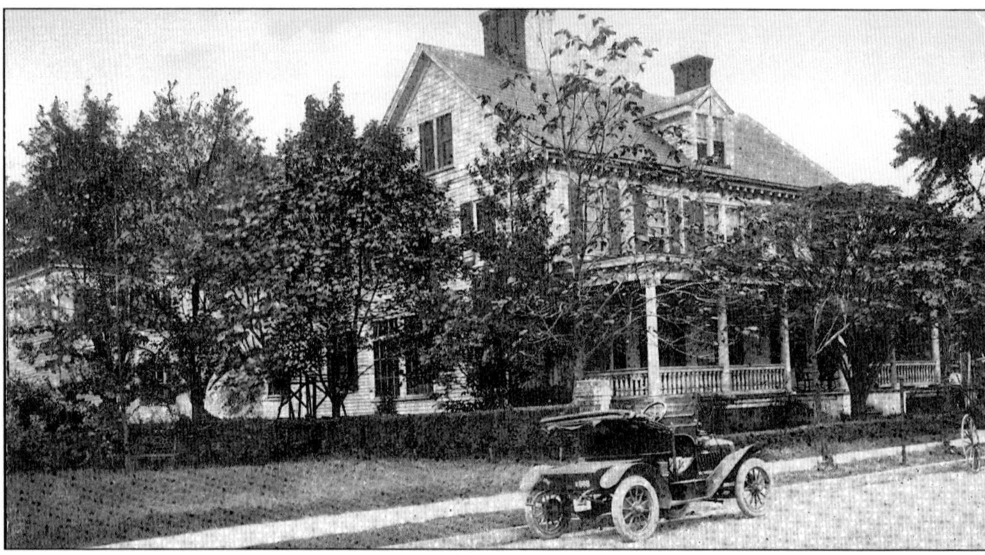

The King's Daughters Hospital in Portsmouth, Virginia, was featured on this divided back postcard, printed by Louis Kaufmann & Sons of Baltimore, Maryland, in 1905. The card was given the series number A25187. King's Daughters was begun by the Circle of the King's Daughters, a ladies' charitable association chartered in 1899 by the women of Trinity Episcopal Church. The charter specified that a hospital or medical clinic be provided within the city limits of Portsmouth. The hospital moved into the Schmoole residence at 824 Emmett Street, shown here in 1903, and there it remained until the first Portsmouth General Hospital was opened in September of 1914. The house subsequently became a home for the aged and the earliest precursor of Emily Green Shores, a present-day retirement residence on Westmoreland Avenue.

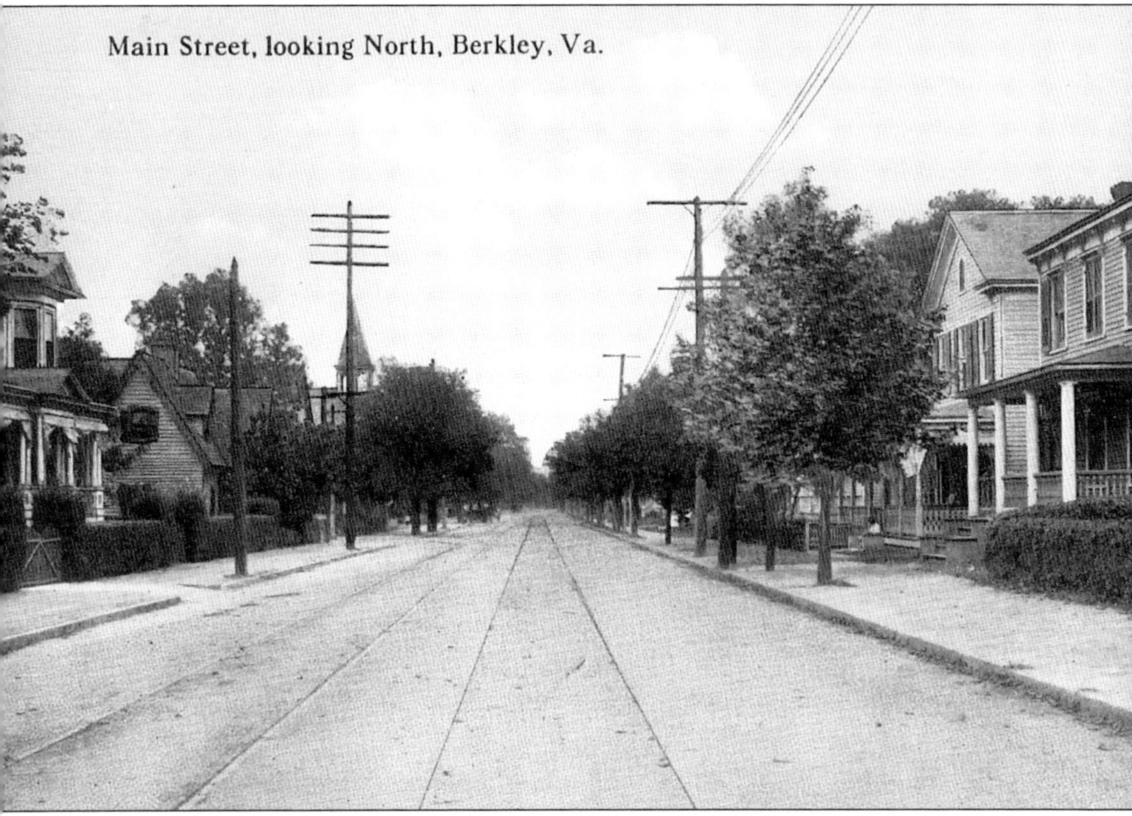

Main Street in Berkley, looking north, was photographed in 1910, hand colored, and run on a divided back penny postcard, also manufactured by Louis Kaufmann & Sons. The series number assigned to the image was A25194. Berkley's earliest known name was Powder Point. When William Byrd passed through the area in 1728, he documented his travel to Powder Point, an area he observed was already a careening ground for ships. The name "Powder Point" came about in 1700 when the little settlement was chosen to house the first powder magazine outside the town of Norfolk. Between 1790 and 1801, Berkley was called Washington Town or Point, when the county courthouse was located there. Perhaps the greatest distinction the people of the town may have boasted was of being one of the first places in the nation named for the Father of Our Country, George Washington, nine years before his death. One of the first streets in the town was also named for Washington (subsequently known as Walnut Street) and another, for patriotic reasons, Liberty Street. The latter street was subsequently known as Chestnut Street, but it should not be confused with the location of today's Liberty Street. The town was seriously proposed as the location of the nation's capital before the site overlooking the Potomac River was chosen. Shortly before 1800, the town was also called Ferry Point because of the ferry dock at the foot of Liberty Street (Chestnut) which connected to the county dock in Norfolk. Herbertsville is also a name associated with Berkley. After the Civil War, however, Herbertsville was developed by Lycurgus Berkley (1827-1881), who incorporated the town now bearing his surname in 1866. The city of Norfolk annexed Berkley in 1906. The oldest and most historic part of Berkley disappeared when Interstate 464 was cut through the neighborhood in the 1980s.

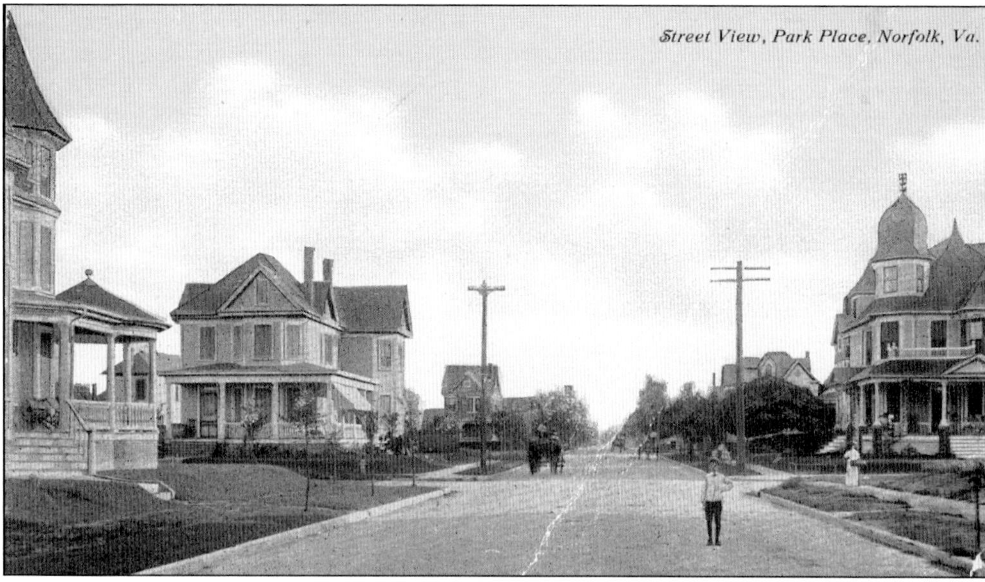

This divided back penny postcard depicts a street scene from Norfolk's Park Place neighborhood. It was produced by Louis Kaufmann & Sons of Baltimore, Maryland, from a photograph which was hand colored. The series number of the card was A4369. The photograph to produce the card was taken about 1910. The city of Norfolk expanded its boundaries with the Park Place annexation of 1902. This annexation took in the neighborhoods of Park Place, Colonial Place, Riverview, plus a portion of what was west of Colley Avenue.

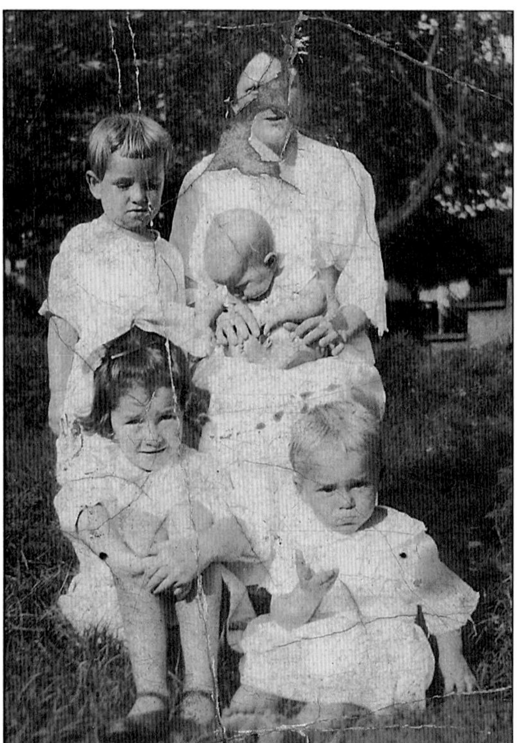

Edna Izora Bell Fentress, born on October 14, 1882, and wife of Herbert Maitland Fentress (born July 29, 1889, and died February 7, 1964), posed with four of her children in the summer of 1920, in the side yard of the family's house at 513 West Twenty-ninth Street in Norfolk's Park Place section. The Fentresses would eventually have ten children, nine of whom lived to adulthood. The children in the picture, listed counter-clockwise, are as follows: Herbert Maitland Jr. (otherwise known as "Buster" to his brothers and sisters), standing next to his mother; Mildred Ione; and Richard. Edna is holding Lanetta. Mildred, the oldest of the couple's children, was born June 7, 1913. The children's father owned Herbert M. Fentress & Company, a produce business on Roanoke Avenue.

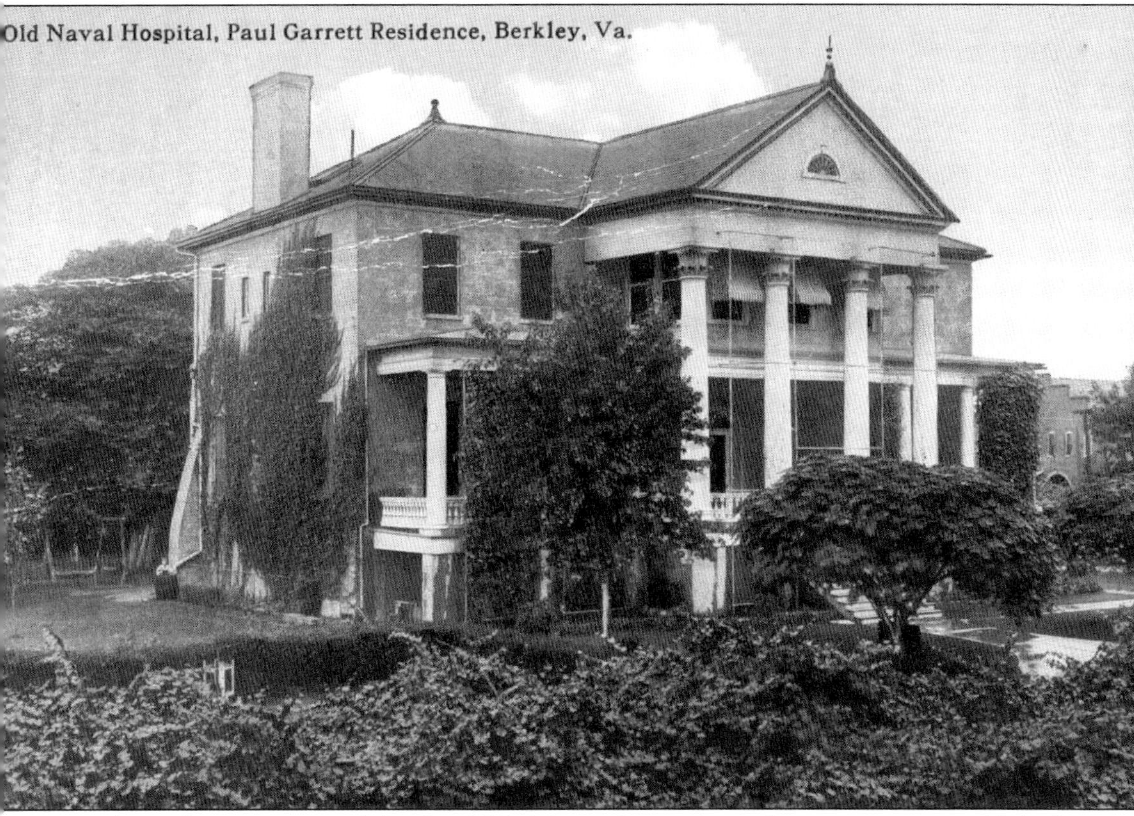

In the early 1800s, one of the first U.S. Marine hospitals in the country was established at the foot of Chestnut Street in Berkley. During the Civil War, the building was used by Confederate and Union troops as a barracks and hospital. Shortly after the war, it became the Berkley Military Academy, and, by the late 1800s, the Ryland Institute for Girls. The building was later occupied by Paul Garrett and his family, who converted it to their home about the time Garrett opened his winery next door to the house in late 1903. The Garrett and Company's winery remained in operation until 1916, when Prohibition was enacted. When the winery building was subsequently destroyed by fire, the Garretts moved out of Berkley, and the house and winery properties were sold to the Imperial Tobacco Company. During WW I, Imperial Tobacco Company graciously opened the house as a recreation hall for servicemen. After the war, the house was divided into apartments. It was in these postwar years until the end of Prohibition that numerous bootleggers' stills were found—off and on—throughout the house. The house was eventually razed to make way for the downtown tunnel connecting Norfolk and Portsmouth. When this postcard was printed in 1910, Paul Garrett and his family occupied the house.

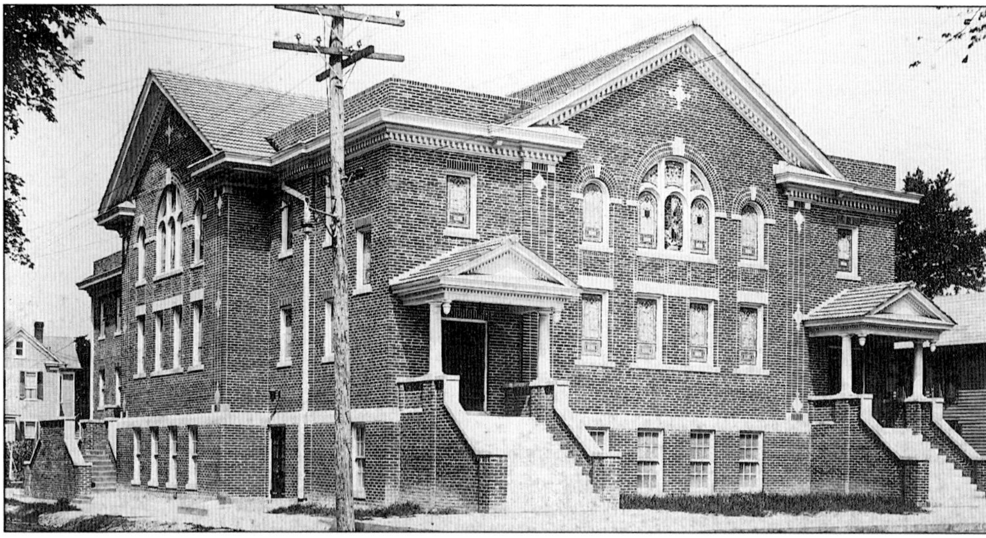

South Norfolk Christian Church, a landmark at the corner of Guerriere Avenue and Jackson Street, was photographed by Edgar A. Caffey on July 21, 1926. Caffey owned and operated a photography studio at 251 Granby Street in Norfolk.

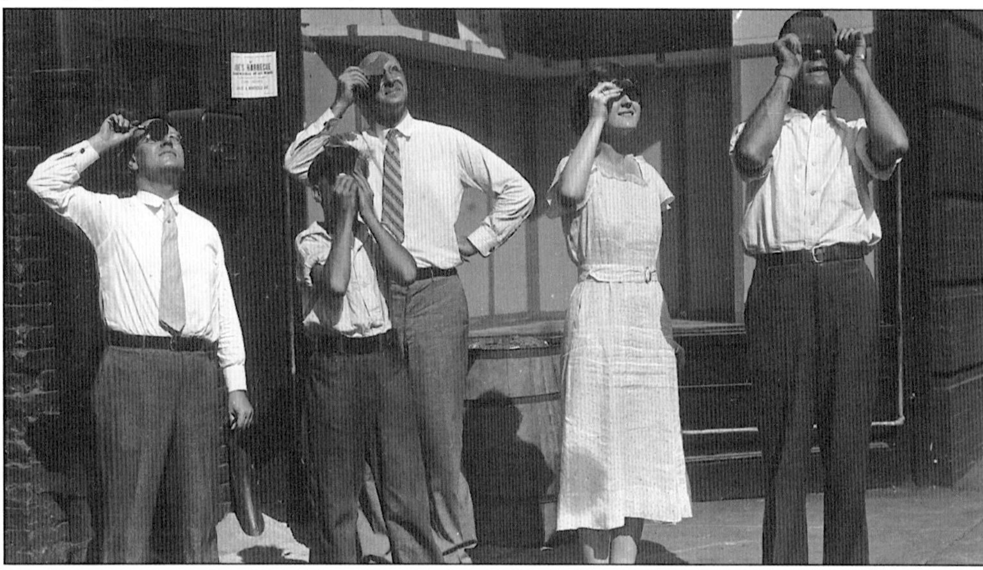

As the moon crept between the sun and the earth on August 31, 1932, and caused a partial solar eclipse, tens of thousands of Norfolkians paused from their afternoon work to gaze skyward through smoked glasses, film negative, and other glare-eliminating devices to watch. This group was photographed on Granby Street by Charles S. Borjes. The heat of the day did little to prevent crowds from venturing into the streets even as the thermometer registered 100 degrees. One of the most amusing incidents to occur during the eclipse was the fellow whose pair of smoked glasses burst into flames. The embarrassed gentleman, who never revealed his name, had only slightly tinted glasses and no smoked glass to sufficiently view the eclipse. He took a match and started to smoke his glasses. His celluloid frames responded heartily to this treatment, catching fire, and going up in flames with a sharp hissing sound and a flash that caused the man to drop them and run. This was probably more exciting to watch than the actual eclipse. (Charles S. Borjes, photographer.)

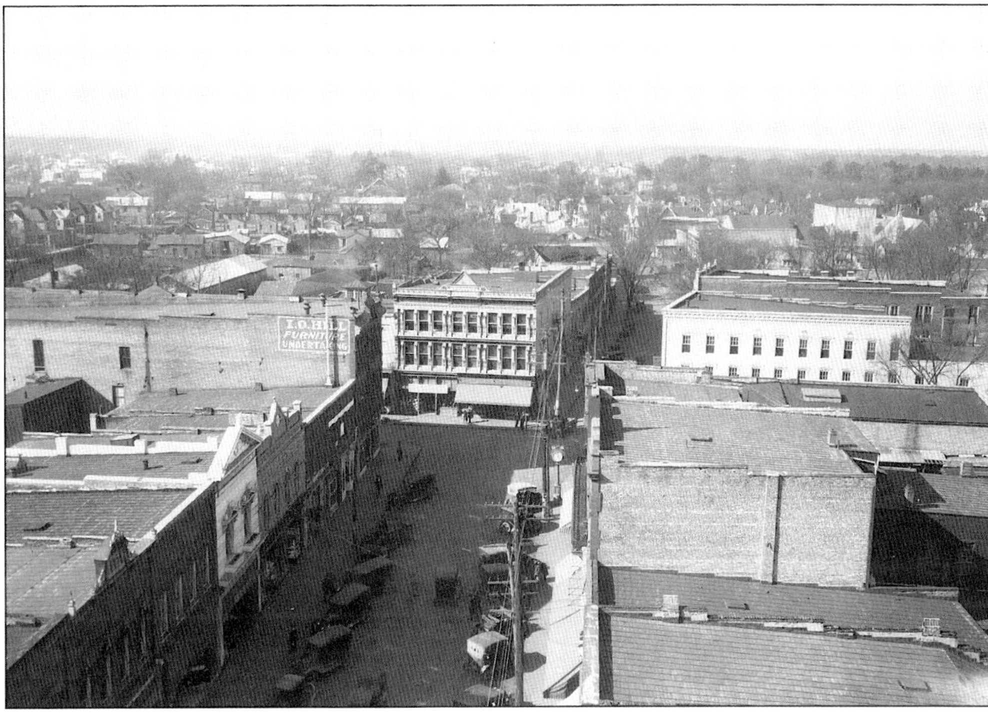

Charles S. Borjes photographed downtown Suffolk (above) and the city's Academy of Music (right) in 1927. The Academy of Music sat at the corner of Main and West Washington Streets. Built between 1890 and 1891, the building first served as the City Market, then the city hall. As time went on, an 824-seat theater was installed upstairs, and the structure housed not only city hall downstairs, but the Academy of Music in its upper floors. Like so many of the nation's legitimate theaters and music houses, the advent of motion pictures spelled the academy's demise. This beautiful building was razed in the 1960s.

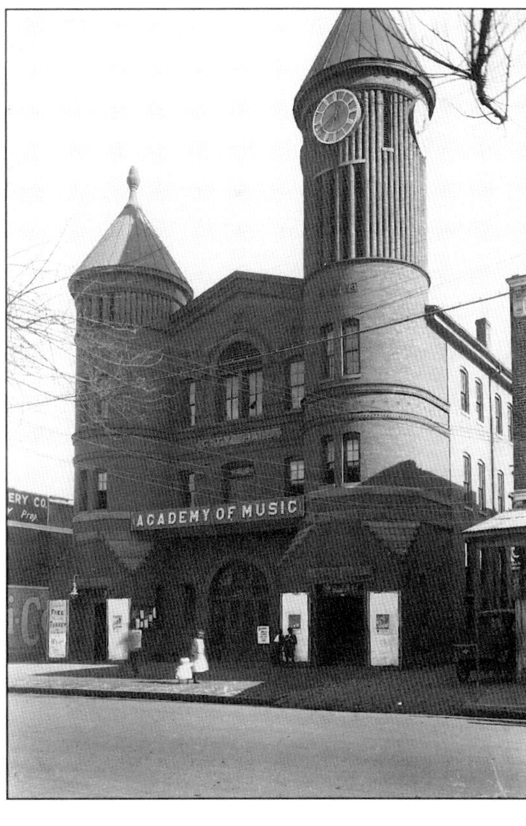

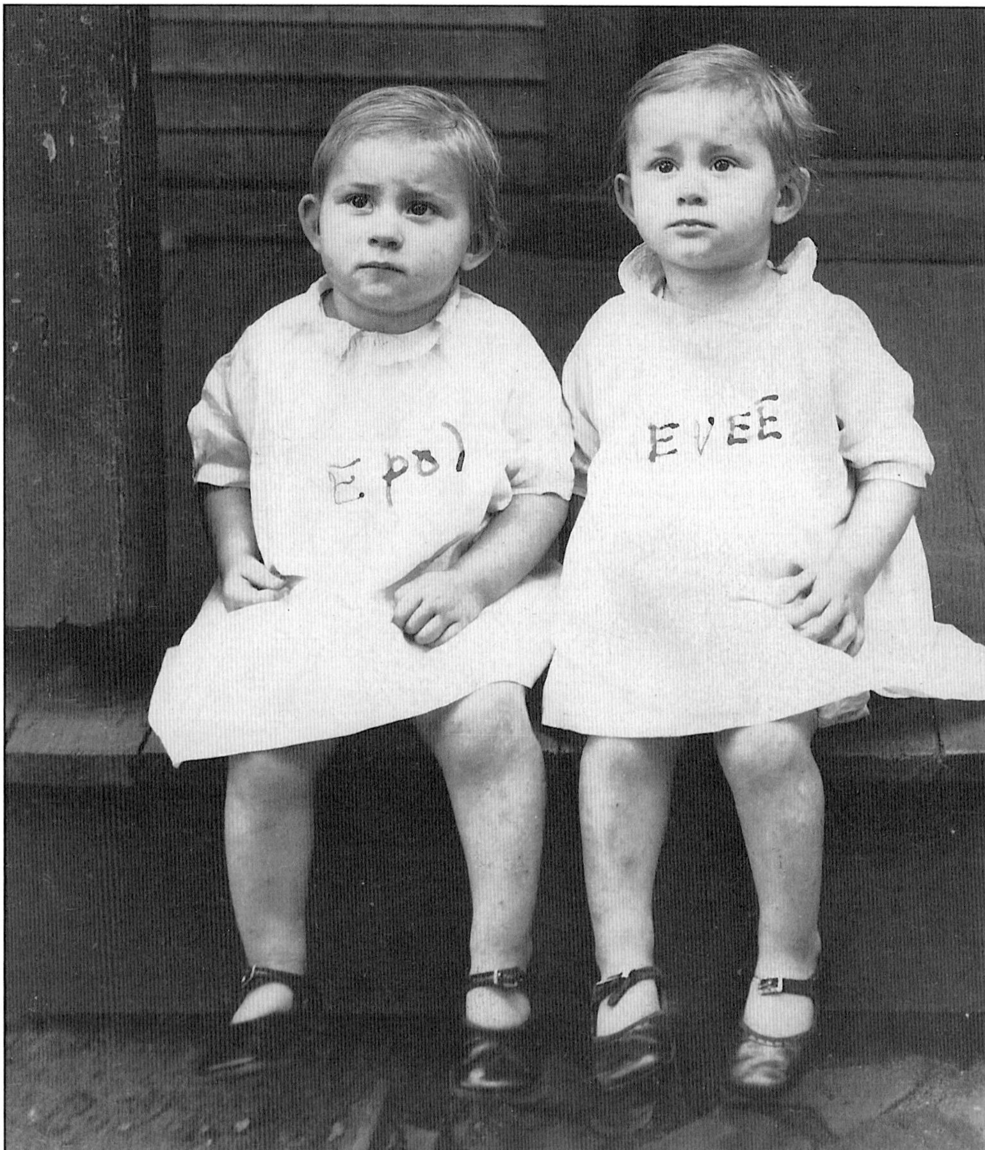

Ibolya Violet (left) and Eve Veres (right), twin girls born on January 16, 1933, to a Hungarian family living upstairs in John T. and Mary Beulah O'Reilly's house at 405 Park Avenue in the Brambleton section of Norfolk, are shown on the back porch of the house in the spring of 1935. The twins were the third and fourth children of Vince and Emerene Gerovicky Veres. Their older siblings, Leo (1929-1930) and Iren (1922-1923) had already passed away when this picture was taken but are buried alongside Eve, who died of pneumonia on April 10, not long after this picture was taken. On Eve's marker are the words which so clearly express the love and affection of her doting parents: "Oh, our dear little Angel / Though you have left us / You shall always live in our hearts / Safe in the Arms of Jesus." Ibolya means "violet" in her parents' native Hungary. Vince Veres was born on February 9, 1901, and his wife, Emerene, on April 7, 1906. He eventually went to work for and retired from the Ford Motor Company, Norfolk plant. Emerene passed away on March 3, 1969, and Vince, on December 9, 1987. (Photographer unknown.)

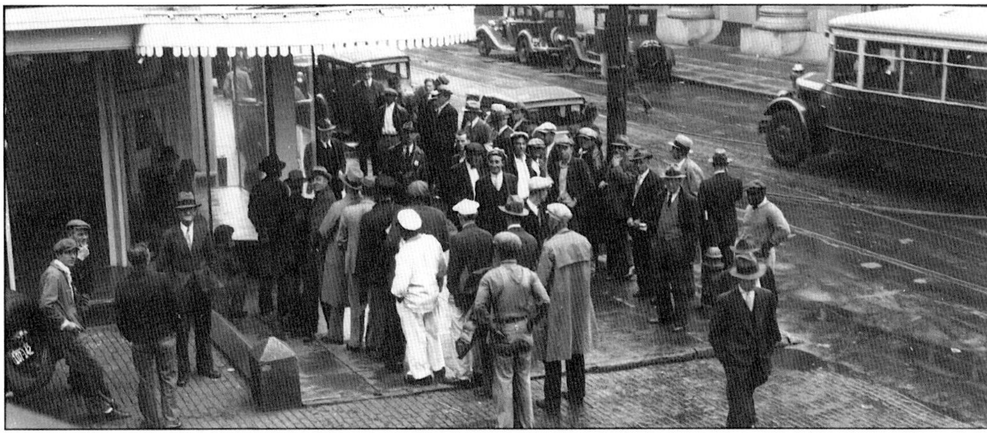

Legal liquor returned to Norfolk on May 28, 1934, as Prohibition ended. After an absence of nearly 18 years, Norfolk's two state-operated liquor stores, one on West Main Street and the other on Church Street, opened for business to lines of patrons that wrapped around the block. The Virginia Alcoholic Beverage Control Board also opened a store at Twentieth Street and Atlantic Avenue in Virginia Beach a couple of days after the Norfolk stores opened. (Charles S. Borjes, photographer.)

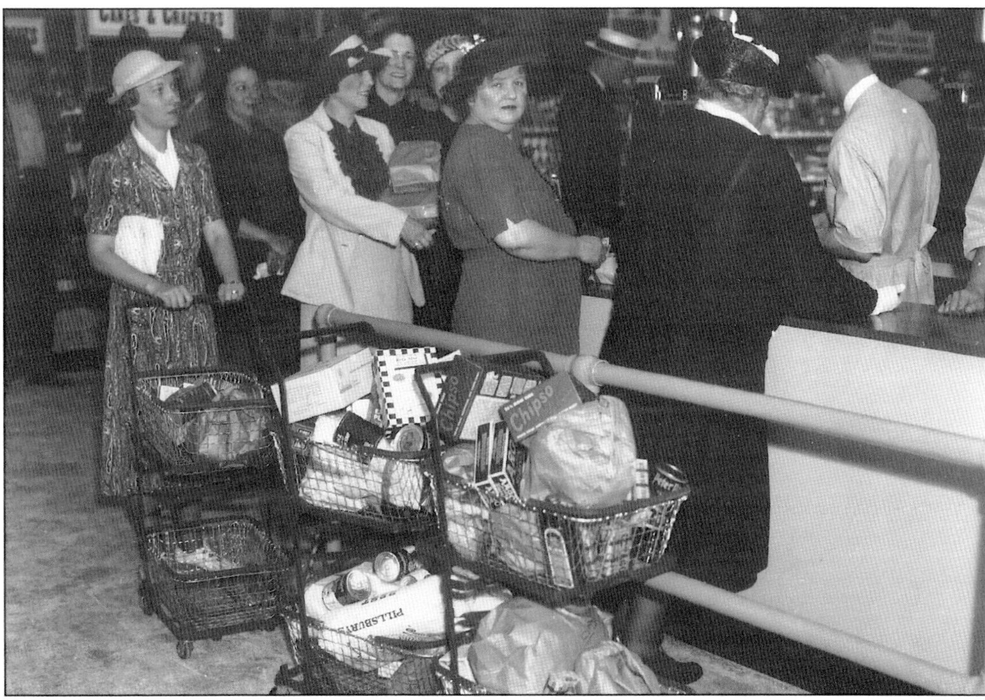

These ladies are doing their grocery store shopping at the Big Star on Monticello Avenue on its opening day, June 2, 1938. Big Star opened two stores in Norfolk, the first at 1700 Monticello Avenue and the other on Colley Avenue at the corner of Harrington Avenue. The stores were managed by Percy L. Edmonds. Norfolk had never had a self-service-style grocery store where all the items were within easy reach—each marked with a price to show patrons exactly what they had to pay. Big Star's advertised prices certainly reflected the times. Ten pounds of Florida sweet oranges sold for 29¢, a pound of Land O'Lakes butter went for 30¢, and a 50-ounce can of Webster's tomato juice was only 15¢. (H.D. Vollmer, photographer.)

The last of the early glory-seeking aviators, Douglas "Wrong Way" Corrigan delighted the world with his "wrong way" flight from New York to Dublin, Ireland, on July 17, 1938, in a rebuilt 1929 Curtiss J-1 Robin that he had bought from a salvage yard for $310. There was more than a simple dash of deviltry to Corrigan. There was a certain distillation of Irish mockery and the traditional insolence of a Texan that made Corrigan one of the great anti-heroes of the 20th century. Born in Galveston, Texas, in 1907, Corrigan learned to fly in 1925. He considered himself privileged to have been able to help weld the Ryan monoplane his hero, Colonel Charles A. Lindbergh, would fly from New York to Paris in May of 1927. Corrigan's admiration for Lindbergh's achievement spurred him on in his quest to make his own solo transatlantic flight. Eleven years after Lindbergh made history, Corrigan was ready to make his own. He made a non-stop flight from California to Roosevelt Field in New York in mid-July of 1938. At Roosevelt Field, Corrigan requested approval for a transatlantic flight from New York to Dublin. His request was promptly denied. After studying his maps and the weather for a trip back to California, Corrigan climbed into his airplane and wired the pilot's door shut with bailing wire because the handle was missing. The world next heard from Douglas Corrigan as he stepped nonchalantly out of his plane in Dublin asking, "Just got in from New York, where am I?" Corrigan would maintain that he had read his compass wrong or that it simply malfunctioned. Though aviation authorities in the United States suspended his pilot's license, it did not last long because the 31-year-old became an overnight sensation. By the time he arrived back in New York, Corrigan was greeted with a ticker tape parade bigger than that accorded Lindbergh—and a new nickname, "Wrong Way." Douglas "Wrong Way" Corrigan later became a test pilot. He was married to Elizabeth Marvin, a childhood sweetheart, on the first anniversary of his famous flight . Corrigan passed away on December 9, 1995, at the age of 88.

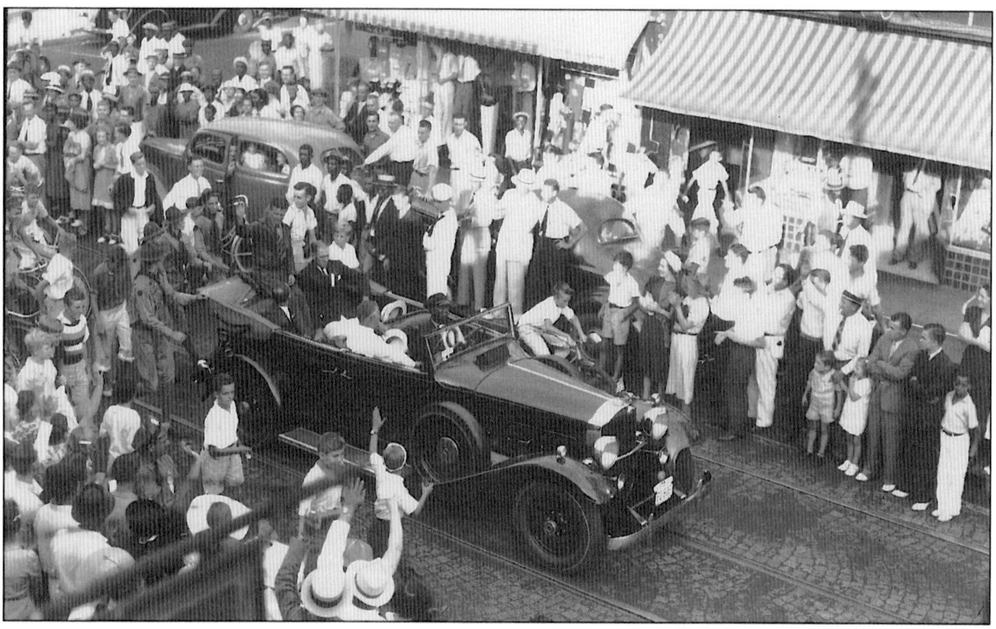

Douglas "Wrong Way" Corrigan arrived at Glenrock Airport on August 30, 1938. His motorcade leaving the airport was choked by throngs of fans eager to get a glimpse of the nation's newest—and unassuming—hero. The streets of downtown Norfolk were mobbed as the aviator made his way down Granby Street and eventually up City Hall Avenue to Bank Street, where he accepted a key to the city from the mayor. (Charles S. Borjes, photographer.)

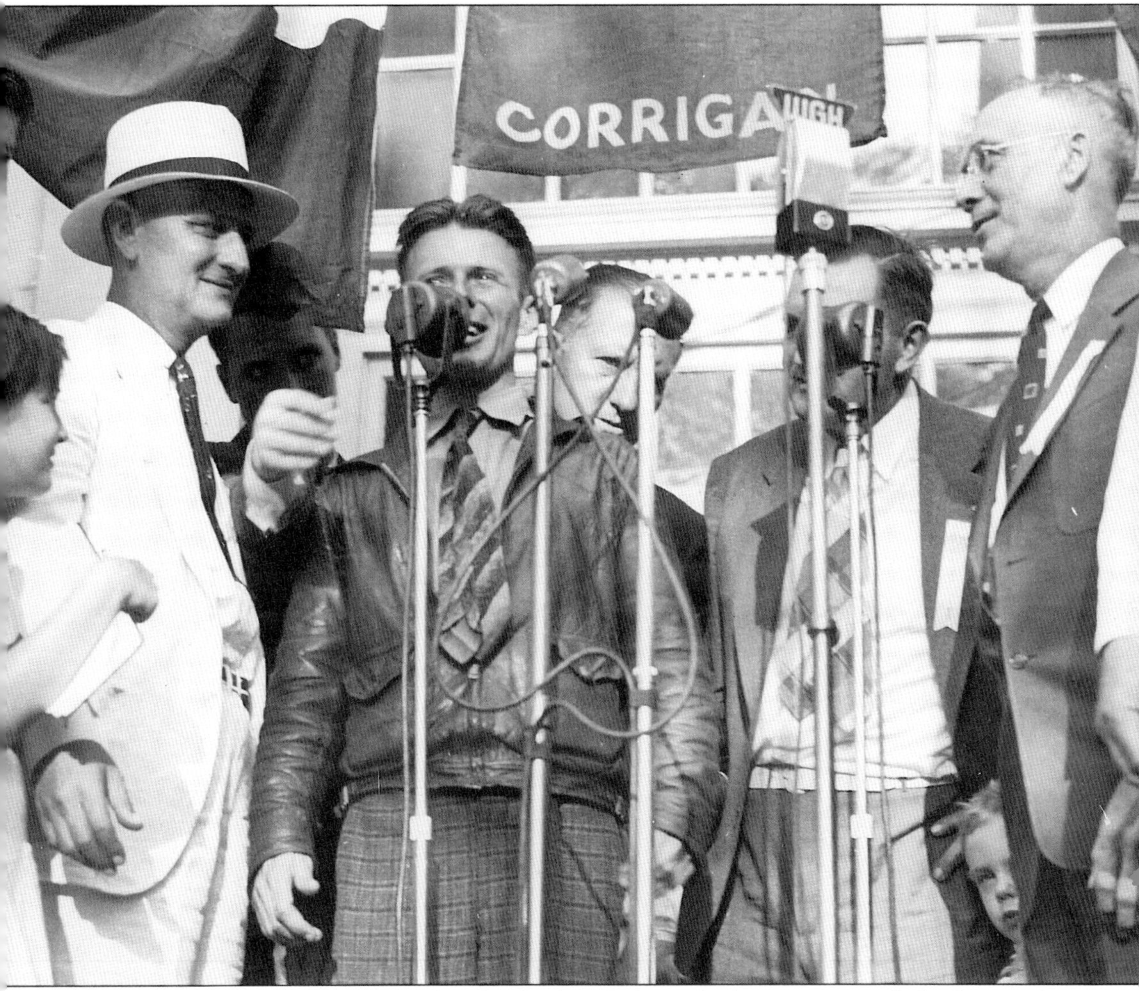

Douglas "Wrong Way" Corrigan (in the leather flight jacket) was presented the key to the city of Norfolk by Mayor John A. Gurkin (standing directly behind Corrigan) on August 30, 1938. Corrigan first came to Norfolk in 1931 when he was on the barnstorming circuit. His association with the area would prove a long and happy one, though perhaps riddled with moments of excitement from time to time. Coming back from North Carolina one day in 1933, rain got into the engine of Corrigan's Eagle Rock biplane and forced him to the ground in a field alongside Virginia Beach Boulevard. Corrigan's piloting skills saved him and a passenger, his brother Harry, from being seriously hurt, but Harry's arm was broken, and the Eagle Rock was stripped of its wings. The plane was one Corrigan purchased from the old Norfolk Aviation Club. (Photographer unknown.)

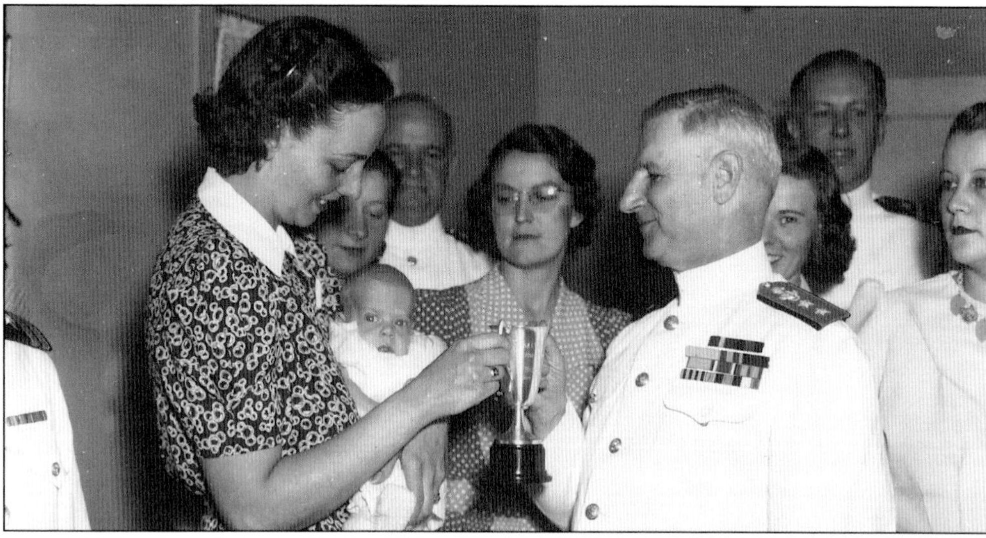

Mrs. E.W. Lovejoy (left) holds her baby son as Rear Admiral Joseph K. Taussig presents the baby with a silver loving cup, the gift of Rear Admiral Ben Moreell, for whom the Navy housing development of Benmoreell was named, on June 4, 1941. The baby, Michael Ervin Lovejoy, was born on April 7, the first child born to parents living at Benmoreell. Rear Admiral Moreell had promised the loving cup to the first child born at the complex. Neighbors and other naval officers were present at the Lovejoy home, 359-A Allen Street, for the ceremony. In the picture, to the rear, is Captain Thomas N. McCloy, personnel officer of the Fifth Naval District. The officer just behind Rear Admiral Taussig is Lieutenant Commander J.M. Bolt, his aide. The baby's father, E.W. Lovejoy, was a machinist's mate, first class, attached to the USS *Ranger* (CV-4) and could not attend his son's party because he was deployed. (Charles S. Borjes, photographer.)

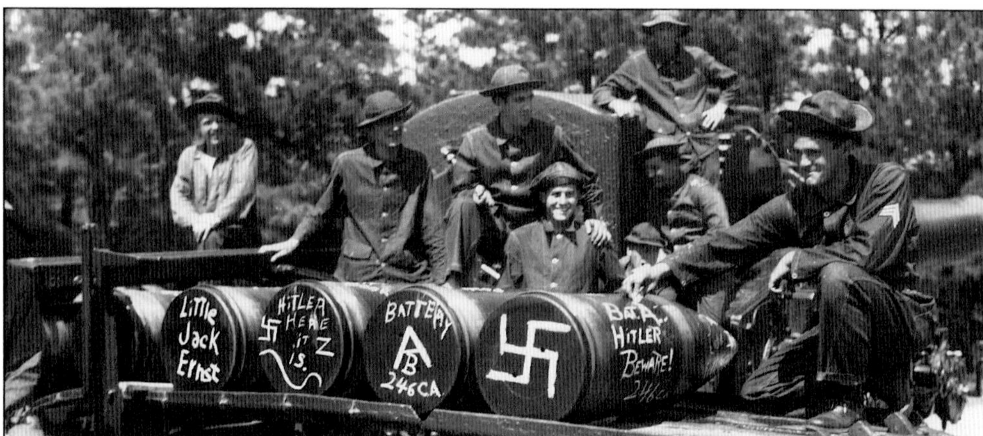

Troops of Battery A, 246th Coast Artillery at Fort Story participated in the first scheduled target practice from the Walke battery since 1928. Completed on October 24, 1924, at a cost of $700,000, only 25 16-inch rounds had ever been fired from the huge emplacement when this picture was taken on June 10, 1941. The 35-foot-long barrel of Gun No. 1 weighed 197,000 pounds, while the howitzers carried an overall weight of about 705,000 pounds. A 40-foot foundation of steel-entwined concrete was built around these behemoth guns to provide stability. Soldiers did nothing to hide their animosity toward the Germans. They consigned 16-inch shells to everyone from Adolf Hitler to Davy Jones's locker. (Charles S. Borjes, photographer.)

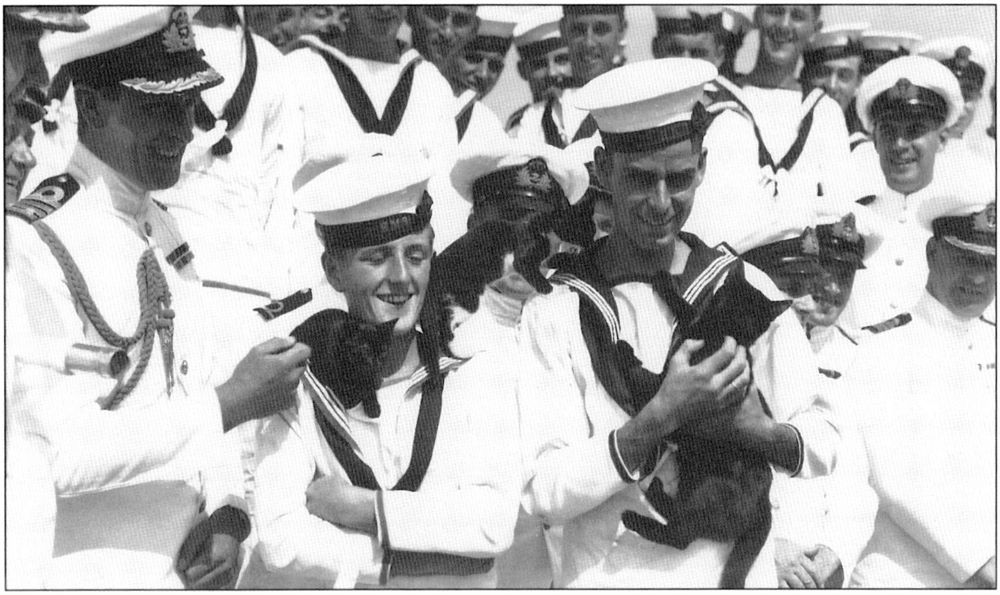

Captain Lord Louis Mountbatten of the Royal Navy, cousin of King George VI of England, assumed command of the British aircraft carrier HMS *Illustrious* on August 28, 1941, in a simple ceremony held pierside at the Norfolk Naval Shipyard in Portsmouth, Virginia. The *Illustrious* was undergoing repairs for damages she received during an attack by German and Italian dive bombers in the Sicilian channel in January of 1941. Mountbatten noted in his remarks, "It is a great thrill for me to take command of a ship with such a fine fighting record. I am looking forward to getting back into the war to hand a few more knocks to the Germans and Italians." This picture by Charles S. Borjes showed the lighter side of Mountbatten's inspection of his ship and crew as he inspected the cats of the *Illustrious*.

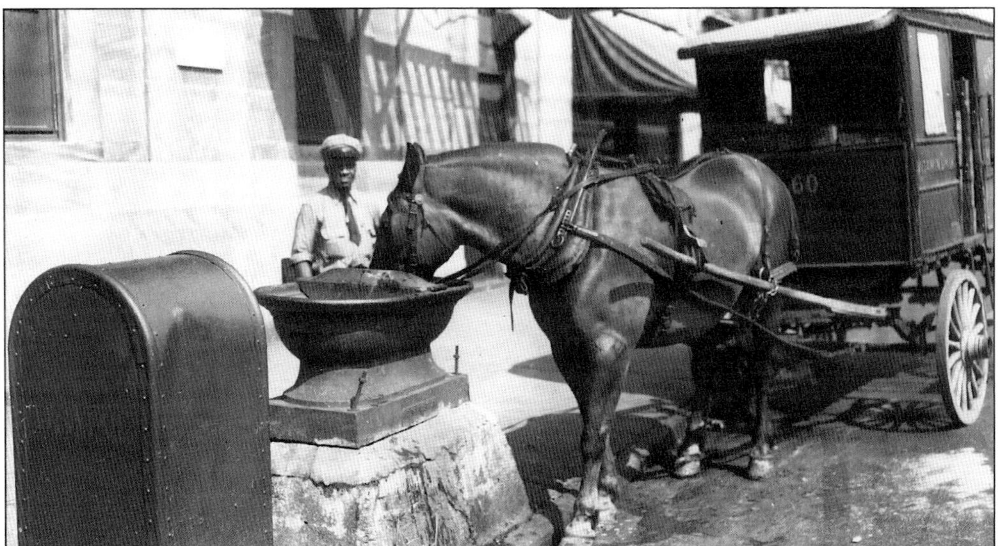

A Rosedale Dairy horse paused in the heat of summer's day to take a drink, August 5, 1949. Rosedale Dairy was headquartered at 929-931 Monticello Avenue. Harry F. Wall was Rosedale's president, and T.S. Lawrence served as its vice president and treasurer. (Charles S. Borjes, photographer.)

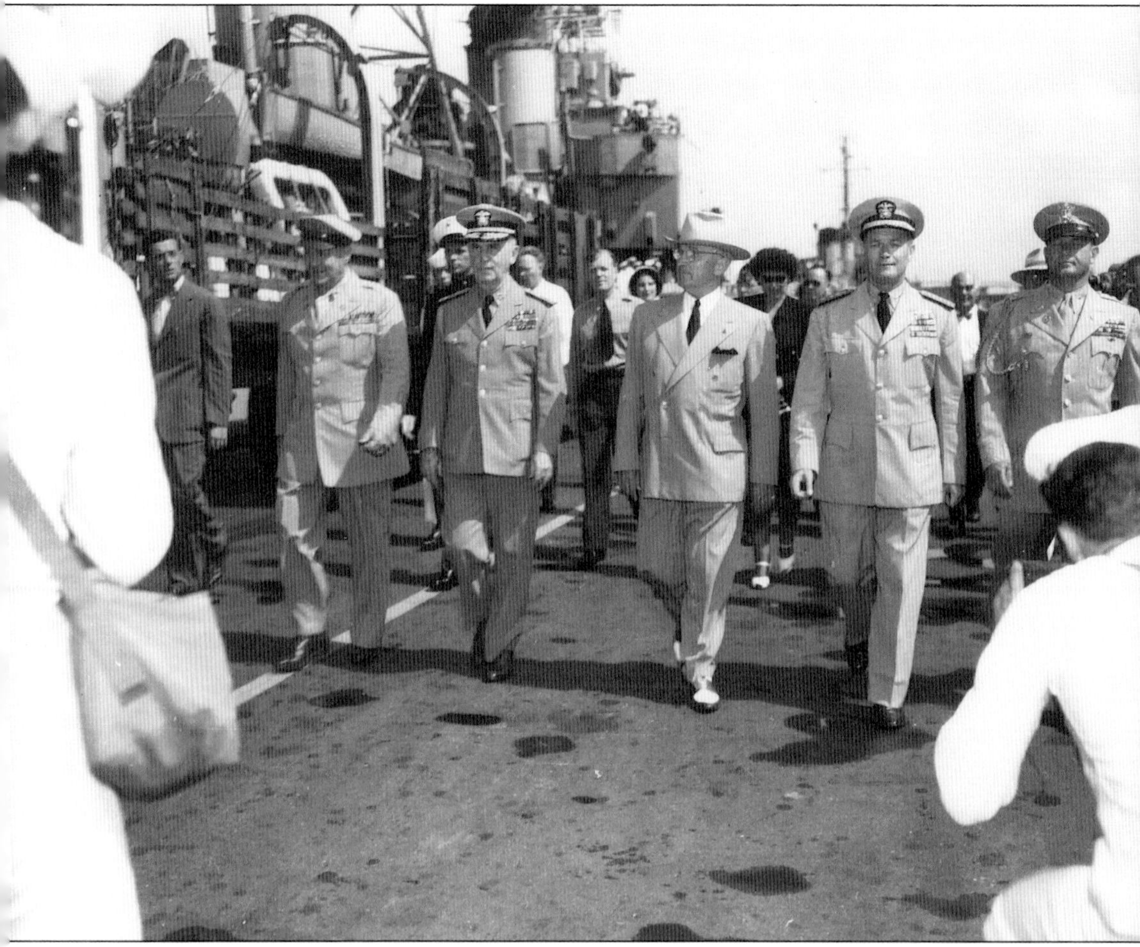

President Harry S. Truman made a brief visit to Naval Station Norfolk on September 19, 1947. Truman, returning from a diplomatic visit to Rio de Janiero, Brazil, aboard the battleship USS *Missouri*, had not totally enamored all her crew. One sailor quipped, "All this trouble for a farmer" as the ship neared Pier Seven. When told what the sailor had said, Second District Congressman Porter Hardy Jr., accompanying the president, replied with a smile, "Now that's really fitting. The farmer's an important man in our country." As Truman was piped over the side of the "Big Mo," he was supposed to head directly across the pier for the presidential yacht *Williamsburg*, but instead he headed landward toward the hundreds of happy children and wives of the Navy men on the task force that took the president and his family to Rio de Janiero and back. President Truman was almost immediately surrounded by talkative children. It was at that point he did the unexpected—Truman stayed and talked to the children and their mothers for a few precious moments. President Truman's gesture drew applause from the *Missouri's* crew and created a lasting impression on the sailors' families which would last a lifetime. (Charles S. Borjes, photographer.)

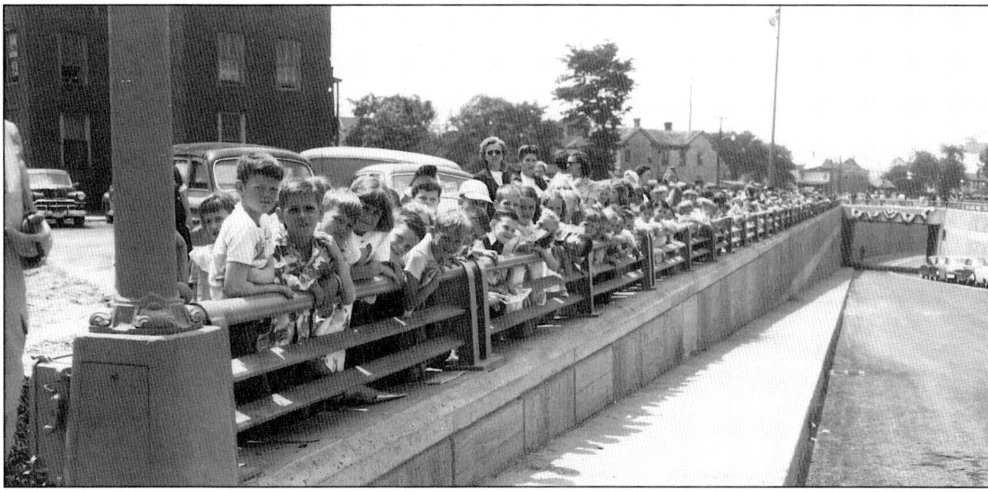

The opening of the Norfolk-Portsmouth Tunnel on May 23, 1952, heralded the arrival of Virginia's first subaqueous tunnel, a two-lane 3,300-foot toll facility under the Southern Branch of the Elizabeth River. Governor John S. Battle addressed a crowd of more than 2,000 who came out to see this important link between the two cities. On opening day, automobiles—and people on foot—by the hundreds passed through the tunnel lying 90 feet below the surface of the river. (Charles S. Borjes, photographer.)

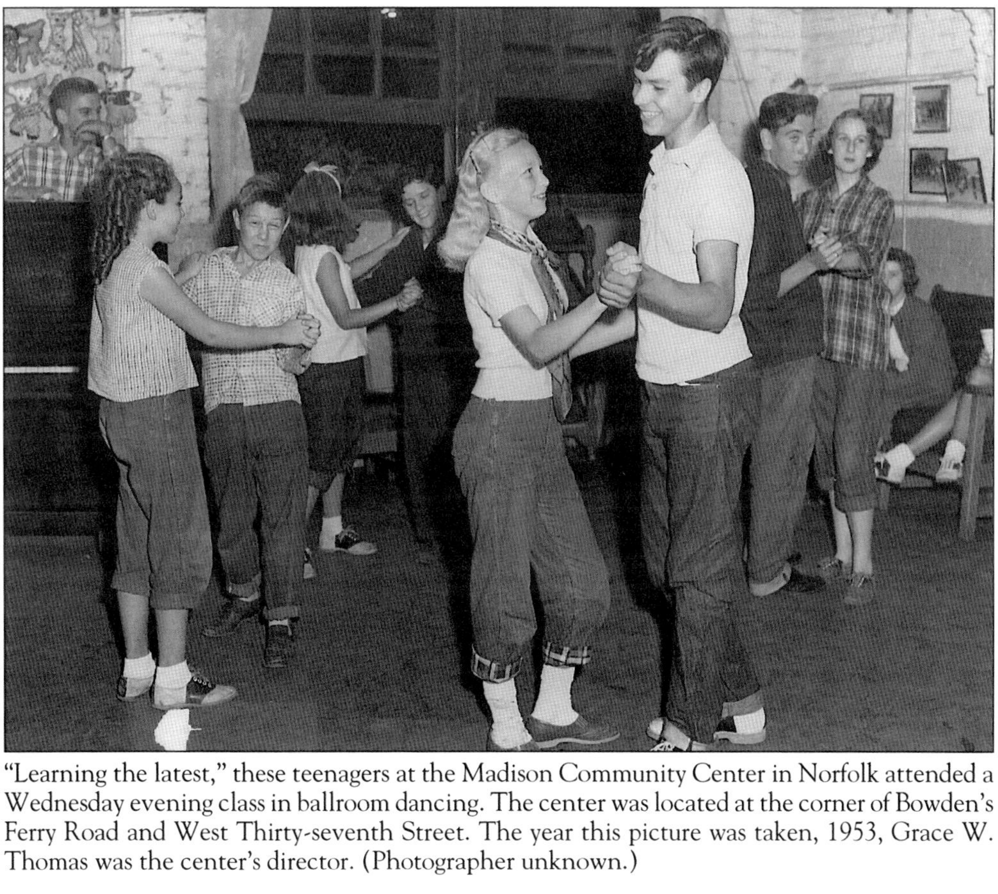

"Learning the latest," these teenagers at the Madison Community Center in Norfolk attended a Wednesday evening class in ballroom dancing. The center was located at the corner of Bowden's Ferry Road and West Thirty-seventh Street. The year this picture was taken, 1953, Grace W. Thomas was the center's director. (Photographer unknown.)

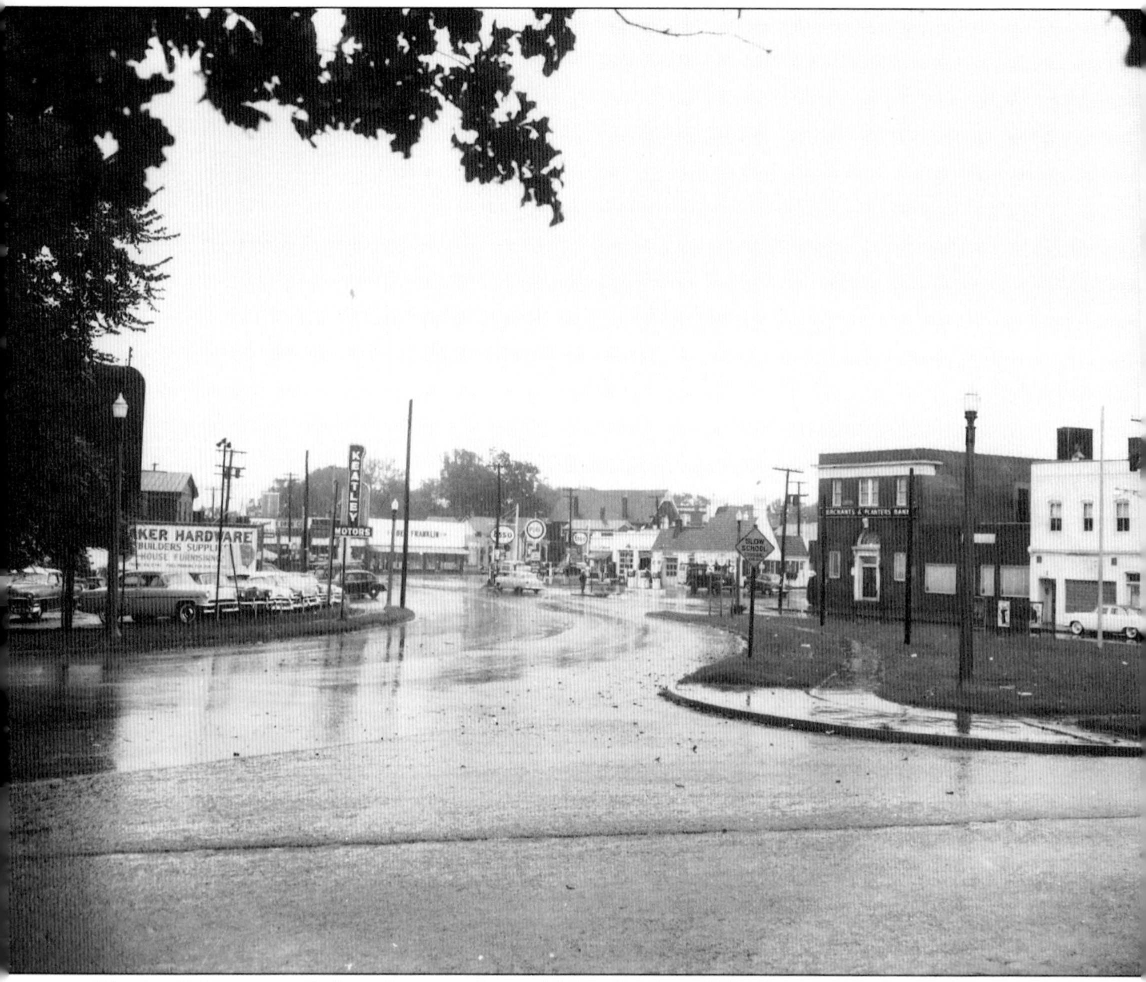

Charles S. Borjes took this photograph in old South Norfolk looking toward Poindexter Street from the steps of the Municipal Building in 1954. The town of South Norfolk was incorporated in 1919. The town became a city of the second class in the Commonwealth of Virginia three years later, able to administer its municipal affairs, but was not fully independent of the county court. South Norfolk did not become a city of the first class until 1950, and it was at that time that the city was granted its own corporation court. The Berkley and Campostella sections of the city of Norfolk defined South Norfolk's northern boundary while to the east and west, it was bounded by the Washington District of Norfolk County, to which South Norfolk once belonged. The southern boundary of South Norfolk was originally Jones's Creek at the Virginian Railway's bridge over the southern branch of the Elizabeth River, but in 1950, this area was expanded to include the village of Portlock and the Money Point industrial area and eastward to encompass Indian River. South Norfolk ceased to exist as an independent city in 1963, when it was absorbed in the creation of the city of Chesapeake.

Twelve

School Bells and Fall Leaves

"Hush, Summer! It is my time now,
And have my say I will, I now!
Here I have sat in perfect quiet,
Listening to this unseemly riot
'Twixt you and Spring—she coolly showing
How all good things to her are owing,
And you with natural heat contesting
Her claims, and your own right protesting."

—From *The Seasons*, 1873
John Thomas Watson, American poet (1822–1905)

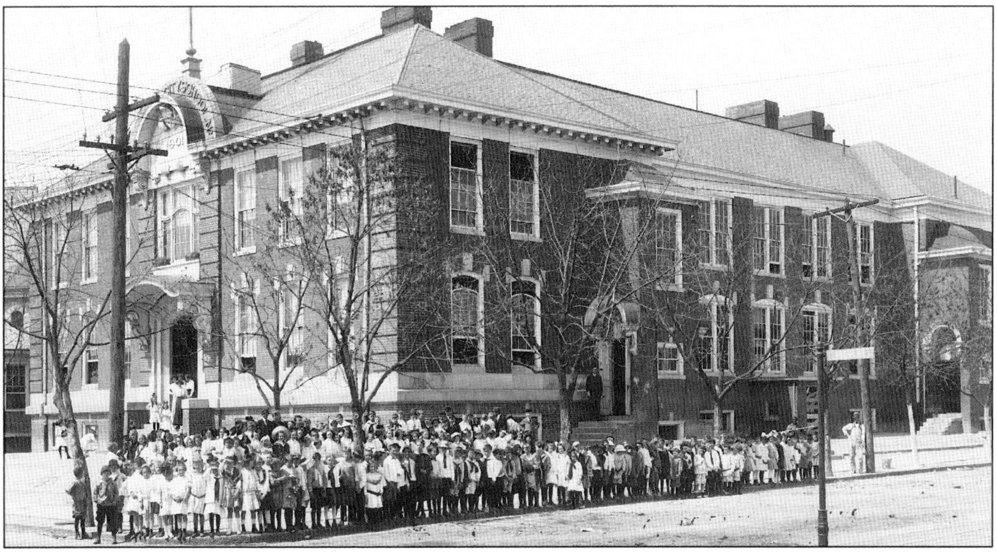

The Atlantic City School No. 2, renamed Robert E. Lee School in 1912, was photographed by Harry C. Mann *c*. 1908. The building, constructed in 1901 and located at the corner of Graydon and Moran Avenues, was in Norfolk's Atlantic City section. The principal was George L. Fentress. Atlantic City was annexed by the city of Norfolk in 1890. At the time of its annexation, Atlantic City encompassed both sides of Colley Avenue southwest of Olney Road and extended from the Norfolk and Western railroad terminal at Lambert's Point and touched the railroad tracks at Twenty-third Street all the way to Elmwood Cemetery. The area was so extensive that three new public schools were built in Atlantic City after 1900: Atlantic City No. 1 (Patrick Henry), the school building shown here, and Atlantic City No. 3 (John Marshall), located on Omohundro Avenue.

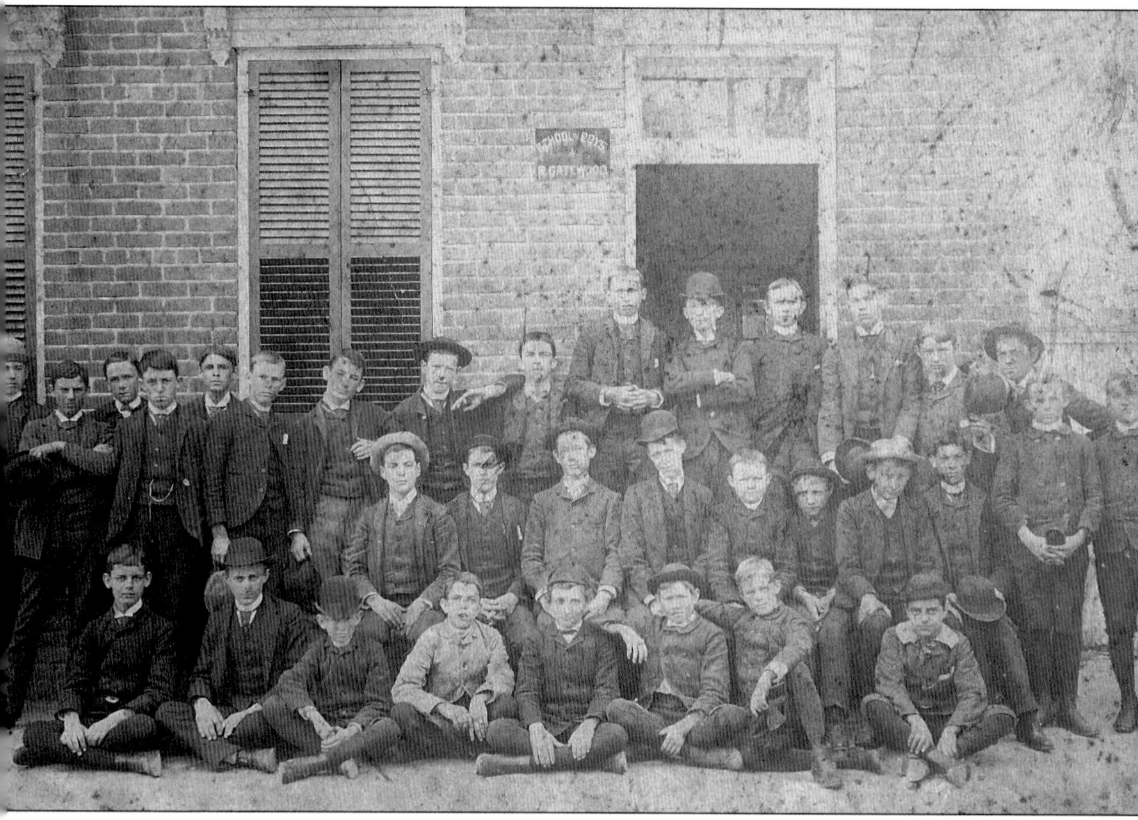

The picture shown here was provided by a descendant of the Weston family of Norfolk. It shows the Robert S. Gatewood School for Boys at 233 Bute Street as it appeared about 1883. From left to right, the students in the photograph, are as follows: (front row) E. Keeling, W. Jones, H. Bell, H. Nebling, H. Roberts, Oscar F. Smith, D. Merritt, and W. Butte; (middle row) A. Coke, A. Borland, W. Moore, E. Scott, W. Hankle, P. Jones, J. Umstadter, W. Culpeper, W. Davis, and Cary Parks Weston; (standing, back row) R. Kyle, E. Cunningham, L. Broughton (son of instructor Alex Broughton), S. Baldwin, J. Desendorf, T. Hoggard, G. Boush, L. Merritt, C. Pollard, W. Old, W. Herd, H. Old, J. Grice, F. W. McCullough, and T. Gwathmey. The school was operated by an Episcopal minister, the Reverend Robert S. Gatewood (1829-1909). Gatewood was a chaplain in the army of the Confederate States of America from 1861 to 1865. He became headmaster of the old Norfolk Academy in September 1865. In 1877, the city of Norfolk tried to take over the academy in the belief that it was intended for public education. The attempted takeover failed, and Norfolk Academy continued as a private institution. Gatewood retired as Norfolk Academy's headmaster in 1882, but it was, of course, a retirement short-lived. He opened his school for boys on Bute Street in 1883. The school remained open until his death in 1909. (J.J. Faber, photographer.)

Pretending to be Pocahontas, Hildegarde Lucas Chamberlain posed for photographer William Freeman at his 176 Main Street studio about 1895.

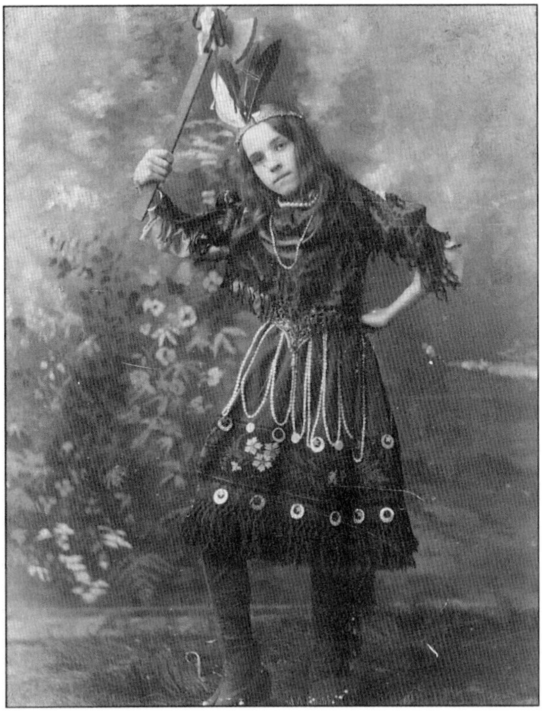

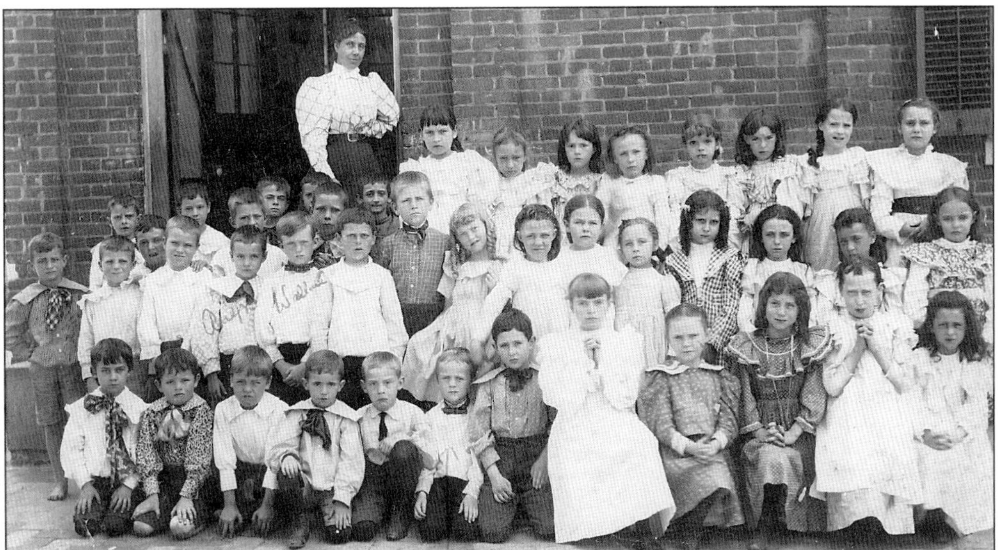

Lucy A. Hall (standing in the doorway) was rector of the Bank Street School, a little two-story schoolhouse for boys and girls on Bank near Charlotte Street. The first grade class, shown here with Miss Hall as they appeared in 1898, met on the first floor of the building. The Bank Street School was built in 1877 and, even at the time the picture was taken, had only one teacher in addition to Miss Hall. Students attended from September 15 until the last Friday in June. The children in this picture were the last to attend school in the old building. The same year this photograph was taken, the school board elected to sell its four oldest school structures, of which this was one. It was subsequently razed, and the children sent to the Triangle Building, where they took their classes until a new elementary school was built.

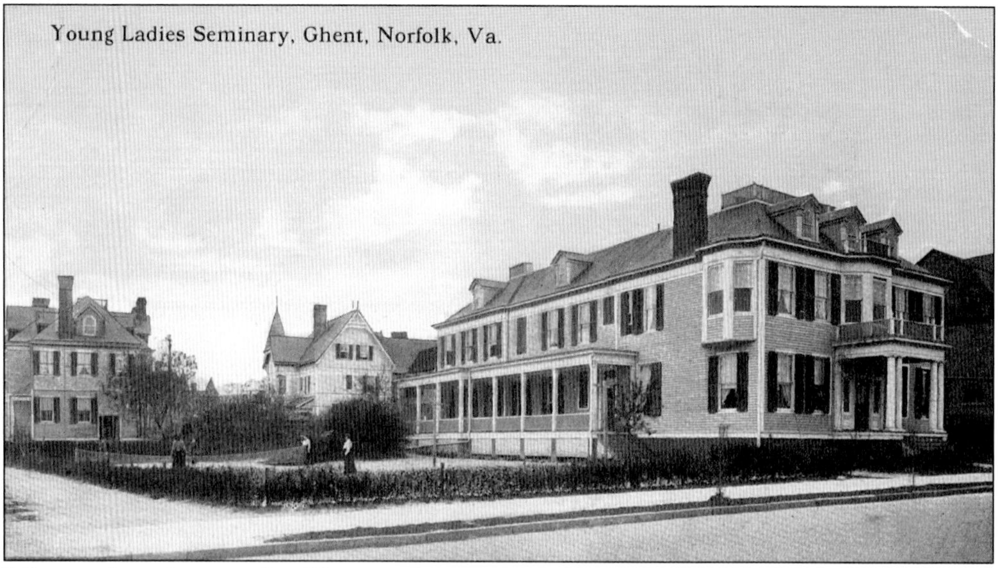

"This is where I go to school," wrote a young woman named Gladys to her friend, Josephine Watson, of Providence, Rhode Island, in 1904. The divided back, hand-colored postcard was published by Louis Kaufmann & Sons, of Baltimore, Maryland, as Series No. A23360. The school was the Leache-Wood Seminary, which had moved from its location at 138 Granby Street (with a large addition fronting Freemason Street) to Fairfax Avenue, Ghent, in September of 1900. The Leache-Wood Seminary remained at this site until it closed for good in 1917. The school was founded in 1871 by two remarkable women, Irene Leache and Anna Cogswell Wood, but in 1898, two years before it moved to Ghent, the school was bought from Leache and Wood by Agnes Douglas West.

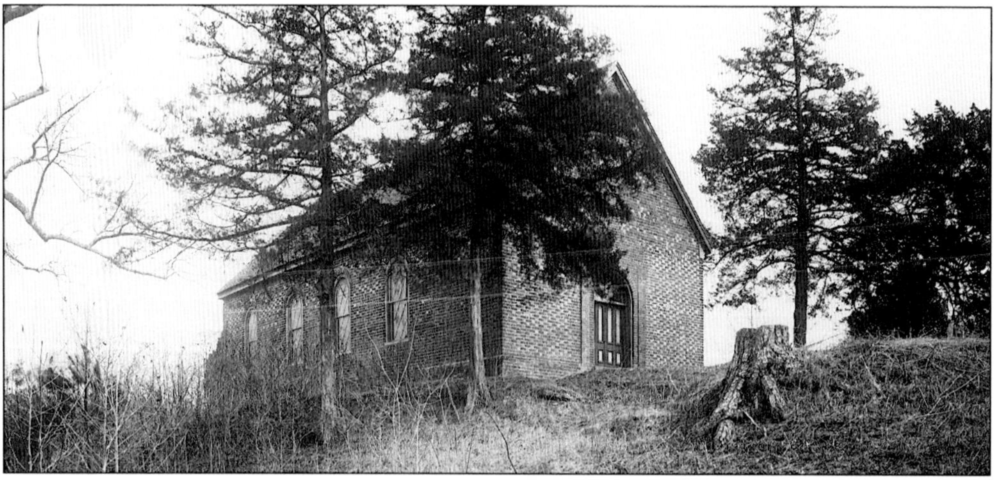

St. John's Church (shown here), located near Chuckatuck in old Nansemond County, was constructed in 1755 and is the third church to stand on the site. Originally called Chuckatuck Church after the Native American word meaning "crooked creek," the building was abandoned by its parishioners a half-century after the American Revolution but reconsecrated in 1826 under its present name. During the Civil War, Union soldiers plundered the church, ruining most of its original interior woodwork. The church was restored around the turn of the century. Nansemond County ceased to exist in 1974 when it was merged with the city of Suffolk. (Harry C. Mann, photographer.)

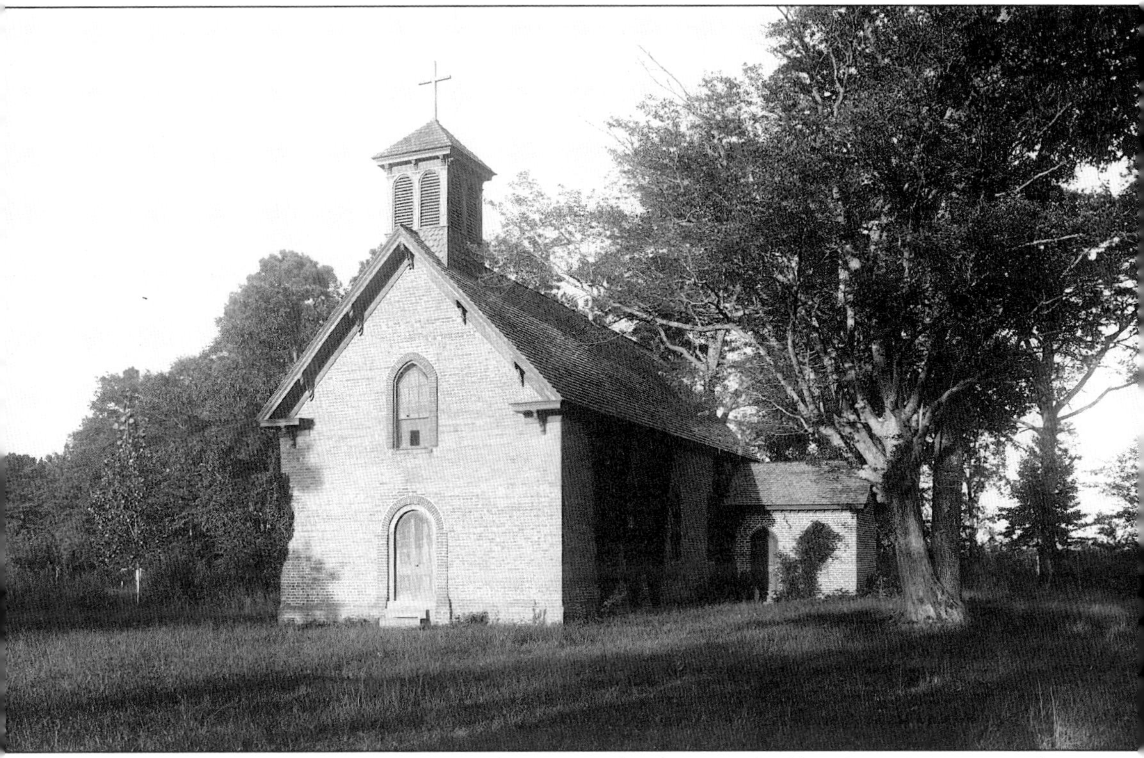

The third Eastern Shore Chapel of Lynnhaven Parish, photographed by Harry C. Mann in the summer of 1907, was located at the far southern end of Great Neck, as it extended south of Oceana, on lands granted in 1657 to William Cornick, son of Simond Cornick, who arrived in Virginia in 1650. William Cornick's home, called Salisbury Plains Plantation, was acquired by the U.S. Navy in 1952 (as was the chapel) for the expansion of Naval Air Station Oceana. A contract for construction of this third chapel to be built within a half mile of Salisbury Plains was awarded to Joseph Mitchell by the parish vestry October 1, 1753, and construction completed on March 12, 1754. The chapel was painstakingly constructed by Mitchell, believed to have built the first schoolhouse in Norfolk in 1761, and his workers. Unlike most Colonial period houses of worship, it is interesting to remark that the interior paint was not white but sky blue, a reflection of the color of the heavens. Worship was rather peaceful for the congregation of the chapel until the Revolutionary War. A number of prominent members of the congregation were loyal to the British, such as the Cornicks and Colonel Jacob Elligood (who resided at Rose Hall Plantation). Elligood fled to Canada, where he remained, never to return to his plantation in Virginia. During the war until 1785 there was no minister. After the Revolutionary War, only visiting clergymen ministered to the congregation, as it shifted from the authority of the Church of England to what was then called the New Protestant Episcopal Church. The Reverend Anthony Walke, who lived only a quarter mile from the chapel, became the first postwar minister in 1788. He remained until 1800, but returned, again, in 1812 and stayed a little over one year. During the Civil War, Union troops used the Eastern Shore Chapel as a barn for their horses. It was not until 1880 that the building was fully restored by parishioners. Reverend John Wales was the minister of the chapel when this picture was taken. The last service conducted here occurred on January 27, 1952. The Navy later razed the chapel but paid to move the congregation and its cemetery to part of the property belonging to the Hillwood Estate on the north side of Laskin Road at its intersection with Virginia Beach Boulevard. The fourth Eastern Shore Chapel was completed almost 200 years to the day of its predecessor.

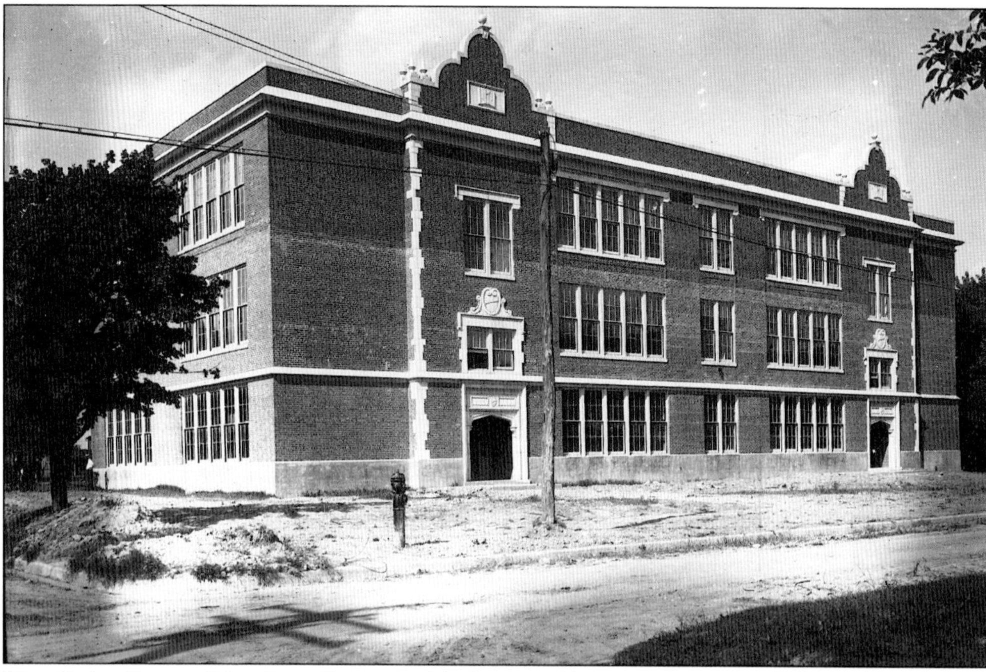

The Duke Street School in Portsmouth's Prentis Place was new when Charles S. Borjes photographed it on September 2, 1926. The new school building took the place of two buildings, one on Elm Avenue and the other on Lincoln Street, which were closed after Duke Street School was completed. The school year in Portsmouth began on September 10 that year. Harry A. Hunt was superintendent of schools.

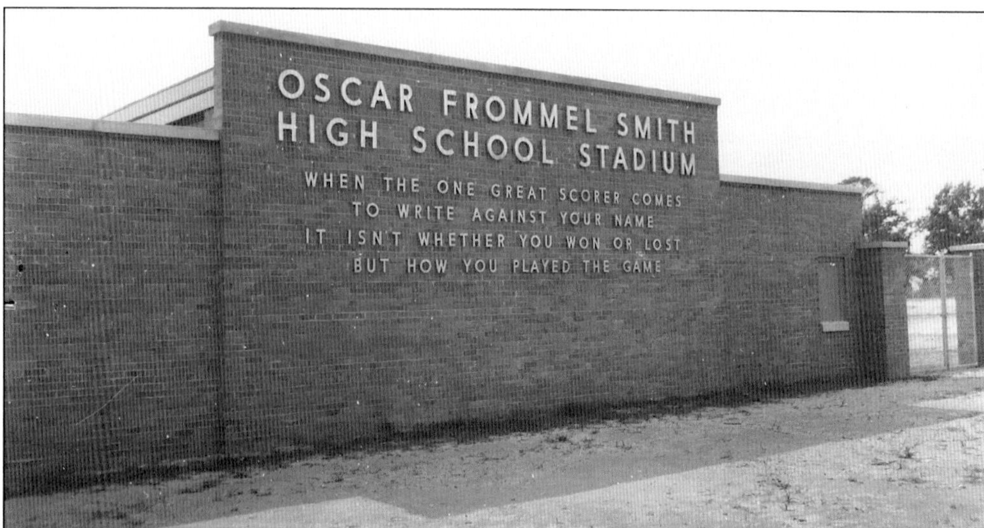

The message on the sign in front of Oscar Frommel Smith High School's newly completed stadium in South Norfolk caught photographer Charles S. Borjes's eye on June 29, 1955. Attributed to Grantland Rice, the eye-catching and heart-stirring words gave athletes and fans something fundamental to think about as they entered the stadium, completed for $80,000 and ready for the first football practice in the fall.